GOVERNING THE DISPLACED

GOVERNING THE DISPLACED

Race and Ambivalence
in Global Capitalism

Ali Bhagat

CORNELL UNIVERSITY PRESS   ITHACA AND LONDON

First published 2024 by Cornell University Press

Library of Congress Cataloging-in-Publication Data

Names: Bhagat, Ali, 1991– author.
Title: Governing the displaced : race and ambivalence in global capitalism / Ali Bhagat.
Description: Ithaca [New York] : Cornell University Press, 2024. | Includes bibliographical references and index.
Identifiers: LCCN 2023032725 (print) | LCCN 2023032726 (ebook) | ISBN 9781501773600 (hardcover) | ISBN 9781501773617 (paperback) | ISBN 9781501773624 (epub) | ISBN 9781501773631 (pdf)
Subjects: LCSH: Refugees—Government policy—European Union countries. | Refugees—Government policy—Africa, East. | Racism—Social aspects. | Equality—Social aspects.
Classification: LCC JV6346 .B53 2024 (print) | LCC JV6346 (ebook) | DDC 325/.214094—dc23/eng/20230809
LC record available at https://lccn.loc.gov/2023032725
LC ebook record available at https://lccn.loc.gov/2023032726

To Shabnam and Huzefa

Contents

Acknowledgments

I owe so much of this book to the incredible guidance of Susanne Soederberg, whom I am lucky to call a friend. In later years, Genevieve LeBaron pushed me to forge on and has been incredibly supportive and wonderful. I could not have completed the book without the help of my dearest friends Marc Calabretta, Nadège Compaoré, and Rachel Phillips, who were with me every step of the way. In no particular order I would like to thank Nik Heynen, Marcus Taylor, Beverley Mullings, Pegah Rajabi, Ahad Bhagat, Villia Jefremovas, Margaret Little, Lama Tawakkol, Michael Clark (University of Pittsburgh), Laura Vaz-Jones, Martin Danyluk, Mat Paterson, Andrew Nguyen, Sarah Sharma, Jacob Robbins-Kanter, Gavin Fridell, and my department at Queen's Politics, without which I would not have been able to complete this book. I would also like to thank my former colleagues at the University of Manchester including the CGP and GPE clusters with a special shout out to Veronique-Pin Fat for her mentorship.

A special thanks to Jim Lance for believing in this book and for seeing this project through.

Above all, I owe much of this book to those who shared their time and expertise with me during my fieldwork. I was lucky to have made many connections with relevant social justice NGOs who helped shape some of my thinking around forced displacement in contemporary capitalism (BAAM, RCK, DRC, and UNHCR), I interviewed people who continued to face forced displacement and while there is no satisfying way to acknowledge the extractive process of research, I am forever indebted to those who took the time to speak to me.

This book was funded through an IDRC Doctoral Research Award which fostered an affiliation with Professor Luke Obala at the University of Nairobi, Ontario Graduate Scholarship, and a WC Good Memorial Fellowship. It was also funded by a generous subvention from Saint Mary's University.

GOVERNING THE DISPLACED

GLOBAL DISPLACEMENT AND RACISM

We left Nairobi's Westlands area for a queer refugee safehouse many miles from the city. The safehouse was hosting an event, and a few of its residents were participating in a film discussing queer migration in Kenya. I do not want to give you, the reader, the impression that this book is about queer refugees explicitly, but I start at a queer refugee safehouse because it sparked my understanding of fantasy as an element of refugee governance. I feel that this often-hidden subset of refugees illustrates both the politics of abandonment vis-à-vis state violence and the potential joys of community. Indeed, it might be useful to think about refugee survival and governance as queer experiences. To follow Natalie Oswin, perhaps queerness can be subjectless—tied to both the politics of love and belonging and the tensions of struggle and violent exclusion as well. Twinning refugee experiences with queer ones allows us to think about the politics of belonging—a key impetus of this book.

My first thought after arriving at the safehouse was how utterly far and isolated this place was from central Nairobi. Some months later I asked a representative from a nongovernmental organization (NGO) that runs these safehouses about this, and they told me they wanted to keep these safehouses anonymous and far away to protect residents from the potential of homophobic violence. This is difficult to digest because, in effect, these safehouses keep queer people and queer communities invisible; however, many of the residents I spoke with felt much safer behind the high walls of the safehouse.

In reflecting on this contradiction, I invite you to think about how queer refugees (mostly from Uganda) arrive in Nairobi and eventually move to these

1

safehouse communities. Indeed, these spaces exist only because of a heteronormative/homophobic state and society that target queer people; however, we should also reflect on the netted practices of urban refugee governance in general. In both Paris and Nairobi, refugee governance entails the intersection of states, NGOs, international and national organizations, various charities, private citizens, and often corporate actors. For better or for worse, a queer refugee safehouse exists in the time and space of various governance mechanisms and helps us understand refugee governance in general on a range of imperfect, exclusionary, and sometimes survival-enabling policies and practices that are often incongruent with wider liberal framings of refugee rights.

I pick up on this throughout the book, but for now I want to emphasize that the material practices of refugee governance are informed by immaterial fantasies that surround the prospect of refugees entering the borders of a nation-state. These fantasies are undoubtedly grounded in imaginaries of race and ethnicity, and I contend that refugees are often framed in the terminology of a crisis because they challenge the racial (and supremacist) visions of a nation-state. For instance, the war on Ukraine has resulted in millions of refugees, but only refugees from the Middle East and Africa are framed as undesirable. The leader of Spain's Vox Party recently claimed, "Anyone can tell the difference between them [Ukrainian refugees] and the invasion of young military-aged men of Muslim origin who have launched themselves against European borders in an attempt to destabilize and colonize it"[1]

The fantasy of the refugee subject is disconnected from the humanity and lived realities of those who are forcibly displaced. It was through my visit with the residents of the queer safehouse that this preoccupation with fantasy and the refugee experience arose. My definition of fantasy is twinned to ideological power where states and society enact policies and justify them on the basis of some preconceived notions of morality and nation. The fantasy disappears contradictions and exists on the register of the immaterial while having decidedly material consequences. I dive deeper into this in subsequent chapters, but for now let us return to my day with the safehouse's residents.

As part of the day's activities, the residents of the safehouse and other guests participated in a series of role-playing games, led by a theater scholar. We played some icebreakers and shared common issues based on collective queer experiences. The usual topics, such as coming out, self-discovery, and sexual experiences, enabled a universal vocabulary.

One particular moment has stayed with me. I participated in a role-playing game with three residents of the safehouse: Shaziya, Joyce, and Justice. Our task was to create three tableaux prompted by the word *hope*. The first scene involved a secret affair between two men (Justice and me) in what was narrated as Kampala, Uganda—the hometown of many of the refugees in the safehouse. While we held hands, Joyce (Justice's sister in the play) secretly observed the scene unnoticed. In the second scene, the mother character (Shaziya) found out about her son's sexuality and his same-sex relationship, resulting in him being forced out of his home and out of Uganda. The moment of forced displacement in our discussion and in the tableaux was rushed in the sense that it was not spelled out for me why it was so obvious that the discovery of Justice's sexuality would result in his mother immediately disowning him. I read this as some expression of lived reality and a comical moment of play. Joyce's character betrayed Justice, and while the whole scene was intended to be melodramatic and humorous, the deep cuts of this betrayal resonated with those in the audience who had to leave everything behind because of their gender identity or sexual orientation. The scene ended with Justice exclaiming, "I am a gay now! I can do whatever I want!" I continue to read this assertion as a choice to break free from the heteronormative traditions of his family. Indeed, these words reflect the overarching fantasy of queer liberation, and they might in fact be words Justice never got to say. The statement itself is curious; the indefinite article *a* in front of *gay* aligns Justice with some form of global queer other. He accepts that he is one of *them*, and at the same time, the existence of a universal gay other is also a fantasy—something that exists overseas, far away, and in a distant place and has filtered its way through the pipeline of the internet, films, and various NGOs, but a thing, nonetheless, that feels out of reach.

The final scene was rife with contradiction. Justice and his lover (a role Justice volunteered me to play) reunited in America as Justice held a baby (we used a watermelon) to symbolize happiness, hope, and an escape from homophobic Uganda. At the same time, we were also at Shaziya's funeral, and Joyce decided to forgive Justice for his alleged transgressions. The scene was both a marriage and a funeral encapsulating opposite events that represented an unbridled fantasy for Justice. The play was just that—a place to enact fantasies that seem impossible but, in some ways, reflect on the hopes of relocation.

In developing this book, I spoke to queer and straight/cisgender refugees. The deep desire for a life away from both Nairobi and Paris cut across many of their stories. There always seemed to be a proverbial promised land that offered better rights, better livelihoods, and safer surroundings, pointing to the cyclical and never-ending features of displacement where race and class haunt those who are forcibly removed. My experience with the safehouse residents made me think about how fantasies drive the refugee experience. While the role-playing was revelatory of the desires of someone like Justice, who wanted retribution from his homophobic mother, reconnection with his sister, and a family life with a man he loved, what is missing here is why some of these desires are perennially out of reach. Justice's desires are oppositional to those of states and an increasingly antimigrant society. If refugees fantasize about relocation, do states fantasize about the potential of refugees? Are refugees destabilizing the nation? Are they a new source of labor? Are some deserving and others not?

In considering these questions, I aim to intervene in dominant understandings of refugees as passive recipients of aid divorced from the social realities and lived experiences of work, shelter, and political belonging in contemporary racial capitalism. Capitalism is a tricky word, and I use it to refer to two things. First is the dominant logics of capitalist governance that bolster private interests and profits over human life. By this I mean a systemic tendency to devalue the lives of the poor and marginalized particularly on the grounds of social difference where race becomes the governing logic of displacement management. Second, and related, I am referring to contemporary capitalism at the level of the urban scale where refugees—despite the fact that various governments and societies might not actively consider them workers—are often folded into or excluded from the material spaces of life in the realms of housing and labor market access.

Indeed, the dominant images of refugees involve boats on the Mediterranean, encampment, death, and violence. Truly, this is part of the lived experiences of many refugees, but many more live in urban areas and must navigate difficult terrains of housing and labor market access in spaces that are increasingly antimigrant. Therefore, I situate refugee governance and survival in the city and in so doing also hope to shed light on how the poorest, most marginalized, and forgotten people survive in various sites and spaces of relocation.

Throughout this book, I am preoccupied by two related threads: fantasy and survival. Therefore, I center this intervention on two key questions: What are the fantasies that make up refugee governance? How do refugees survive upon relocation to major urban centers, if they manage to make it there? For answers, I look at refugee governance on multiple scales—transnational, national, and urban. The urban is where Paris and Nairobi emerge as sites of survival and contestation and where refugee governance is rendered most visible. I follow this line of inquiry because refugees are misfits in the global political economy of migration. Refugees are not workers (though they must work). Refugees are not considered enslaved people (though they definitely face detention and forms of unfree labor). And refugees are considered beneficiaries of human rights and international regulations (and yet, face abject exclusion and violence). Situating refugee governance under capitalism requires us to understand the overall system in which refugees exist and yet also account for the ways in which forcibly displaced people survive at the fringes of this system. With this tension in mind, I am concerned here not only with the material dimensions of exclusion but also with the undergirding logics of refugee governance that are untethered from profits, bottom lines, and formal work. Despite this, persistent desires for exclusion, accumulation, austerity, productivity, and self-reliance exist on multiple scales of refugee governance.

Refugees often face abject exclusion or some form of economically justified reasoning for inclusion. For example, the Jordan Compact on refugees is frequently described as a pioneering effort of integration where refugees are provided work permits. Its key objective is to enhance refugee self-reliance—an explicit commitment to valorizing refugee labor for the purposes of development. Recent reports have indicated, however, that migrant workers in Jordan face deplorable labor conditions, including forced labor and degrading treatment.[2] While the Jordan Compact illustrates a state's commitment to some form of integration, Viktor Orban's Hungary has infamously enacted the Stop Soros Law, which threatens anyone assisting refugees with a one-year jail sentence.[3] With the arrival of Ukrainian refugees, Orban's government echoes other Far Right figures in the European Union (EU) who are using Ukrainians to further highlight that nonwhite refugees threaten European values and nationhood.

The term *refugee* is contentious. The United Nations High Commissioner for Refugees (UNHCR) defines a refugee as a person who has fled their country because of a well-founded fear of persecution on the grounds of race, religion, nationality, social grouping, or political stance. In this book, however, I make little distinction among asylum seeker, refugee, and irregular economic migrant. I do this to move away from reifying state categories of status and value. I differentiate from the word *immigrant* only insofar as refugees (or those who seek asylum) are navigating an often-varied set of systemic barriers. I see the refugee experience, on balance, as occupying intersectional positions of marginality that differentiate this group from others. At the same time, the experiences of immigrants of color, the extant poor, and other marginalized groups should not be minimalized. We are part of the same system of oppression with various incongruencies and potentialities, but by differentiating between the groups I am hoping to provide some granularity to the refugee experience.

Global displacement has reached unprecedented levels—the number of people fleeing their homes has doubled in a decade.[4] At the same time, the deadly Mediterranean Sea Route contributes to widespread loss of life, continuing the violence of the so-called European refugee crisis in 2015. This has prompted a simultaneous response from the EU to accept some refugees while curbing all sorts of migratory flows from the Middle East and sub-Saharan Africa.[5] While media attention continues to focus on Europe, the numbers in Africa are staggering, with 2.5 million refugees held in camps in Ethiopia, Kenya, and Chad alone.[6] These numbers are no longer shocking as the media coverage of mass death has desensitized viewers to the spectacle of forced migration and created a passive tolerance toward the displacement of dark-skinned people, particularly at Europe's shore. So far, global displacement is untethered from the goings-on of capitalist logics and state welfare and has been considered a phenomenon caused by mismanagement, conflict, and social instability in the global South. Refugees are thus treated as if removed from capitalism, but this is simply untrue.

In developing this conception of the refugee fantasy that emerges amid neoliberal logics of austerity, I pay attention to the ways in which both the political Left (liberals so to speak) and the political Right (and the rising alt-Right) frame refugees. For instance, the body of Aylan Shenu (Alan Kurdi) made global headlines after he drowned in September 2015. The image of this child alerted the world to the brutalities of forced displacement and contextualized the Syrian refugee crisis. Since then, however, refugee life has become devalued owing to rampant xenophobia and the rise of alt-Right populism not only in Europe but also the world over. Various politicians have called for the closing of borders under the auspices of affordability. In 2016, then French prime minister Manuel Valls said, "[France] cannot accommodate any more refugees . . . that's not possible."[7]

The fantasy operates on the register of the immaterial, but it only arises because of the material circumstances that contextualize refugee governance. For instance, Kenya has managed refugees in its camps and urban spaces for close to three decades; however, with diminished aid funding and the pivot of global attention to Europe, politicians in Kenya have echoed similar sentiments of xenophobia and economistic rejection as their European counterparts. Amnesty International's deputy director for East Africa, Michell Kagari, has publicly stated that "refugees are caught between a rock and a hard place. Kenyan government officials are telling them they must leave by the end of the month [December 2016] or they will be forced to leave without any assistance."[8] It is not coincidental that fantasies surrounding refugees as destabilizing agents emerge during heightened economic insecurity.

In 2022, Kenya pivoted toward a Jordan Compact style of self-reliance. In an about-turn, the government decided to allow refugees to seek employment and issued work permits[9]—previously unheard of for the majority of refugees in Kenya during the time of my fieldwork in 2018. Regardless of this shift, refugees continue to struggle to validate their documents, find work, and secure housing; in effect, self-reliance is a framework that absolves the state and various institutions of the responsibility for governing migrants.

Refugees struggle to survive not only because of the systemic and institutional contexts of economic insecurity but also because of how the refugee becomes an ideological construction. The refugee emerges as a phantom character that needs to be managed for the purposes of economic and cultural stability. This fear strikes at the heart of the so-called refugee crisis. The framing of refugees as those in crisis while also presenting a crisis through regional instability is explored in this book as a trope. Using crisis terminology to refer to refugees flattens extant issues of inequality amid rising homelessness, job insecurity, and political division. Indeed, it is capitalism itself that should be understood as crisis prone and unmanageable. As the mayor of Leipzig, Thomas Fabian, puts it, "I don't like to use the term refugee crisis. We don't have a refugee crisis. We have a housing crisis."[10]

The mayor's statement points to the key puzzle of this book. Namely, there is global recognition of increased internal and international forced displacement due to conflict, climate change, poverty, and persecution, and yet, despite this unprecedented movement of people, refugees have been undertheorized within the context of global capitalism in either policy or scholarly works. Refugees are rarely recognized as workers, entrepreneurs, home renters, and part of the fabric of everyday life.

In trying to understand the everyday lives of refugees amid multiple scales of systemic exclusion, *Governing the Displaced* places the EU, France, and Paris in conversation with East Africa, Kenya, and Nairobi. The urban scale of analysis features extensively because it is where the everyday politics of survival play out, namely on three axes: shelter, work, and some form of political belonging. These three prongs of access (Ribot and Peluso 2003; Newell 2006) dovetail with systemic inequalities that have been present since gradual welfare retrenchment in Europe in the 1980s, which has only been exacerbated since the Great Recession in 2008. In East Africa, and Kenya specifically, the legacy of structural adjustment has shaped housing and labor access for the extant poor and, thus, has affected refugee life for almost three decades.

While the Right seeks to prevent refugees from entering regions and states through border securitization and jingoistic rhetoric, the mainstream perception of liberals such as Justin Trudeau and Angela Merkel is that these types of governments and leaders welcome refugees with open arms. However, most asylum cases in the EU have been rejected—in 2021, only some 34 percent of claims were accepted on the first instance.[11] Even when people are accepted, the lack of available welfare in terms of housing and employment leads many refugees to some form of poverty. These policies appear to appease both the political Left and Right—they allow only a few select refugees to enter, and these refugees fall outside the purview of state responsibility. Refugee acceptance thus exists in the realm of appearance, but the materiality of survival is avoided. This is because the refugee represents a particular fantasy in capitalism where these groups are passive recipients of aid, apolitical, and extant only in distant geographical locations. They are forgotten and abandoned, but urban social realities of refugee relocation in both Paris and Nairobi challenge these fantasy-driven conceptions. In recent times, refugees have posed a threat to the nation, hence divergent responses from the political Left and Right.

I take inspiration from such dialecticians as Louis Althusser, Stuart Hall, Slavoj Žižek, and Jodi Dean in understanding refugee governance at the level of ideology, which is always inseparable from capitalism. Ideology serves to smooth over inequalities and inherent violence in capitalism by gaining consent from workers. In contending with various processes such as detention, deportation, surveillance, and survival, I place refugee governance in the intertwined politics of race and class. The fantasies of refugee governance are tied to the material and lived conditions of relocation from Kenya's refugee camps to the streets of Paris. Refugees do not fit into current logics of capital accumulation, and the rhetoric from Prime Minister Valls and Kenyan government officials indicates that refugees are considered unaffordable. At the same time, refugees do relocate and they do survive, and in doing so they exist at the fringes of urban capitalism—a population of greater marginality than the extant poor.

The book thus contributes to emerging debates in migration studies (Rajaram 2017; Morris 2021; Bhagat 2022) that are embedded in critical political economy. In so doing, I seek to deepen debates surrounding Marx's relative surplus population by marrying these conceptions with theories of racial capitalism, abandonment, and social reproduction—the key topic of inquiry in chapter 3. Here, people such as Gargi Bhattacharyya, Susanne Soederberg, Ruthie Gilmore, and Robbie Shilliam point us to a retheorization of capitalism that takes seriously the impacts of social difference and its various exclusions. In terms of its contributions to the "real world," this book emphasizes that policies surrounding refugee governance are not removed from political and economic circumstances and that the key policies that manage refugee survival are based on fantasies that unite the political Right and Left. In their neutral guise, these policies appear divorced from the historical circumstances that drive urban inequality in major cities of refugee relocation. By placing refugee governance and survival in capitalism, this book provides a wider commentary on social life at the edge. In so doing, I hope to shed light on forms of structural, epistemic, and everyday violence and the ways in which survival is both constrained choice and an infinite number of radical acts performed by those who are forgotten in global capitalism.

To answer the two leading questions and summarize the key contentions of this book, I argue that refugees emerge as fantasy subjects in contemporary capitalism. An examination of their lived realities reveals various features of organized abandonment and survival in both exclusion and acceptance. Refugees must thus be understood as a population beyond surplus labor power as theorized by Marx, because their survival is irrelevant to nation-states. Regardless of the fact that refugees represent a population of experimentation, inclusion, and exclusion, the extant logics of austerity, accumulation, and race thinking structure refugee survival. The refugee fantasy is rooted in ideological ambivalence. It operates for both the political Left and Right, where the former governs through rights and the latter through racism and exclusion.

Racial Capitalism and Surplus Populations

Following Robin D. G. Kelley's foreword in *Black Marxism*, where "capitalism and racism, in other words did not break from the old order but rather evolved from it to produce a modern world system of 'racial capitalism' dependent on slavery, violence, imperialism, and genocide" (Robinson 1983, xiii), I explore refugee governance as a set of violent processes underpinned by the systemic brutalities of always-racialized capitalism. What is now known as the migration crisis is reflective of the racism that has always lurked insidiously behind the liberal veneer of equal opportunity and humanitarianism. Refugees survive in between the political fissures of the alt-Right and a seemingly gentler and accepting liberalism. We do not have to look too far to see these contradictions in play. Lest we forget, Democrats (rightfully) chastised Republicans for draconian antimigrant rhetoric and policies, only to have Vice President Kamala Harris tell Guatemalan migrants, "Do not come. Do not come. The United States will continue to enforce our laws and secure our borders. . . . If you come to our border you will be turned back."[12] The contemporary context of Ukranian refugee acceptance and fast-tracking in Canada along with the closure of the Roxham Road crossing is further illustrative of racial bias in refugee acceptance. In short, Canada's acceptance of Ukranian refugees (a resoundingly good policy) is occurring at the same time that both Canada and the US (led by alleged champions of refugees Justin Trudeau and Joe Biden) are making it illegal for asylum seekers to cross from either side of Roxham Road—a move that refugee rights' groups are calling a violation of human rights. Instances of border closing and increased migrant surveillance are happening the world over and thus, I contend that refugees are racialized subjects that represent divergent yet contemporaneous fantasies for the political Right and liberal Left, and I develop this through the first key theoretical thrust of this book—refugee governance as fantasy.

Refugees are simultaneously portrayed by the media, policymakers, and governments as destabilizing agents referred to metaphorically as disastrous circumstances such as floods and swarms, among thinly veiled racial references of barbarism. On the flip side, refugees are potential sources of labor and present opportunities for states to display benevolence in line with liberal premises of freedom and human rights. Both xenophobia and passive humanitarianism mask the social realities of shelter and labor insecurity in cities such as Paris and Nairobi. The fantasy is a central ambivalent logic of refugee governance—a Janus-faced regime that justifies the acceptance of some refugees while committing many more to deportation and death. Refugee governance rests on the profitability of refugees in both real and abstract terms. They face disciplinary pressures to become productive members of their societies of relocation, joining those who already struggle to find formal employment. In effect, these sorts of disciplinary pressures only serve to obfuscate the lack of welfare support for the preexisting poor, let alone refugees.

To deepen this theorization of the fantasy in relation to survival, I highlight a supporting theoretical concept—disposability. I ground this concept not only in Marx's relative surplus population but also in Melissa Wright's (2013) framing of disposable bodies as unwanted, used, and outside the purview of state welfare. Disposability captures the potentiality of labor (and entrepreneurship) where refugees could be a useful stock of low-wage work or consumers in future generations. The potential for refugees to turn themselves into so-called productive citizens is a disciplinary force that parallels the fantasy that surrounds refugees and works to place them outside of welfare responsibility. That is to say, if refugees do not find meaningful work or become entrepreneurs, they are rendered disposable. In turn, refugees are blamed for their inability to survive, and these logics are motivated by the fantasy of the productive refugee despite the lack of available long-term shelter or formal employment in Paris and Nairobi.

Race and capital dovetail with refugee survival in variegated ways. To survive, refugees must engage with some aspects of a wider capitalist society. They attempt to work. They need to engage in some form of rental relations. They attempt to start businesses. And they are treated as bodies requiring mass surveillance for the purposes of profit accumulation through various modes of surveillance and border securitization. The refugee is simultaneously a homogenous racial other and a disambiguated category where many other groups receive varied treatment according to preconceived racial attributes. For example, at the height of the Syrian mass displacement, these refugees received the highest rate of acceptance in Europe, whereas refugees from Africa are still framed as opportunistic or irregular economic migrants. Often the country of origin determines the authenticity of the asylum claim; however, the struggle for survival appears at various stages of relocation.

The social realities of relocation are most evident on the urban scale as 60 percent of the world's twenty-six million refugees live in urban areas.[13] Despite the increasing presence of refugees in urban environments, scholarly and policy literature continues to emphasize the camp while ignoring emerging issues such as homelessness and cyclical urban displacement. While debates of abandonment—the framing of certain racialized groups as indifferent to global capital existing in abandoned spaces (Povinelli 2011)—have some resonance as they pertain to the treatment individuals receive in refugee camps, I go further to show how camps, border sites of detention, and cities are interlinked.

Refugee survival occurs in multiple spaces and on multiple scales and is defined as the netted practices of states, NGOs, private actors, and various social services (see also Mitchell and Heynen 2009). For example, refugees in Kenya—who do not have adequate welfare support—turn to credit to pay for daily necessities. Credit is offered by institutions such as the Mastercard Foundation and Kiva and fintech companies such as Vodafone-backed M-PESA. Refugees are managed by international organizations, policed by national-level government, and live in informal settlements, where they face xenophobic violence.

While refugees are forced into social relations of debt and housing insecurity, their ability to make ends meet points to the inherent resistance necessitated in an understanding of survival—an active and lived response to systemic and everyday pressures of life in urban capitalism. For example, the Paris case illustrates the disciplinary force of refugee labor in the context of urban austerity and the diminishing capabilities of the welfare state. In Nairobi, refugees disciplined through financial inclusion/exclusion are also illegal subjects outside of camp spaces. In both cases, refugees are among the most marginalized people in society and are included at the fringes of urban life, in piecemeal ways, as they struggle to survive.

Setting the Stage

Survival is embedded in fantasy in three important ways: First, neither the political Left/Right nor the pro-refugee/antirefugee discourses address the material necessities of refugees upon relocation. Second, refugee survival hinges on their potential as workers or consumers, but the lack of available and long-term secure employment gives this notion an illusory or phantasmal quality. The desire to put refugees to work is mismatched with the actual realities of production on the ground, where issues like language training, work and housing availability, and racial discrimination are considered. Third, refugees represent divergent utility in rejection and acceptance for states. Alt-Right populists scapegoat refugees to bolster ahistorical and homogenous cultural nationhood prevalent in both Kenya and France, as well as Europe and East Africa more widely. Simultaneously, many states also view refugee acceptance as a humanitarian responsibility but ultimately the multiscalar nature of refugee survival points to the futility of these discourses of acceptability that are not grounded in policies that secure work, shelter, and political belonging. In short, refugee acceptance in the realm of humanitarianism does ideological work. Some refugees are seen as deserving of residency and status, but many more are placed in detention or perish en route to refuge.

To understand refugee governance and survival, I look at two cities—Paris and Nairobi—that are hotspots of refugee hosting in the European Union and East Africa, respectively. There are numerous hosting hotspots around the world, but these two cities are emblematic of the important themes that contextualize this book: race, exclusion, and the tensions between liberals and a nationalist Right. Though this is not a comparative study, placing these two cases in conversation shows how a country with a robust welfare system like France still fails refugees. Kenya is the opposite, with little to no welfare support for refugees in urban settings, and yet informal networks of survival emerge as both a useful avenue for kinship and an expression of social exclusion and violence.

My fieldwork in Paris confirmed that many undocumented or so-called irregular migrants turned to France and Paris to find social housing and other welfare assistance. Germany and France receive a disproportionate number of asylum claims, and France sees about a 10 percent increase in the number of refugees each year; the number of refugees in the country is estimated at five hundred thousand—the majority of which head to Paris at some point in their journey.[14] Kenya has managed displacement since the early 1990s, with the influx of refugees from Somalia leading to the setup of the Dadaab and Kakuma camps. Many refugees have lived in these settlements for three decades, and with ongoing closures, many of the residents are choosing to try their luck in Nairobi. Estimates of urban refugees in Nairobi are inaccurate, but even the modest approximation of eighty-one thousand makes Nairobi a hotspot.

While I flesh out the justification for these cases in more detail in chapter 1, here I want to highlight the crosscutting tensions of race, antimigrant sentiment, and the variegated struggles for political belonging, shelter, and labor in both cases. The book is situated within dynamic migration events—long-standing and chronic displacement in the Horn of Africa and the more recent European migration event commonly referred to as the European migration crisis (Bhagat and Soederberg 2019). These two cases vary in terms of colonial history, policies of welfare retrenchment/structural adjustment, and the treatment of racialized people. In placing these cases in conversation, I seek to show the similarities of refugee governance in these disparate cities.

Fieldwork for this book took place over twenty-four months in 2017–2018 in the two respective cities of Paris and Nairobi. I conducted eighty formal interviews but also had countless conversations with NGO workers, consultants from think tanks and international organizations, charity workers, private sector actors, and refugees. I also interviewed various government officials at multiple levels and conducted participant observation with some of these organizations. Fieldwork was necessary not only to understand the thus far unexplored urban contexts of refugee survival but also to find out how the global refugee regime functions. Paris and Nairobi are undoubtedly different, but fantasies surrounding refugees and the resultant policies have transnational salience. The empirical contribution of this book seeks to unearth the various dimensions of refugee life under capitalism and, at least to my knowledge, differentiates this work from other projects.

Instead of a direct comparison based on conventional approaches rooted in causality, I follow Salter (2013) in aims for this type of post-positivist work to center itself for the purposes of legibility. I am thus less interested in most-similar/most-different approaches because we already know that Paris and Nairobi are vastly disparate spaces. What intrigues me and thus forms the methodological thrust of this book is convergence amid variegation. Here, Squire's (2017) work on migration governance in the United States and Europe buttresses the work of critical geographers like Hart (2018), who shows us the methodological utility of a relational comparison that brings together processes of similarity and difference across a varied geographical terrain. I hope to add to these methodological conceptions by placing the global North and the global South in conversation as the convergences between seemingly disparate spaces pertains to refugee governance in contemporary capitalism.

I organize the remaining eight chapters of this book as follows: chapter 1 provides the contextual support, engages with extant literature in migration studies, and provides definitional foreground particularly surrounding refugee governance in this current neoliberal moment. Chapter 2 presents the first theoretical prong—what I am calling fantasy—by contending with Marxist theories of the state, neoliberal statecraft, and the utility of ideology through psychoanalytical critiques of capitalism. Chapter 3 adds to the theoretical conception found in the previous chapter by contending with disposability and engaging with debates in Marx's surplus population and raced labor. I assert that the refugee experience mirrors queer conceptions of liminality, thereby highlighting refugees as quintessential queer subjects.

Chapter 4 deals with encampment, detention, and casting out at the frontiers of Europe. Here I place the current migration event in historical context and also provide an analysis of the legal infrastructure that governs EU migration. I emphasize the irrationality and incompatibility of right-wing xenophobia and left-wing humanitarianism, especially as they relate to material resources of survival in the EU-27, and focus on bordering and ongoing displacement that further casts refugees as disposable people.

Chapter 5 links refugee governance in the EU to issues of survival on the streets of Paris. In mirroring the preceding chapter, I provide a historical background of Paris's disdain for the poor before moving on to the French particularities of neoliberalism. I then draw on my fieldwork in Paris to illuminate issues of shelter, income, and belonging that refugees face daily. At the same time, I emphasize forced displacement as an ongoing process—one that refugees do not escape by arriving in a major urban center such as Paris. High rents, unemployment, and lack of resources at the city level intensify the struggle for survival upon relocation.

While chapters 4 and 5 focus on Europe, chapter 6 centers on Kenya and its hosting of refugees for close to thirty years. The chapter is concerned with the ways that refugees are increasingly seen as a burden as media attention has pivoted to Europe and international aid money has dried up. In turn, some refugees are removed from Kenya's camps and returned to Somalia. Meanwhile, neoliberal policies have shifted from welfare in encampment to integration, thereby opening up camps to private actors, microfinance agencies, and fintech-driven solutions for poverty alleviation. In mirroring EU policies, this chapter is similarly focused on detention, deportation, and surveillance.

In the penultimate chapter, I look at embodied disposability in Nairobi, where refugees are made de facto illegal people. I first provide an overview of the particularities of neoliberal restructuring in Kenya and Nairobi before moving to a discussion of shelter, labor, and political insecurity by asking, Who does a city belong to? In so doing, I examine housing precarity, ongoing displacement in Nairobi, and various strategies of survival that hinge on loans, and highlight the liminality of refugees who are simultaneously seen as security and economic threats while also being forced to hide as illegal and marginalized subjects in urban space.

I conclude the book by returning to key theoretical concepts such as fantasy, liminality, and disposability to draw connections between refugee survival governance in Paris and Nairobi.

THE LOGICS OF REFUGEE GOVERNANCE UNDER CAPITALISM

This book sits at the intersection of global political economy, urban geography, and refugee studies. I follow a multiscalar approach, in a methodological and practical sense, that pays attention to the transnational, national, and urban contexts of refugee governance and survival. Not only do I aim to link distant geographical spaces like refugee camps and border sites to Paris and Nairobi, but my field-based research includes interviews with and participant observation of actors who also operated at various sites and scales in the global political economy of migration.

It goes without saying that migration and refugee governance are big business. For example, a think piece that appears on the website of the Organisation for Economic Co-operation and Development is titled "Refugees Are Not a Burden but an Opportunity." Some of the opportunities of welcoming refugees are framed under dividends where refugees will perform underpaid and undervalued work, provide workplace diversity and skills, contribute to public finance, and also assist in overseas development through remittances.[1] On the exclusion side of the coin, migrant surveillance is providing a new market for technology companies assisting in border control through the use of drones and facial recognition technology.[2] The global is not "out there" in abstraction and legible only to economists and technocrats. Instead, and as feminist political economists such as V. Spike Peterson, Nancy Fraser, and Isabella Bakker remind us, the everyday and indeed the material politics of survival in spaces like the household (and the body) should be part of how we understand capitalism. This is because the refugee crisis is not a crisis at all. In fact, the mass movement of people is a phenomenon that is here to stay with upcoming social and climate insecurity worldwide. Displacement is only ticking up, and the word *crisis* seems to imply a temporary and shocking event. Europe's crisis is far from over, and I contend that this is a crisis of capitalism with particular emphasis on the urban scale, where the politics of survival are most visible. As Susanne Soederberg and I (Bhagat and Soederberg 2019) have argued, the refugee crisis is a trope because it obscures the fact that capitalism—by nature—is itself crisis prone. Situating refugees in global capitalism thus requires us to be attuned to the everyday issues of survival from country of origin to relocation.

While I discuss the role of the fantasy in refugee governance, it is important to note that the legal construction of a refugee continues to shift. The definition is not straightforward and is not applied universally. Indeed, the nation-state determines who is deemed a refugee. The 1951 Geneva Convention was limited to Europeans displaced by the Second World War, but this constraint was removed in 1967. As Fitzgerald and Arar highlight, "Refugee numbers are flawed and can be intentionally misleading. These numbers serve political purposes: to advocate for increased aid or influence admission policies. . . . The categorization of refugees is malleable both from above and from below. State labels are not necessarily transferable. The same person who is a 'refugee' in Kenya could be a 'guest' in Jordan, an 'asylum seeker' in Germany, a 'migrant worker' in the United Arab Emirates." (2018, 391). Arguably, the figure of the refugee is a legal construction based on international protocols and national state priorities and directives; however, I take a constructivist approach in understanding how refugees arrive as global actors from localized violence, conflict, or persecution. The concept of the fantasy that I discuss in the following chapter is thus tied to the political-economic undercurrents that characterize contemporary capitalism.

For now, I want to flag that refugee rights were denied to colonized subjects. The system of refugee governance as we know it—backed by international laws and legal protocols—could be read as a commitment by European and other Western nations toward other Europeans first and foremost. This is no longer unequivocally true; however, the rhetoric from Far Right politicians in the EU implicitly supporting Ukrainian refugee integration while banning African and Middle Eastern people indicates that a wider racial project might still be at play. Dark-skinned colonial subjects—as indicated by, say, the Windrush Scandal in the United Kingdom (UK)—continually threaten the coherency of the nation-state in ways that so-called Europeans do not. Refugee governance as it stands represents a racial hierarchy that overlays perceived economic benefit and/or detriment. Harsha Walia perhaps puts it best in *Border and Rule*: "Classifications such as 'migrant' or 'refugee' don't represent unified social groups so much as they symbolize *state-regulated* relations of governance and difference" (2021, 24).

Like everybody else, refugees need to survive outside the legal fantasy realm of humanitarianism, liberal prescriptions of acceptance, and possibilities of citizenship. These fantasies (the ideological backbone of chapter 2) are important, but for now it is important to dwell on the physical realm of survival—that is, the obvious but often ignored question of what refugees must do to get by when they arrive in major urban centers. For me, the city is also where the border, survival, and circuitous displacement play out. Refugees in Paris and Nairobi hold the stories of survival through encampment, detention, and various precarious forms of movement.

I frame refugee survival on three prongs: shelter, work, and political belonging. Shelter and work are interrelated aspects of survival, and most refugees are unable to find long-term housing or a stable job that pays for their daily necessities. In Nairobi, this has meant an overreliance on credit and other forms of informal lending. In Paris, this has meant cyclical street living and ongoing displacement. The third category, political belonging, is slightly more elusive to define. I propose political belonging instead of citizenship because often refugee status by means of formal documentation is not enough to secure the everyday dimensions of survival. Moreover, political belonging also points to the ways that states and societies of relocation treat refugees. For the most part, refugees in both France and Kenya are unwanted despite potentialities of labor and international appearances of acceptance. Not only do most displaced people face rejection as their claims are being adjudicated, but they also face violence and exclusion in their societies of relocation.

Neoliberalism and Refugee Governance

The neoliberal context of forced displacement is of central importance to this book for two reasons: First, neoliberalism undergirds the disciplinary logics of refugee governance, accumulation and austerity, which I unpack below. Second, neoliberalism provides the material and immaterial features of the refugee crisis that affect how refugees are perceived and how they are governed en masse. The recent history of global displacement has also taken place within the context of the Washington Consensus. This is true for the displacement of Afghanis, Somalis, Syrians, Iraqis, South Sudanese, Rohingyas, and now Ukrainians. While I am not arguing that global displacement is a consequence of neoliberalism, it is worth considerable attention that solutions for refugee assistance take place within a wider neoliberalized framework of development and global assistance.

I define neoliberalism as market-oriented governance and emphasize the undergirding logics of market-driven metrics that affect social reality on multiple scales. States, various domestic and international institutions, and many aspects of society have adopted neoliberal logics of governance that are attuned to metrics of profitability, productivity, and cost cutting even if they are public authorities. Refugee governance is no exception; even under liberal auspices of human rights, refugees are governed under premises of austerity and accumulation that are intertwined features of neoliberal-led development. For instance, the development of refugee camps in Kenya coincides with structural adjustment programs in the country. In Europe, more recently, increased deregulation and austere forms of management since the 2008 recession and the eurozone crisis have further affected European policies toward migrants. Not coincidentally, refugee crises—on the urban scale—emerge in contemporary (crisis-prone) capitalism because of extant issues in social housing, labor insecurity, and rampant xenophobia: parallels to the three prongs of refugee survival that I am interested in here.

Undoubtedly, neoliberalism is a contested term, and we have arguably entered an era of post-neoliberalism where market rule requires re-regulation and a return to some form of embeddedness with the state (Macdonald and Ruckert 2009; Peck, Theodore, and Brenner 2011; Alami and Dixon, 2020). The fallout from the 2008 Great Recession has revealed the role of state intervention in protecting the interests of capital, pointing to the relevance of the colloquialism "socialism for the rich." Regardless of these scholarly contestations, I do not abandon the term *neoliberalism*, because the neoliberal project has always involved an active contract between the state and private interests. While the balance continues to shift, we cannot forget Peck and Tickell's (2002) insights surrounding neoliberalism (or neoliberalization) as a process of both generalizable and specific features. Neoliberalism does not appear in the same form in every city the world over, but localized neoliberal projects are embedded in a wider network of neoliberal logics. That said, recent political discourses surrounding socialized medicine, the canceling of student debts, and living wages in the United States are evidence of shifts and cracks in the neoliberal hegemony; however, these movements have also paralleled intensified commitments to security-led dimensions of the state.

Perhaps what Bruff (2014) refers to as authoritarian neoliberalism best captures the types of state-led exclusionary strategies that refugees face. Refugees are increasingly governed by border security measures, the shutdown of camps, biometric surveillance technologies, detention, and ongoing deportation. Kenya's camps are continually under threat of being dismantled, and those refugees who flee to urban environments like Nairobi face police threat and relocation. Meanwhile, EU policies of keeping refugees away from its borders—what I call prevention in chapter 3—have resulted in detention in Libya and Turkey, which are funded to prevent refugees from entering the EU in the first place. When refugees do make it to major cities in Europe and East Africa, they are not met with a consistent or coherent welfare strategy but rather rely on a piecemeal and splotchy network of NGOs, charities, and local government agents. Shelter and work are particularly difficult to find because of extant homelessness and the legacies of structural adjustment in Paris and Nairobi, respectively. All this is to say that the neoliberal context has not disappeared—it assembles the political and economic landscape that refugees enter upon relocation.

What are the governing logics of neoliberalism? I contend that these can be captured in a dialectical tension between *desires* for accumulation and austerity. These in turn impede refugee survival. Accumulation, in the classical Marxist sense, is understood as the piling up of capital through the exploitation of workers. Workers provide surplus value, which, in turn, is the key logic that allows capitalism to persist, or what Harvey (1982) rightfully names as the crisis of overaccumulation. I go beyond the Marxist notion of capital accumulation tied to worker exploitation, simply because refugees are not always framed as workers—they are not always able to sell their labor power on the market unequivocally. As I discuss in chapter 3, refugees go beyond Marxist conceptions of the relative surplus population and are rendered disposable or abandoned in the global market of migrant workers.

Despite this, the logic of accumulation persists even when no formal work is available to refugees. Therefore, accumulation is understood in this book as a phantasmal logic in capitalism, where it operates as a disciplinary force. In its desire for efficiency and profit, capitalism is unable to absorb the very surpluses it produces. It is useful to think of accumulation as largely nonsensical, endless, and looping. As Dean, using Freud's conception of the drive, reminds us, "Lacking an end or a limit, capitalism pushes on, in a relentless, nonsensical circuit. . . . Capitalism cannot be reduced to our desire for it. Rather, capitalism persists as a system of practices in which we are caught" (2013, 139). Accumulation operates as an inescapable logic that provides the bedrock for refugee governance. It means that refugee assistance must be framed within extant logics of cost and benefit as opposed to human life. Refugees are accepted insofar that they can contribute to this overall illogical process of accumulation even though they may not find lucrative jobs or become entrepreneurs. The point of framing accumulation as a disciplinary logic, however, is to assert that it *does not* matter that refugees are workers; rather, it shows us that even humanitarian aims like refugee assistance are trapped in these compulsions and fantasies of accumulation.

Running concurrent to accumulation is austerity—a key policy agenda of neoliberalism if we keep in mind structural adjustment and welfare retrenchment. On the urban scale, which is relevant to refugee governance in Paris and Nairobi, austerity refers to the downward pressures of responsibility, debt, and deficit through budgetary constraints that flow from national to urban levels of government (Peck 2012). Austerity dovetails with neoliberalism as a complex, contradictory, and unevenly applied ideological and disciplinary force rooted in logics of welfare retrenchment (Roberts and Soederberg 2014). Accumulation and austerity are two sides of the same coin. They are compelling logics that fuel aims of economic growth while placing the burden of poverty on devolved forms of government and the poor themselves. I contend that states are less concerned with the actual profitability of refugees, but a focus on the costs of refugee management—within austerity governance—has buttressed racialized policies of exclusion in both France and Kenya. Accumulation and austerity characterize refugee governance within austerity neoliberalism.

For example, Italy's deputy prime minister Matteo Salvini went on record to tell five hundred thousand migrants to "pack your bags. . . . My interest is to work in order to reduce the number of people arriving and increase the number of deportations. This is not easy to do . . . but in the coming weeks we want to give new signals to cut costs and durations."[3] This statement exemplifies the dangerous combination of racism and austerity, where refugees are viewed as costly and unwanted. In contrast, German chancellor Angela Merkel's "We can do it!" campaign relies on a liberal Left approach centered on refugee acceptance in the face of international legal and humanitarian commitments. This is not a bad thing; in fact, a strong case can be made about the violence of borders and nation-states as constructs in and of themselves. However, what the liberal Left approach rooted in "rights"-based rhetoric fails to contend with is extant issues of social insecurity in countries and cities of relocation in the first place. Both the Paris and Nairobi cases show that refugees, regardless of whether they are meant to be in the city, struggle to access the material conditions of survival. This is not simply a result of a refugee crisis but is built into the system of deregulation, privatization, and welfare retrenchment that has made urban centers in particular prone to crises. As disciplinary logics, accumulation and austerity obfuscate the pressures of everyday survival and instead either prevent refugees from entering the country or ignore, police, and/or render them invisible if they do manage to arrive in urban centers. This tension leads me to my first prong of survival: political belonging.

Political Belonging

I use *political belonging* instead of *citizenship* to go beyond liberal rights discourses and fetishized elements of refugee governance like statehood and citizenship status. These are important artifacts that signify refugee life and rightful location; however, their overemphasis obfuscates the everyday challenges of refugee survival from camps to border sites and cities. The human rights perspective of refugee governance, where the refugee subject requires humanitarian assistance, stems from Hannah Arendt's *Origins of Totalitarianism* (1951 [1991]), where she argues, "We become aware of the existence of a right to have rights (and that means to live in a framework where one is judged by one's actions and opinions) and a right to belong to some kind of organised community, only when millions of people emerged who had lost and could not regain these rights because of a new political situation" ([1951] 1991, 296–297). Arendt calls this the "Right to have Rights," and not having this right—that is to say, not being identified as human—entails "the loss of the relevance of speech, and the loss of all human relationship . . . the loss of a community willing and able to guarantee any rights whatsoever" (297). Undoubtedly, these passages resonate with the current moment of global displacement, where the rights of many refugees—asylum, freedom from torture or degrading treatment, and life, liberty, and security, to name a few[4]—are violated at various stages of encampment and relocation.

In her essay *We Refugees*, Arendt provides a prescient warning for Europe when she writes, "The comity of European peoples went to pieces when, and because, it allowed its weakest member to be excluded and persecuted" ([1943] 2007, 297). Arendt warns about the framing and treatment of the refugee subject as less than human. In effect, denying refugees rights is a slippery slope to authoritarianism across the political spectrum. These perspectives on refugees as stateless people without rights are particularly relevant at the site of the refugee camp—a space previously framed as removed from society. While Arendt's work is conscious of the fact that rights do not always result in better living circumstances, I question whether these rights are futile in and of themselves, particularly if they are disconnected from wider issues of inequality in capitalism. Critics of Arendt's work point out her blind spot on the racial violence toward Black people in the United States in her conception of a post-totalitarian society, for example (Owens 2017), and a serious undertaking of this critique involves a recognition of capitalism's racist constitutions.

While Arendt points to the importance of human rights as a way to recognize who is considered part of the people and who is not, I am more concerned with the ways in which refugees and the marginalized find a way to access political belonging in the capitalist context. Thus, I pose a counterquestion: What difference does it make if you have arbitrary rights if you cannot survive? I ask this because the social reality of refugee survival I witnessed on the ground in Paris and Nairobi involves ongoing housing insecurity, lack of proper work, and, regardless of appropriate documentation, a marginalized position in French and Kenyan society. Importantly, I am not denying that sometimes citizenship and appropriate papers confer some privilege. I opt for the term *political belonging* as opposed to *citizenship* because it necessitates an acknowledgment of the material conditions of survival outside of prized (and perhaps fetishized) documentation and state-ordained statuses of legality.

In so doing, I follow insights from Anne McNevin (2013, 190), who powerfully asks, "How do we avoid conflating the failings and imperfections of the human rights regime with the limits of human rights struggles?" and thus describes irregular migration or the asylum regime in particular from the starting point of ambivalence. On the one hand, refugee claims based on human rights reify a system that includes border control, surveillance, and exclusion. On the other hand, the asylum claims also provide a counternarrative and dislodge the hegemonic power of the state, opening up avenues for alternative political positions and—importantly, for me—the possibility of survival (see also Mezzadra and Neilson 2012).

I also see the migration system as trapped in political ambivalence between liberals and antimigrant right-wingers on the level of the state, and between abandonment and survival at the level of the body. Here Brett Neilson's (2018) conception of migration as currency is helpful—indeed, many migrants can access only piecemeal forms of belonging if states can see capitalist valorization through the exploitation of migratory movement. In the EU and in Kenya, migrant acceptance and detention are tied to some form of monetary exchange and, as Neilson's work illustrates, the power of the capitalist system in structuring mobility.

I deepen the concept of political belonging in line with the lived realities of struggle and once again emphasize the urban as the place where the politics of ambivalence and the border are rendered visible. As David Harvey argues, "The right to the city is far more than the individual liberty to access urban resources: it is a right to change ourselves by changing the city. It is moreover a common rather than an individual right since the transformation inevitably depends upon the exercise of a collective power to reshape the processes of urbanization" (2008, 1). Through this, political belonging—which encompasses documentation and the trials of accessing citizenship—is married to shelter and labor-based survival. This analysis, rooted in the political economy of everyday life, adds depth to understanding refugee survival.

Even the refugee camp—read as an urban space, of which I believe Dadaab and Kakuma in Kenya easily qualify—can be understood beyond the confines of what Giorgio Agamben (1998) referred to as bare life. Agamben's concept dates back to ancient Greek concepts of *bios* (political life and the manner in which people live) and *zoe* (simply the biological fact of life).

Refugees have *zoe* (bare life), but the camp does not allow them to have *bios* (enjoy the quality of life being lived). They are thus abandoned people in a purgatory space. Refugees are undoubtedly racially maligned groups, but the contemporary refugee camp is not so disconnected from the material realities of everyday capitalism. The camp is not entirely a state of exception; in fact, it becomes a space of capitalist expression and experimentation. For example, the Kalobeyei settlement in Kenya, discussed in chapter 4, is a new avenue for financial inclusion through pilot programs by Mastercard and Western Union. In keeping the urban scale of analysis in mind, the refugee camp can be read for its definitive urban features—political economies of shelter, entrepreneurship, and finance grounded in the material reality of survival.

Importantly, even if international aid has dried up and the refugee camp continually faces threats of obliteration, the fact that queer refugees in Kakuma held a pride parade in 2018 is illustrative of the transformative potential of refugees in a space where their sexual and gender identities expose them to homo/transphobic violence.[5] The camp is no utopia for queer rights, but it is through the frameworks of rights that queer visibility and refugee resistance are rendered visible. The material and immaterial features of resistance, survival, and abandonment thus situate my reading of refugee life.

Shelter and Work

The lived realities of survival rest on shelter and work (or entrepreneurship) at various sites and scales of refuge. I emphasize shelter and work because scholarship on the survival of refugees in urban areas is scarce and the majority of scholarship focuses on documentation for urban refugees (Crisp, Morris, and Refstie 2012; cf. Grabska 2006; Kibreab 2003). Documents matter, and the scholarship importantly points to the successes and failures of various solutions to the now unavoidable urban refugee integration question. Documentation sometimes leads to better material circumstances, but the central issue is that many refugees in Paris and Nairobi are undocumented and need some form of shelter and work at various stages of the displacement. A preoccupation with documentation as a key to survival ignores the context of capitalism and refugee positionality therein. Understanding refugee survival in effect teaches us something more about how capitalism treats (and disposes of) the most marginal people, particularly in urban settings.

Shelter access is intimately tied to working-class exploitation and inequality in capitalism. Here, Friedrich Engels's *Housing Question* (1872) reminds us that sheltering working-class people without addressing the exploitative mode of production based on surplus-value extraction is futile. Centering housing in refugee governance necessitates an analysis of low-income rental housing as a commodity in capitalist society and a contested site of survival where 1.2 billion people live in rental accommodations worldwide (Soederberg 2018). In their important article, Aalbers and Christophers argue that "private rental markets are, for instance, usually the only segment that is accessible to the lion's share of newcomers to a housing market, including intra and international migrants, young people, ex-prisoners, and others" (2014, 382). Rental housing is thus one important prong of refugee survival in both Paris and Nairobi. The two cities provide empirical evidence for the ways in which refugees struggle for shelter security. The Paris case reveals the issues of welfare retrenchment and social housing, while in Nairobi refugees live in informal settlements. Soederberg (2018) emphasizes both primary and secondary forms of exploitation that link to Engels's key contention. Workers are exploited in the primary wage relation, but housing—particularly rental housing—offers a secondary source of exploitation with rising rental rates in many of the world's major urban centers. Refugees are of course unable to access long-term work and must still be able to afford exorbitant rents in cities like Paris and Nairobi.

Centering housing also poses a challenge to liberal conceptions of refugee acceptance. Since refugees are not formally workers who are immediately seen as warehouses of value, the various issues of street living, homelessness, and shelter insecurity are ignored under the premise of humanitarianism. As Engels reminds us, even giving people homes will not solve the crisis of shelter insecurity, because the former is rooted in the inequalities in the mode of production. Austerity politics not only makes it hard for the poor to access all sorts of government subsidies, but also maintains the fantasy of the refugee. There are those who deserve welfare and those who do not. Most refugees are rejected as inauthentic and, thus, undeserving of assistance. This is true even for those who make it to Paris or Nairobi, where they are unable to pay rent or find work.

The third interlinked prong of survival thus relates to work or income, where refugees, as racialized subjects, face marginality and exclusion in the two cities of interest in this book. As I will detail later, the Paris case shows us how refugees are framed as deviant migrants who take away valuable resources owed to Parisians. The rhetoric is embedded in the Far Right stance of people such as Marine Le Pen, who urged the closure of borders. These tendencies have not disappeared with the Emmanuel Macron presidency, where France's migration policies are caught between Far Right pushes for increased deportation and the actual need for France to incorporate cheap (racialized) migrant labor. Ambivalence is continually at play. In Nairobi, the refugee has posed a more chronic threat, related to the neoliberalization of the refugee camp through dismantling or the removal of aid. The neoliberal logic of accumulation appears as a disciplinary force in order to ensure compliant refugee subjects who should not (and cannot) rely on any form of state assistance in an era of permanent austerity. Work or entrepreneurialism reminds us of the dialectical logic of austerity and accumulation—you cannot have one without the other. I theorize about this type of survival in chapter 3 in relation to labor concepts of disposability and surplus.

Paris and Nairobi in Global Refugee Governance

So why Paris and why Nairobi? In simple terms, these cities are exceptionally different. Their colonial histories differ, the refugees of majority managed in both France and Kenya differ, and the time frames of the two refugee events, while overlapping, wax and wane in different decades. I stress here that this book is not a traditional comparative study. Instead, I employ crosscutting themes that unite these disparate cases. The political economies of survival surrounding belonging, shelter, and work are variegated; however, the overarching context of authoritarian neoliberalism persists in the EU and East Africa. The cities are further joined by societal hostility toward refugees despite various international and national protocols that favor some form of refugee acceptance. While I pay attention to the variegated experiences of neoliberal refugee governance in both cities (along with their respective states and regions), I am particularly interested in how these vastly different places converge.

France is second only to Germany in the number of refugees it receives—a number that has only increased since the ongoing closure of the so-called Calais refugee jungle[6] (don't miss the racialized discourse here!). France received a record one hundred thousand asylum requests in 2017 and had a rejection rate of 75.4 percent.[7] Undoubtedly, many of these refugees end up on the streets of Paris, and although the real number of refugees remains fuzzy, this might be linked to what Soederberg (2018) calls an erasure of vulnerable populations. Paris continues to attract many refugees from sub-Saharan Africa and the Middle East, and many of these people live on the streets. Regardless of the fact that France rejects more asylum claims than it accepts, many refugees are still awaiting the processing of their claims. Because they receive only minimal housing and other forms of social assistance, refugees often end up on the streets of Paris in informal housing. They face constant harassment by police and turn to informal types of work—symptomatic of system-wide shelter and labor insecurity in the EU.

Since 2006, homelessness in Paris has risen by 50 percent, and the number of forced evictions by 33 percent. The poor and working poor who cannot afford housing in the city are forced to relocate to *banlieues* (Abbe Pierre Foundation 2018, 4). Shelter and work are linked issues of survival and are undoubtedly raced and classed, where one-fifth of Paris's poor experience severe overcrowding (16).

Wacquant's *Urban Outcasts* (2008) provides a historical account of the development of the Parisian banlieues as working-class and racially heterogenous zones where 80 percent of people in the Parisian metropolitan area reside.[8] The banlieues are discursively constructed as derelict spaces of violence and social decay. For example, an article in the right-wing news outlet *National Review* titled "France's No-Go Zones: Assimilation-Resistant Muslims Are the Real Refugee Problem" describes how these spaces are portrayed outside of French identity—an antithesis to the modernity of Paris.[9] These spaces are seen to be impervious to French nationalism, thereby requiring intense surveillance matched with reduced welfare. Refugees, echoing Roy's (2017) notion of racial banishment, are subsequently banished from Paris "proper," as well as from the banlieues and from Île-de-France, pointing to their deeper racialized and marginalized positions as they struggle to survive. I return to the interconnections between refugees and the creation of banlieues in chapter 5, but for now I emphasize refugee survival as part and parcel of a long history of capitalist development that simultaneously requires the labor of the poor to physically build the city but also works to actively expel them (Harvey 2003). Paris is often colloquially referred to as the modern City of Light, and this image is incongruent with widespread street living and shelter insecurity. Refugees, framed as disposable people in chapter 3, are outside this need of labor. They exist on the fringe—invisibilized and erased.

The current refugee "crisis" in Paris cannot be divorced from the wider context of the EU and a historical approach to dealing with refugees in the first mass movement of people into western Europe during the breakdown of the former Yugoslavia, which produced 2.3 million refugees. Of these, around 1.8 million people sought asylum in such countries as Germany, Austria, France, and Sweden (World Refugee Survey 1994; Cohen 1995). As the high commissioner for refugees at the time, Sadoko Ogata, said, "The plight of the displaced is increasingly desperate . . . [and] the burden on the host countries is becoming unbearable."[10] The region responded through burden-shifting arrangements contingent on preventing the flow of migrants regardless of the ethnic cleansing of Croats and Muslims in the Yugoslavian area. Indeed, this historical moment reflected similar trends of xenophobia and showed the tendency of European states to return migrants to their countries of origin.

In the 1990s, Germany accepted the most refugees (three hundred thousand), followed by Austria (seventy-four thousand) and Sweden (fifty thousand), while France accepted a meager seven thousand (Barutciski 1994). Many Bosnians were treated as temporary guests in their host countries, and by 1998 most of them had been returned (Martinovic 2016). EU policies focused on border security and relaxed their conditions for temporary visas only upon international pressure. Even then, the borders were not entirely open for refugees from Bosnia-Herzegovina, resulting in further precarity for refugees in the 1991–1996 conflict-based expulsion (Barutciski 1994, 33). It is important to recall from this snapshot that the treatment of refugees was, and continues to be, underpinned by a shifting logic of race where some refugees are authentic and deserving while others are not. That many refugees were returned and were given only temporary residence in host countries emphasizes issues of access particularly to political belonging.

There are clear parallels between the management of refugees in the early 1990s and this current moment of increased migration. The number of migrants since January 2014 has led the EU to intensify its border security measures in an effort to limit the mobility of refugees and thus maintain the appearance of a fair allocation of refugees per member state. The EU gained the power to draw up new legislation for asylum seekers through the Treaty of Amsterdam (1999), thereby establishing the Common European Asylum System (CEAS), explored in more depth in chapter 4. This was followed by the Treaty of Lisbon (2009), which required the CEAS to have a uniform status of asylum and subsidiary protection, a common system of temporary protection, common procedures for the granting and withdrawing of uniform asylum or subsidiary status, standards concerning reception conditions, and the determination of how member states become responsible for asylum seekers. While I deepen this discussion—and the inherent tensions that emerge from the CEAS—it is important to note that everyday survival in Paris is linked to the national and regional scales of refugee governance in the EU. In this moment of heightened authoritarianism in neoliberalism—where racial exclusion, surveillance, and terrorist and security threat dovetail—racialized refugees in particular have many more barriers even before arriving in a city like Paris.

Unlike the EU, the East African Community (EAC) has witnessed chronic, gradual, and long-term refugee displacement. Kenya is the economic powerhouse of the EAC, and it is the center of migration management with many international organizations operating out of Nairobi. While I narrow the book's focus on refugee governance in the neoliberal era, it is important to note that Kenya only gained formal independence in 1963, so the colonial violence that haunts the region and produces the conditions for conflict, poverty, and, ultimately, more refugees cannot be avoided. Compared with the EU, the East African region is far less integrated, and refugees, while still facing intense surveillance, contend with piecemeal and contradictory governance policies that are highly variant depending on the country of relocation. This variance is hinged on the language of the African Union (AU) Convention on Refugees. While the legal document maps onto the Geneva Convention, Article 2(1) says, "Member States of the AU shall use their best endeavors consistent with their respective legislation to receive refugees and to secure the settlement of those refugees who, for well-founded reasons, are unable to return to their country of origin" (AU 1969).

Kenya, Uganda, Tanzania, and Rwanda are the refugee-accepting regions of the EAC, and each represents what a combined report by Samuel Hall and the African Centre for Migration and Society (2018) refers to as regional migration regimes. Uganda has the most progressive regulations in terms of refugee mobility as many refugees are given documentation and allowed to find employment in major urban centers such as Kampala. However, ongoing antihomosexuality legislation makes Uganda a refugee-producing nation, and, interestingly, many queer people claim asylum in Kenya despite its anti-LGBT laws. I explore this further in chapter 7, but it is important to note here that international human rights values are not adopted unequivocally and that there are tensions in regard to the degree of queer acceptability within an overarching context of heteronormativity.

Despite its antihomosexuality bill, Uganda is seen by the international community as a best-practice case because it allows refugees to formally integrate into Ugandan society. In contrast, Kenya, Tanzania, and Rwanda practice encampment. The UNHCR promoted encampment as the key strategy to deal with refugees in the EAC, particularly in the 1990s and 2000s, as aid could be organized and directed without much state interference if camps were set up outside major urban centers. It is only when the aid dries up, and UNHCR's attention is divided among sub-Saharan Africa, the Middle East, and Asia, that self-reliance and integration become important policy directives.[11]

At present, Uganda hosts the largest number of refugees (1.47 million), with Tanzania and Kenya hosting 350,000 and 415,000 refugees, respectively. Rwanda hosts the smallest number with 172,000; however, refugees from Uganda, Rwanda, and to a lesser extent Tanzania continue to seek entry to Kenya in search of job prospects (UNHCR 2018a). These numbers are, of course, somewhat unreliable as many urban refugees remain unaccounted for.

Refugee hosting is fraught with tensions concerning global aid. As Kairu (2018) highlights, the Ugandan state's exaggeration of refugee numbers in order to gain more international aid lines the pockets of government officials. Despite consistent levels of global aid, Tanzania has pulled out of the United Nations' comprehensive refugee response framework, citing a lack of available funds while continuing to hold refugees in its western province for nearly four decades. Similarly, Kenya continues to threaten the closure of Dadaab refugee camp in order to levy for more aid funds. Refugee life, particularly in camps, is disposable, and the logic for encampment as the predominant management strategy is based on the promise that the global community, along with the UNHCR, would bear all responsibility for camp management. In some cases, refugees are lucrative for stimulating revenue not only for the state but for multiple actors who have recently seen the camp as an untapped market.

Unlike the EU, which follows rigid guidelines, the EAC operates under loose premises such as the equal treatment of nationals of other partner states and the sharing of information across borders (Samuel Hall and African Centre for Migration and Society 2018). Despite being far less integrated, the EAC predominantly functions as a liberalized trade regime that prioritizes border security and economic growth. Like the EU, the EAC views refugees as economic threats that require surveillance. Refugees also exemplify the porous nature of borders in the EAC—a positive aspect as it pertains to economic growth and regional stability but an inherent contradiction as it also facilitates the movement of people in so-called unregulated (irregular) ways. It is difficult to guarantee freedom of movement to some people in the region when refugees are seen as a looming threat.

The Kenyan case, and Nairobi in particular, is an important site of inquiry in this moment of neoliberalism owing to the pressures of austerity that are threatening the closure of refugee camps. While Kenya still practices encampment, the government has done an about-face and has committed to providing refugees with work permits in an unprecedented pledge to integration. In turn, many more refugees are intermingling with the urban poor in Nairobi, necessitating a response from multiscalar actors in the city, country, and beyond. Exclusion of refugees and the ethnically heterogenous poor is evident in Kenya through the presence of mega informal settlements such as Kibera in Nairobi, paralleling the duality of the Paris banlieues in a stark way. Kenya has held half a million refugees in its Dadaab and Kakuma camps for close to three decades, and the UNHCR (2017a) estimates that sixty-seven thousand refugees live in Nairobi today owing to the ongoing dismantling of the Dadaab camp. Chronic displacement and refugee hosting coincide with the era of structural adjustment where Kenya was among the first countries in the world to adopt these measures. The legacy of structural adjustment has resulted in the lack of welfare resources, increased rental and home ownership prices, and wide-scale urban poverty. Refugees, particularly on the grounds of perceived racial and ethnic difference, were de facto illegal subjects. Although it is unclear whether this holds true with the new comprehensive refugee response framework in Kenya as of 2022, refugees still face undue police targeting and surveillance.

Only 5–10 percent of sub-Saharan Africa's urban population can afford even the cheapest type of formal housing. Kenya also has a housing shortage, and the World Bank suggests that the country is experiencing a housing deficit of two million units with 61 percent of urban households living in informal settlements. Other countries in the East African/Horn of Africa region have comparable numbers in informal settlements (e.g., Uganda at 63.5 percent, Tanzania at 65 percent, Rwanda at 68.3 percent, and Ethiopia at 79.1 percent). However, Kenya is the stablest and wealthiest economy in the region, and Nairobi ranks among the top five growing cities in Africa (the other cities are Lusaka, Lagos, Accra, and Cairo). Despite Nairobi's position as an economic powerhouse, it remains one of Africa's most unequal cities. Sixty percent of Nairobi's three million people—a reflection on the national scale—live in informal slum housing.[12]

In Nairobi, most refugees lack the legal permits to live outside camps (some groups are more persecuted than others), and so they have no choice but to occupy the same informal settlements as the already burgeoning poor in the city and compete with them for material resources. Informal settlements, then, become a site of both solidarity and communal sharing as well as spaces of intense racialized violence—the latter a feature of authoritarian neoliberalism. The Kenyan state owns 90 percent of the land in Kibera and other slums with private landlords owning and renting out the remaining 10 percent to locals and refugees alike.[13] Refugees, who reside in these areas illegally, are charged a premium for rent to dissuade the landlord from disclosing their status to the authorities. Nairobi, in contrast to Paris, does not have a sustainable affordable or social housing program, and the state's promise to build these units does not include refugees. In terms of both work and shelter, refugees must fend for themselves. To build homes, start businesses, and tend to their families in the most precarious spaces in the city, many look to microfinance and other forms of aid supplied by NGOs on a piecemeal basis—a topic I delve into in chapter 7.

In closing this chapter, I return to the key pillars that provide the architecture for this book: understanding refugee governance under capitalism requires a multiscalar approach where cities cannot be separated from their national and transnational contexts. In so doing, two dominant logics of austerity and accumulation structure neoliberal refugee governance. Refugees are often framed as people needing humanitarian attention, but even this sector is not cushioned from the governing logics that exclude refugees from the camp to the city. Despite this framing, refugees must portray some form of capitalist valuation in order to be treated justly. At the same time, the humanitarian regimes of asylum are disconnected from the three prongs of survival that affect refugees on the urban scale: shelter, work, and political belonging. These three prongs compose the messy social reality of relocation that is often ignored by the political Left and Right. They also point to the heart of the refugee crisis trope, which frames refugees as damaging to nation and culture while avoiding the fact that neoliberal-led development was what caused widespread social insecurity in the first place. Refugees overlay onto extant inequalities, and thus the fantasy of the refugee subject emerges.

THE FANTASY

Why the fantasy? Because the word contends with the imaginary and the improbable, and for people like Jacques Lacan, the imaginary order was akin to a fraud. The fantasy is the realm of surface appearances that are inherently deceptive (Bowie 1991). The fantasy denies the antagonisms of capitalism; it smooths over social ruptures to produce a wholeness (Dean 2011). The fantasy is ambivalent. It is oppositional and intertwined in racial capitalism, stripped away from (yet still tethered to) the material realities of survival and operating at the base instincts of society where economic and racial insecurities become encapsulated by those refugees who are seen to threaten the nation and way of being. I am struck by Herbert Marcuse's (1966) theorization of repression as a "basic ambivalence" in relation to competing images of dominance and liberation. Refugees encounter a "basic ambivalence," where they are simultaneously marked populations deserving humanitarian assistance while many more of them face exclusion, harm, and death. The refugee fantasy operates on two levels: On the one hand, the refugee is noble, benevolent, and deserving. On the other hand, the refugee is inherently destabilizing, a thief, and fraudulent.

The fantasy allows us to observe contradictions between domination and liberation that are brought together through the illogical nature of accumulation and austerity that undergirds refugee governance in capitalism, as discussed in chapter 1. Dean's (2013) Freudian explanation of capital accumulation as an inescapable compulsive and looping logic that underpins all forms of governance in neoliberalism provides useful foreground. Refugees are managed under a neoliberal neurosis (Wilson 2013) with profit and loss calculations that support authoritarian policies under the guise of humanitarianism. In brief, the key argument presented here ties the management of refugees to the material and ideological dimensions of capital and race. With this aim in mind, this theoretical conception of fantasy allows us to better understand the institutional apparatus of refugee governance in the EU and East Africa. This chapter and the next operate in tandem—they capture the systemic pressures and everyday lives of refugees. It goes without saying that refugees are global actors. This is evident in camps that may be geographically distant from major urban centers but are somehow increasingly penetrated by global financial actors, as I show in chapter 6. That refugees are often forcibly moved across borders to various spaces of detention or are left to survive through policy directions of self-reliance at the level of the city further illustrates the multiscalar nature of global displacement.

Fantasy and the Neoliberal State

My understanding of the capitalist state is rooted in the state debates from the Conference of Socialist Economists. While an overview of these contestations exceeds the purpose of this book, I am interested in one particular thread forwarded by Clarke (1991), which is the concept of capital in general. Capital in general foregrounds the disciplinary logics of neoliberalism—austerity and accumulation—and I hope to provide a rereading of this concept as it relates to ideology. In a nutshell, capital in general points to the overarching capitalist orientation of refugee management, especially in relation to the institutional apparatus of states and international organizations that manage so-called refugee crises. The conception of the capitalist state deployed here is not a functionalist one and instead relies on understanding the state as a regulative agency that manages the social relations and antagonisms of capitalism (Clarke 1983; Picciotto 1991). As Holloway (1994) suggests, the state appears as a form external to social relations, but it is fundamentally a relation between people.

In emphasizing the state *form*, then, we are returned to the realm of appearances and imaginations. Indeed, the state is imagined to be a legitimate and unquestioned authority, but it is, and has always been, continually challenged by a multitude of social antagonisms, including race and class. In this state form, the state exists to promote the reproduction of capitalist social relations, but it also conceals social cleavages (race and class for our purposes here). I twin capital in general with the logics of refugee governance insofar as to understand how seemingly noncapitalist state functions like refugee management and integration are still haunted by the logics of value extraction and labor valorization.

Speaking to capital in general, the state does not always *appear* to act in the interests of capital accumulation, often catering to the needs of workers and other social groups. However, as Harvey reminds us, "the capitalist state must, of necessity, support and enforce a system of law which embodies the concepts of private property, the individual, equality, freedom, and right which correspond to the social relations of exchange under capitalism" (2001, 274). What is evident from Harvey's conception of the capitalist state is that liberal fantasies of equality, freedom, and rights have always been endemic to the reproduction of the capitalist state. Just because capitalist states appear to favor the interests of refugees in legal terms does not mean that refugee life is valued—this is how the capitalist state maintains an image of benevolence, neutrality, authority, and fairness. The state decides who is an authentic refugee, who deserves justice, and who is allowed to relocate to cities like Paris and Nairobi.

This is why capital in general is a useful tool for us to understand refugee governance, because even when the state is appearing as a benevolent actor, the implicit aim—whether consciously or not—still reflects on the key aims of protecting, managing, and upholding the interests of capital above all. Thus, for the fantasy of the capitalist state to persist, some refugees must be accepted under liberal preoccupations with rights and freedoms insofar that the social relations that maintain capital accumulation remain unchallenged. The refugee crisis is only seen as a crisis because it challenges the various social contracts that have allowed neoliberal capitalism to persist unfettered in the face of housing- and labor-related crises in Europe and in East Africa.

Refugees are thus seen as a tipping point where extant issues of poverty can no longer be blamed on the individual failures of people. Accepting refugees en masse necessitates more robust commitments to welfare for all people, and this is inherently threatening to capital. Hence, so-called refugee crises have dovetailed with rising jingoism, antimigrant sentiment, and xenophobia under the fantasy that states simply find refugee welfare unaffordable. Even if some refugees are accepted, they are permanently noncitizens who consume resources and make up what Shilliam (2018) refers to as the undeserving poor. The refugee subject and refugee crises are thus fantasies that distract from extant issues of social insecurity and bifurcate working-class solidarity. Indeed, neither liberals nor the political Right is interested in challenging the systemic inequalities of capitalist accumulation. Instead, the former focuses on rights and the latter on jingoistic exclusion with austerity at the forefront of its political directives. This ambivalent fantasy in turn obfuscates the plight of refugees who do relocate while also avoiding actually existing crises in capitalism.

Capitalism by itself is not self-sufficient nor is it self-regulatory, and so the state is partly mandated to create and sustain conditions for accumulation to take place; the state is still separated from production, but it must ensure that production is sustained (Jessop 1990). This separation means that the interests of workers and the management of social insecurity are always part of the capitalist state project. Three overlapping state forms of neoliberalism are pertinent to this discussion and emerge as extensions of capital in general: workfare, debtfare, and prisonfare. In turn, these forms of the neoliberal state also influence policy directions of refugee governance. In identifying these, I aim to shed light on the ideological power of the capitalist state undergirded by neoliberalism's disciplinary logics: austerity and accumulation. The neoliberal social contract between worker and capital is motivated by fantasies of equality, individualism, and justice where people experience poverty only because they are unable to work hard and navigate beyond their social circumstances. Thus, it is not shocking that refugees face similar ideological pressures upon relocation.

Workfare states arise as an accumulation regime and a mode of social regulation under the impetus of putting the poor back to work. As Peck highlights, workfare is part political ideology, part moral crusade, and part of a new welfare retrenchment strategy and lies "at the emblematic centre of the contemporary attack on the principles and practices of the welfare state" (1998a, 133). Workfare becomes a popular strategy owing to the ideological elements surrounding labor productivity and the value of "hard work"—key dimensions of the neoliberal state apparatus that implicitly attack the poor.

Regarding refugees, an EU paper on labor market integration suggests that refugees would bring useful skills and boost economic growth in their new countries of relocation—an asset to the labor force.[1] Refugee integration into the workforce is reminiscent of workfarist models that emphasize a "no-frills, high-volume, low-cost means of enforcing work participation and work disciplines" (Peck 1998b, 535). Darrow (2015) tells a workfarist story of settlement organizations responsible for integrating refugees into the US labor market. Refugees face a high barrier to entry, and with limited resources for the organizations themselves, refugees are unable to find long-term and meaningful work. Workfare's persistence is due to ideological elements of hard work, self-reliance, and freedom that become entrenched in Thatcherism and Reaganism in neoliberalism's first wave.

Kenya's sudden turn toward refugee integration in 2022 echoes these workfarist directions. Refugees—formerly prevented from accessing work permits—can now integrate themselves in Nairobi, if they find meaningful employment. However, formal employment in general is difficult even for Kenya's citizens to attain, meaning that formal work for refugees is even more unlikely. Workfare buttresses self-reliance as a strategy of refugee integration.

Despite extant logics of refugee life being boiled down to their potential value as workers, it is important to flag that the racialization of refugees sometimes exists outside this economistic reasoning. For example, more than half the population of Hungary opposes refugee acceptance, and this has led to harsh legislation that criminalizes assisting asylum seekers or refugees (see World Economic Forum 2018). I focus on these contradictions later on, but it is worth highlighting that workfarism has produced lingering discipline around work and the resultant utility of refugee acceptance. Whether or not jobs are available, refugees must work, and the potential existence of this work, as the Paris case highlights, is an unquestioned ideological fantasy that masks the hard reality of diminished welfare resources.

Race is central to the emergence of workfare too, and so it is doubly unsurprising that these logics also apply to racialized and unwanted refugees. Lest we forget, Reagan's attack on the poor at the dawn of the neoliberal era included examples of people buying steaks with food stamps and invoked the image of Black women on welfare, thereby conjuring racist stereotypes of predominantly Black women taking advantage of the US welfare system. Workfarism rested and continues to exist on fantasies of undeserving poor people. These thinly veiled racial sentiments fueled the attack on welfare and also popularized welfare-to-work policies. As Prashad suggests, workfare's war on the poor only deepens racialized poverty, where "poverty remains, but the poor have been banished from state care" (2003, 150). In the name of disciplining labor, workfare cannibalized welfare. What remains is fantasy where refugees can allegedly escape poverty through education, language skills, job training, and hard work.

Prisonfare is another aspect of the neoliberal state hinged on disciplining racialized labor. Wacquant (2010) names prisonfare as the extension of the disciplinary penal state. Forced prison labor is justified under workfarist logics of preventing recidivism and providing on-site training; however, postprison unemployment for Black women, for example, sits at 43.6 percent, and recidivism rates coupled with unemployment for the general postprison populations hover around 37 percent in the United States.[2] As LeBaron and Roberts (2010) highlight, carceral institutions and unfreedom are the logics through which capitalism is sustained and reproduced. Various spaces of carcerality exist outside of formal prisons—namely, as spaces that foreclose the future of workers and commit them to lifelong violence. Refugee camps in Kenya or street living in Paris is no different as refugees exist on the margins of capital accumulation. While various appearances of freedom are rooted in humanitarian assistance, refugee survival is still contextualized by the auspices of capital in general.

Prisonfare and workfare are twinned modes of governance where penal logics map onto welfare services too. Prisonfare is relevant to refugees because of the obvious matter of detention at various sites and scales in both Europe and East Africa. Moreover, refugees are viewed with suspicion at all stages of their asylum journey and are constantly monitored and scrutinized for the authenticity of their asylum claims. Refugees are de facto illegal subjects, and this preexisting criminality places them in the circuitous nature of displacement that does not end upon arrival in either Paris or Nairobi. Refugees are also potentially useful sources of revenue in detention. This fact is mirrored by the profitability of US Immigration and Customs Enforcement (ICE) contracts with GEO Group and CoreCivic, which made a combined total of $985 million in 2017.[3] Undoubtedly, the detention business is lucrative, and the rollout of face-recognition and biometric software to further monitor refugees in the EU and East Africa illustrates the potential future profitability of refugees as an experimental group for surveillance technologies that can be adapted and adopted elsewhere.

As I explore in chapter 4, the EU's commitment to so-called development and migration initiatives depends on these logics of deportation and detention— prevention strategies to keep refugees outside of the EU. Refugees are framed as carceral subjects who face intense scrutiny at various checkpoints and border sites.

The third intertwined iteration of neoliberal state form occurs in the realm of finance, through what Soederberg (2014) calls the debtfare state. Tethering workfare and prisonfare together, credit-led accumulation emerged in the 1980s through the rollout of credit cards and other credit-based products to the working poor who, because of neoliberalization on multiple scales in various spaces in the global North and South, can no longer rely on the social safety nets provided by the welfare state (see also Peck and Tickell 2002). The extension of credit allows people to consume while making only minimum payments, thereby incurring higher interest fees and allowing credit issuers to generate a tremendous amount of revenue.

Debtfare works to legitimize, normalize, and depoliticize the immense profit earned from the extension of credit to the poor while also mediating tensions among low-wage work, welfare retrenchment, and social reproduction (Soederberg 2014). When people do not have access to social services, debtfare's most insidious feature becomes apparenty. Namely, people who cannot meet their day-to-day costs based on their own wages turn to credit (debt) instruments to survive. Debtfare thus rests on the disciplinary logic of credit, which is an extension of neoliberal ideologies of freedom and equality so long as the users of credit can pay back their debts (although it is more profitable for credit issuers if users are unable to do so). In the global South, debtfare's logic is supported by development agendas surrounding financial inclusion, particularly through microfinance loans that charge high interest rates to borrowers under the guise that access to credit will transform the poor into entrepreneurs. As Taylor (2012) points out, these types of financial instruments often serve the purpose of consumption smoothing: they manage the costs of everyday life, thereby becoming an ineffective tool for poverty alleviation and serving as a form of palliative microcredit—something that is quite apparent in Kenya too.

For refugee governance, debtfare supports the neoliberal notion of self-reliance in the face of inadequate welfare support, even in cases where refugees are given formal recognition in their states of relocation. Where the Paris case illustrates the disciplinary power of labor vis-à-vis workfarist strategies that are unsupported by the availability of viable employment, the Nairobi case shows the disciplinary power of credit through entrepreneurship. Access to credit is a dominant mode of refugee integration despite the lack of evidence that refugees can transform themselves into successful business owners. In line with debtfare as a normalized and ideologically supported form, the burden of survival is placed on refugees themselves in a sink-or-swim approach to governance. Refugees must successfully access and use credit despite being among the most marginalized people in their societies of relocation. In relation to shelter-based survival, debtfare highlights secondary forms of exploitation as it relates to rental housing—the primary form of housing tenure for refugees.

Taken together, these forms of the neoliberal state appear to solve extant crises in capitalism. They also further new social contracts between the poor and the interests of capital, augmenting and disciplining labor still under liberal conceptions of equality and justice. Work, incarceration, and credit all appear as just solutions in the realm of ideology. These forms mask the real violence of welfare retrenchment and appear as though they are divorced from logics of accumulation and austerity. Like the extant poor, refugees appear as fantasized subjects that need to be managed and regulated, and thus refugee governance takes on these forms of workfare, prisonfare, and debtfare in urban settings too.

Shining a light on forms of the neoliberal state illustrates how austerity governance—felt most palpably at the level of the city as it pertains to shelter and work—allows only a few deserving, authentic, and appropriate refugees into the nation-state. Meanwhile, those who do enter bump into all forms of neoliberal state regulation outside of welfare that are hinged on disciplining refugees as labor even if formal work is difficult to find. The ideological dimensions of workfare, prisonfare, and debtfare rigidify these forms. All three operate on the fantasy of the poor, who require some sort of discipline as a way to manage social insecurity in the face of welfare retrenchment. The fantasy of the refugee is important for the neoliberal state because successful refugees are those who put themselves to work and integrate into their country of relocation in similar fashion to model-minority immigration. At the same time, even with the overall constraints of austerity, it is important for modern liberal states to participate in the international community of humanitarian aid and assistance. This explains why some select refugees are accepted; however, even these groups are not met with robust care or welfare support at urban sites of relocation. This is entirely in line with Harvey's definition of the capitalist state as one that appears benevolent insofar that the interests of capital are protected. Since refugees are mostly redundant to the needs of capital, their acceptance exists in the realm of fantasy and contributes to the trope of the refugee crisis, which is hinged on inauthentic and undeserving groups attempting to access a nation they are not part of. That being said, questions pertaining to the fantasies that make up refugee governance can be answered more fully only while grasping the twinned operation of race and ideology.

Race and Ideology

Race powers the operant fantasy of the refugee subject amid rising xenophobia, concerns over job stealing, and (racially motivated) demographic change in both France and Kenya. In France, the candidacy of Marine Le Pen and even Emmanuel Macron's dog-whistle politics that spur Islamophobia are indicators of rising racial tensions and nationhood in France. In Kenya, Somalis in particular are chastised as terrorist threats to the nation. To understand how race dovetails with concerns about the nation and the refugee fantasy, I connect psychoanalytical theories of enjoyment with theories of racial capitalism. The nation, as a social relation in neoliberal capitalism, demarcates who belongs and who does not. Since welfare is constrained by neoliberal logics of accumulation and austerity, questions surrounding political belonging as it pertains to refugees are of particular importance. In the context of limited welfare, rampant homelessness, and poor access to meaningful work, the refugee subject creates existential dread. Importantly, race contributes to the refugee fantasy as a way to paint the displaced as violent, terror inducing, job stealing, and undeserving.

I start here with the Lacanian concept of enjoyment (*jouissance*),[4] which Dean (2006) defines as an ambiguous excess that sparks desire. It is an intense, excessive, pleasure-pain (xvi). A thorough examination of this concept and its ontological starting points goes beyond the scope of this book, but I raise it here to understand the allure of the nation and the creation of the refugee fantasy. Enjoyment is the illusive extra thing.[5] The thing that supports the various fantasies of neoliberalism. The thing that provides joy in duty (work). The thing that attaches society to the ideological fantasies that support, but are somewhat separate from, capitalism. Dean explains this through two vignettes: a cop giving a ticket to a civilian says, "Sorry about that extra twenty dollars I tacked onto your ticket, ma'am, but, well, it's the law"; a teacher returning a paper to a student says, "These comments I wrote on your paper may seem cruel, but, well, it's really for your own good" (xvi). In short, enjoyment is the perverse pleasure we get from participating in capitalism while perhaps even being aware of its inherent violence. For refugee reception officers in France, for example, rejecting asylum claims on the basis of legality provides a similar sense of enjoyment. The rejection is encouraged by national and international policies and supports neoliberal austerity politics—there is an inherent capitalist logic that this type of austerity-derived enjoyment speaks to.

So, what does it mean to "enjoy" the nation? In response to rising xenophobia as a result of mass migration, Žižek (1993) highlights the theft of enjoyment as a vehicle to explain racism. Enjoyment—the Thing/the stitched-together phantasmas of capitalism—holds the nation together. It fuses national identity where "this Nation-Thing is determined by a series of contradictory properties. It appears to us as 'our Thing' as something accessible only to us, as something 'they', (the others) cannot grasp; nonetheless it is something constantly menaced by 'them' . . . the only consistent answer [to the question of what the 'Thing' is really about] is that the Thing is present in that elusive entity called 'our way of life'" (201).

The theft of "the Thing," then, is the theft of enjoyment tied to a shifting field of cultural practices and myths that give rise to the nation and its associated nationalism. Refugees are framed as "them"—the unwanted and undeserving others—who steal away this enjoyment. However, the nation and the associated racism only arise in the presence of the menacing others—the enjoyment is in fact known only in the acts that disallow others from partaking in the enjoyment of the nation. In terms of racism, Žižek argues that "what we conceal by imputing to the Other the theft of enjoyment is the traumatic fact that *we never possessed what was allegedly stolen from us*" (1993, 203). The refugee is thus a fantasy-based construction that supports the capitalist nation-state. It goes without saying, then, that so-called refugee crises lead to widespread nationalism and racism. The refugee, as thief of enjoyment and threat to the nation, gives rise to rigidified conceptions of the nation itself. The nation exists mainly by demarcating who is not part of it. On the ground, it justifies the poor treatment of those refugees who struggle to access shelter and work because they are barred from political belonging.

As I mentioned earlier, the refugee crisis fuses two divergent fantasies through metalogics of neoliberalism—austerity and accumulation. For Žižek (2016), the dominant narratives of the crisis have the liberal Left outraged at the violence of the Mediterranean Sea Route, while anti-immigrant populists continue to claim that Black and Brown refugees should solve their own problems (as they threaten the European way of life; i.e., they take away enjoyment). Žižek's controversial argument is that "the greatest hypocrites are those who advocate for open borders: secretly, they know very well this will never happen, for it would trigger an instant populist revolt in Europe. They play the Beautiful Soul, which feels superior to the corrupted world while secretly participating in it: they need this corrupted world as the only terrain where they can exert their moral superiority" (17). While Žižek himself it seems is ambivalent to open borders, it is important to highlight how the political Right has been more successful in capturing the enjoyment of its base than the Left. In focusing on the politics that preserve the way of life (not necessarily the material dimensions of survival but a knee-jerk and emotional politics fueled by racism), the Right has won elections in Europe and North America on the basis of anti-immigrant sentiment. Although the framing of migrants as job stealers or as "others" who are incompatible with Western values is easily refuted by the Left, the rejections of these claims in fact continue to energize the Right. In the UK, for example, antimigrant sentiment has fueled Brexit and a thumping win for the Conservatives, who have won districts in Labour Party strongholds. Central to this right-wing shift is the protection of the nation amid the allure of future socioeconomic security by solving crises of immigration and race.

Žižek exposes an important nuance in humanitarian rhetoric that calls for open borders as anti-immigrant sentiment is prevalent and popular not only in the EU but also in refugee-hosting countries such as Kenya. In effect, accepting refugees without addressing extant issues in capitalism is a futile exercise. Left liberalism in the capitalist state allows people to enjoy the empty rhetoric and impossibility (fantasy) of open borders while rejecting many more refugees. It also facilitates strict policies that prevent refugees from accessing the state under the guise of evaluating the authenticity of asylum claims. If refugees are accepted, both the political Left and Right do not address the issues of survival—belonging, shelter, work—upon relocation. The liberal Left's position that refugee acceptance should take place only on humanitarian grounds (thereby ignoring capitalist social reality and real issues of access upon relocation) has been subsumed by the capitalist state. A rejected refugee claim is then justified on the basis of inauthenticity, further obfuscating the calculations of austerity and accumulation that underpin market-oriented governance. In effect, the rejection of certain asylum claimants who are deemed economic or opportunistic migrants is justified under the wider operational framework of humanitarianism. By ignoring capitalism—the cause of and solution to migration crises—many more refugee lives are endangered. Fundamentally, people seeking a better economic life and fleeing their various countries of origin are cast as illegals. Also ignored is the wider history of coloniality and capitalism that has played a part in producing global inequalities.

Missing from psychoanalytical critiques of capitalism and the nation through the theft of enjoyment is a deeper consideration of racial inequality from the position of the racialized and a more concerted effort to understand the twinned nature of race and capital. I am reminded of Homi Bhabha's foreword in Frantz Fanon's *Black Skin, White Masks*, particularly with reference to Europe's inability to contend with or contemplate Black history and, by extension, the experiences of "dispossession and dislocation." Pointing to the urgency of Fanon in contemporary time, Bhabha argues, "The 'social' is always an unresolved ensemble of antagonistic interlocutions between positions of power and poverty, knowledge and oppression, history and fantasy, surveillance and subversion" (Fanon [1952] 1986, xxv). From this, the capitalist state is not only "social all the way through," as those from the Conference of Socialist Economists remind us, but also a series of contradictions, oppressions, and fantasies. *Black Skin, White Masks* shows us how racialized people attempt, fail, and sometimes succeed in translating their humanity to those who oppress them. Alas, as racialized people we might approach but are never fully integrated into the sphere of whiteness, and this applies to the postcolony too, where the governing logics remain steeped in oppression and coloniality. With refugee governance in mind, the mask of humanitarianism allows for more violence in the name of dignity, liberty, and equality. The mask of refugee acceptance also avoids social realities of struggle. In turn, austerity and accumulation are justified reasons for refugee denial.

With further attention to masking, Bhabha quotes Lacan, who writes, "The being gives of himself, or receives from the other, something that is like a mask, a double, an envelope, a thrown-off skin, thrown off in order to cover the frame of a shield" (quoted in Fanon [1986] 1994, xxv). Masking is a two-way street; the white masks adopted by Black people for the purposes of communicating their humanity to those who oppress can be shed, repurposed, and unveiled to reveal a subversive resistance to colonization. Black Lives Matter protests reveal solidarities—not homogeneities—between the struggle of Black people and other marginalized groups on a global scale (Palestinians, Indigenous, even dark-skinned South Asians against the violence of colorism). Refugee survival entails both the brutalities of these lived experiences and the inherent radicalism of surviving, at all costs, within capitalism.

Barbara Fields and Cedric Robinson point to the various ideological idiosyncrasies that arise in the formation and continuation of capitalism. For example, Fields (1990) shows how slavery emerges in the context of US political discourses of liberty and freedom, thereby reifying that Black people are exceptions to these freedoms. In effect, liberalism produces a majority people that should have freedom and rights and undeserving others who are in fact treated as nonpeople. As discussed in this chapter, old adages of liberalism have not disappeared in neoliberalism. Constructions such as multiculturalism and diversity support the discourses of liberty and freedom and do ideological work while racialized others are still targeted by policies of austerity and welfare retrenchment. This point is reminiscent of Hage (2012), who argues that multiculturalism is a fantasy of white supremacy—a set of policies that allows liberal whites to enjoy tolerance and surface-level acceptance (and cultural consumption) of various "others" without entirely accepting them as part of the white settler state. On the other hand, Das Gupta and Iacovetta (2000) show us how right-wing critics of multiculturalism blame immigrants for "stealing away" their society. Both conceptions of society are true and reify one another. For example, Kenya portrays itself as an accepting and multiethnic nation, but Somalis are excluded owing to racializing discourses of violence and incongruence with Kenya's "Western" inclinations. To use a Žižek-style reversal, it is only in the exclusion of targeted groups that the liberal nation finds itself. The liberal nation needs an oppressed other to discipline and glorify while failing to address the material barriers to survival.

The implicit governing code of refugee management follows racist logics of exclusion. According to Hall, "Race is . . . the modality in which class is 'lived', the medium through which class relations are experienced" (1980, 341; see also Robinson 1983). The debate surrounding open borders, authenticity, and legal acceptance is disconnected from the fact that migrants, particularly those from the Middle East and sub-Saharan Africa, do not have access to the material features of survival that allow them to sustain themselves upon relocation. Speaking to Fanonian conceptions of masking, the neoliberal fantasy allows for both violence and acceptance insofar that the racialized other is able to translate themselves into the realm of acceptability—work, entrepreneurship, and integration outside welfare at the level of the city—or passive recipients of aid in distant spaces so they do not steal away enjoyment or threaten the nation. While the political Right undoubtedly denies migrants of their humanity, the political Left conceals its own racism toward refugees. The fantasy of the refugee subject is not congruent with social realities of exclusion—refugees do not always seamlessly adopt so-called liberal values and are far from passive and subservient. Liberal Left acceptance falls apart when refugees "act out" in various ways, such as failing to find work, failing to integrate by learning the language, or, in the worst-case scenarios, committing violence. It is in this denial, where refugees are disallowed to actually be human and falter, that liberal Left dehumanization takes place. Refugee acceptance is thus always tenuous and hinged on some aspect of neoliberal fantasy.

These neoliberal fantasies come undone when we pay attention to racism or what Gilmore calls "state-sanctioned and/or extra-legal production and exploitation of group differentiated vulnerabilities to premature death, in distinct yet densely interconnected political geographies" (2002, 261). In acknowledging that the political Right's refusal of refugees is based on an enjoyment derived from racism that preserves "the way of life," one must also make the liberal Left complicit in the system of racialized capitalism. Melamed (2015) echoes both Marx and Robinson in her suggestion that capital can only be capital through accumulation and that accumulation rests on social relations of inequality in arenas of production and finance through dispossession. Recalling Dean's (2013) conception of accumulation as being illogical yet inescapable is useful here, as capitalism rests on the piling up of raced bodies (see chapter 3), where refugees must be situated in a way that generates some type of value in capitalism. However, this aspect of refugee governance is masked by humanitarianism that seeks to paint a seamless and rosy picture. Instead, racism naturalizes and rigidifies class-based inequalities and maps onto capitalist state forms that extend and legitimize violence toward the working poor (Melamed 2002, 77). Humanitarian fantasies of refugee acceptance and benevolence are mirrored, for example, by policies that determine refugee authenticity. Even once accepted, refugees must attempt to survive by themselves and transform themselves into ideal citizens that match the fantasies of the liberal Left.

Race, ideology, and capital are intimately related. For instance, Hall argues that racism is a set of economic, political, and ideological practices where the racial state is supported by political and cultural legitimacy (1980, 338). Indeed, Robinson's (1983) main contention is that capitalism is racism and that racism predates but also maps onto the social relations of capitalism; therefore, taking global racism seriously as it pertains to the refugee crisis illustrates why refugees are treated the way they are. We simply cannot ignore the fact that refugees are racialized people who are removed from the sphere of whiteness and majority groups in nations of relocation.

Race, like capital, exists in the material and ideological realms too, and capitalism endures, if we take seriously the scholarship of racial capitalism, owing to practices of racialization. In fact, all three modes of the neoliberal state discussed earlier can be understood as elements of what Fields and Fields (2012) call racecraft. Racecraft refers to the construction of the racial state as it is tied to the material realities of production. However, the racial state is imagined and continually articulated through racial thinking, which, like ideology, need only present itself as true. Citing E. H. Lecky, Fields and Fields define racecraft as a thing that "presents itself to the mind and imagination as a vivid truth" (2012, 19). Moreover, the authors argue that racecraft (cf. discussions on the racial state in Omi and Winant 1994) is rooted in material histories of enslavement and production, which made possible the freedom of Europeans and, as a result, Left liberalism and its associated fantasies of freedom, democracy, and liberty.

Only through this colonial violence did the language around race emerge, and this language disguises class inequality while also delegating all sorts of social inequality to the realm of race relations (Fields and Fields, 2012, 111). Bhattacha-ryya (2018) similarly reminds us that capitalism is an expression of racecraft in the economic realm. Capitalist states never name themselves as racist, and yet, even with dominant liberal discourses of migrant acceptance and neoliberal self-reliance, we continue to see overt racial violence. The racial state operates in a way that ignores the existence of racial violence while enacting just the opposite. In neoliberalism, overt racism is demonized and disappeared, but in fact this is ideology at work—workfare, prisonfare, and debtfare show us how the ir-rational logics of accumulation and austerity continue to disproportionately af-fect racialized people.

Indeed, the central purpose of this chapter was to trace, ground, and deepen the theoretical foundation of fantasy, and doing this necessitates an attention to race because refugee governance is inherently a project of managing raced people. So, the fantasy of the refugee subject was first understood in relation to extant neoliberal state forms that have emerged to manage social insecurity in the face of welfare retrenchment. Workfare, prisonfare, and debtfare are driven by ideo-logical imaginaries of the poor, and these imaginaries play out materially and affect the survival of refugees upon relocation.

As LeBaron and Roberts (2010) remind us, the carceral logics of capitalism extend to many spaces outside the prison which I will show in empirical chap-ters throughout this book. The refugee fantasy has political utility and was thus also named as an ambivalent one where the political Right and Left ignore ma-terial conditions surrounding shelter, work, and political belonging while using the crisis as a trope for political ends. This was discussed through the psycho-analytical concept of enjoyment with particular reference to the nation and the theft of enjoyment. The refugee fantasy is the phantom figure that simultaneously threatens the nation while strengthening nationalist unity across the political spectrum. In conceiving the fantasy as both fraudulent and imaginary, we can see how the refugee subject emerges as a mask for extant inequalities in capital-ism. Central to this chapter, then, are the ways in which race supports often vi-olent fantasies and protects the enjoyment of nations. The refugee is the ultimate racialized subject and is particularly dangerous in the face of rising antimigrant sentiment and xenophobia in Europe and East Africa. The next chapter focuses on the embodied experiences of refugees and the ways in which they are ren-dered disposable in capitalism. Race, violence, and exclusion are an important part of how refugees are governed and how they survive upon relocation. Fan-tasy and disposability operate at once and are thus two sides of the same coin, similar to how accumulation and austerity contextualize neoliberal governance.

3

DISPOSABILITY

As mentioned in the previous chapter, I see my two theoretical concepts—fantasy and disposability—operate at the same time. This chapter aims to speak to the embodied experiences of refugees upon relocation at the urban scale. Conceptually, it also helps us understand how refugees become racialized subjects in global capitalism. Disposability is framed not only as a deepened form of Marx's relative surplus population but also in relation to the liminal positions that refugees occupy as they attempt to survive. While the concept of fantasy discussed in chapter 2 speaks to the systemic exclusions faced by refugees en masse, disposability aims to capture refugee survival at the fringes of urban capitalism. I understand disposability through what Ruth Wilson Gilmore[1] and David Harvey[2] (see also Bhagat 2023) refer to as organized abandonment. Refugees face various strategies of abandonment as they arrive and survive in various cities. Refugees are also abandoned through neoliberal strategies of integration that focus on either abject exclusion or self-reliance. In general, my conception of disposability refers to the struggles that refugees endure in their day-to-day survival—that is to say, ensuring their means of social reproduction.

While chapter 2 reflected on the first key question concerning the fantasies of refugee governance, here I shift the focus to the question of survival upon relocation that is still embedded in neoliberal governance. The materiality of survival is also inseparable from fantasies of relocation—the deep desires of freedom, socioeconomic sustenance, and community that are closed to many refugees. Although I was preoccupied with how states fantasize about idealized refugee subjects in chapter 2, it is also worth emphasizing that refugees see Paris and

Nairobi as opportunities for a better life. Thus, it is worth remembering that refugees are *forcibly* displaced—they are forced out of their homes and livelihoods owing to circumstances beyond their control, whether it be conflict, climate change, economic violence, or issues surrounding their sexuality or gender identity. The fantasies of relocation are in opposition to these causes of relocation, and they are disconnected from social realities of street living, homelessness, job insecurity, and an overall lack of political belonging in France and Kenya.

Following this tension between the fantasy and material social reality of relocation, I argue that refugees experience deeper marginality than do the extant poor in both Paris and Nairobi. Unlike those who might fit Marx's conception of the relative surplus population in both of these cities, refugees are either unabsorbed or imperfectly absorbed by capital. The valorization of refugee labor is tied much more closely to the logics (fantasies) of accumulation. Despite this, refugees face disciplinary pressures of work or entrepreneurship (self-reliant survival) that prevail under the auspices of accumulation and austerity. I think about disposability as a deeper surplus than the relative surplus population, namely because the relative surplus population—if we follow Marx—is tied to the general law of capital accumulation. Here, refugees are not tied to capital. There is no capital, just the fantasy of the productive and integrated refugee subject hinged on piecemeal work, poor welfare support, and abject racial exclusion. What we are left with is *logics* of accumulation. Indeed, refugees are so disposable to the needs of capital that their survival in cities like Paris and Nairobi is unrecorded, unaccounted for, and erased.

As I discuss in subsequent empirical chapters, many refugees in these cities end up in a fragmented landscape of welfare. In Paris, this meant difficulty in accessing shelters, finding work, and learning French and therefore facing circuitous forms of displacement to various rural areas in France or even outside the country entirely. It also meant dealing with police violence and state-facilitated displacement. Similar state-led violence occurs in Nairobi too, where refugees are illegal in the city (at least until recently) and they continue to face arbitrary harassment, arrest, and deportation. While the presence of NGOs and international organizations (IOs) is palpable, they are unable to target refugee livelihood in a meaningful way outside of microcredit loans and job training.

Many of these organizations are well meaning and made up of workers who are committed to assisting refugees; oftentimes some of these workers were refugees themselves. In both Paris and Nairobi, the organizations conduct important work, and without them, refugees would be worse off. These initiatives often create a sense of community and support and have resulted in unquantifiable benefits such as psychosocial support, community building, potential safety and violence prevention, and rights-based assistance including legal advice. That being said, NGOs and IOs exist as part of an overall neoliberal fabric *outside* of the state. The result is still a patchy landscape of assistance where many refugees are unable to access long-term and meaningful shelter and work. The embodied fantasy of the refugee subject results in refugees having to transform themselves into potentially useful bodies through either work or entrepreneurialism. In writing this, I do not wish to reiterate a structuralist position where refugees are accepted solely because of some loose association with the extraction of surplus value. Although a business case can be made with regard to refugee acceptance as future consumers and workers,[3] most would agree that refugees would have a marginal impact on overall GDP or other economic measures. Instead, I maintain that refugees are governed on the basis of their *potential*—that is to say, economic growth on one hand, and destabilization and perceived social unrest on the other—and thus, it is unsurprising that the tapestry of refugee assistance upon relocation is splotchy and incapable of ensuring the material dimensions of survival.

I suggest that disposability is a result of an ideological formation that allows refugees to take on the burden of survival for themselves under a wider development agenda of self-reliance. To echo Fanon, the refugee only approaches humanity by emphasizing the brutality of their condition. The ideal refugee subject sheds this past trauma and becomes a citizen in the country. This fantasized subject does not need welfare, does not need assistance, and is, above all, grateful to the benevolent nation-state that accepted them. The responsibility of refugee management, in a pragmatic sense, is passed along to NGOs in cities that have access to only piecemeal funding. Various training programs ultimately have little material use because they are not able to challenge systemic poverty—the inherent crises of capitalism surrounding shelter and work.

The Relative Surplus Population and Crisis-Prone Capitalism

Marx's conception of the relative surplus population is a crucial launching point in my framing of disposability. Disposability refers to an extra violence, a deeper form of surplus that refugees face in their cities/countries of relocation that differentiates them from the preexisting poor or even racialized legal migrants. While many refugees covet formal status, it does not always result in a better quality of life. The roundup of Somalis after the Westgate Mall attacks shows that formal status disappears in the face of an authoritarian crackdown. In this instance, Somali refugees and Kenyan Somalis who had lived in Eastleigh for decades were lumped together as one target-worthy population. Although some refugees are treated better than others—racialization and its perceptions are important here—refugees in general struggle to survive owing to material in-equalities that are based on their country of origin, relevant skills and educa-tion training, preexisting capital, experiences with trauma and violence, lack of kinship ties, and constant relocation. These factors undoubtedly hamper shelter and income access. Refugees are thus differentiated because of their inability to achieve a semblance of political belonging upon relocation.

In *Capital Volume I*, Marx describes the relative surplus population as a pop-ulation produced by capital accumulation where fewer workers are necessary to fulfill the needs of production because of efficiencies at, for example, the site of the factory. Marx writes, "A population of greater extent than suffices for the av-erage needs of the self-expansion of capital, and therefore a surplus population" ([1887] 1992, 435). The relative surplus population or reserve army of labor is necessary for accumulation and expands or contracts depending on the cycles and needs of production.

As Marx writes, "The same causes which develop the expansive power of cap-ital also develop the labour-power at its disposal . . . but the greater this reserve army in proportion to the active labour-army, the greater is the mass of a con-solidated surplus population, whose misery is in inverse ration to the amount of torture it has to undergo in the form of labour" ([1887] 1992, 798). This pas-sage illustrates the relationship between the relative surplus population and cap-italist accumulation. The unemployed masses are necessary for capitalists to control wages—until this population reaches a mass that sends the system into crisis. McIntyre hinges the relative surplus population to the general law of cap-ital accumulation, writing, "The same factors that lead to capital accumulation also cause the production of a surplus labour population" (2011, 1490). Essen-tially, the other elements of capital accumulation—the money form, extraction, and surplus value—are secondary to the production of surplus labor. Capital ac-cumulation *is* the production of the reserve army of labor.

Undoubtedly, this is an important feature of contemporary capitalism, but a purely Marxist conception of refugees as relative surplus populations avoids the social reality of refugee acceptance and rejection on ideological grounds. To avoid this reductionism, I keep returning to the psychoanalytical (but still ma-terialist) conceptions of the reserve army of labor to address why and how refu-gees face particular forms of violence as they travel from their country of origin to France and Kenya. Tomsic, in defining the perpetuation of the capitalist sys-tem, writes, "The only that [thing of importance] that counts is happiness of the system: production for the sake of production, which allows uninterrupted sat-isfaction of the demand for surplus value . . . exploitation appears as a conse-quence of error, corruption of market laws, or it does not appear at all. . . . In truth, exploitation is an expression of the inner contradiction of self-interest"

(2020, 54). Tomsic furthers this analysis in terms of the surplus population, where these people assume "the double role of potential source of wealth (exploitable reserve army of labour-force) and redundant material or systemic waste" (89). In this unsustainable and crisis-prone mode of production, the accumulation of wealth accompanies the accumulation of misery through the production of the relative surplus population (166).

For our conception of the relative surplus population, the psychoanalytical viewpoints show how liberal and neoliberal ideas of the market endure despite the fact that they provide little benefit to workers in the capitalist mode of production. As Tomsic rightly highlights, Marx already detected the elements of compulsion[4] in capitalism's continually repeated oscillation between the drive of accumulation and the drive of enjoyment (Tomsic 2020, 18, as appears in Marx's *Capital Volume I*). This is important in conceptualizing disposability because the inherent nature of capitalism is irrational and oppositional. The surplus population enriches capitalists and facilitates accumulation in the exploitation of not only labor power but also consumers and, in moments of austerity, readily available populations that act as stores of wage-depressed labor. Indeed, the relative surplus population is a great lever of capitalism for this reason.[5]

Marx nuances his conception of the surplus population by including portions of the reserve army of labor that cannot be folded into the workforce—the stagnant, the latent, and the constant, varieties of the relative surplus population. People who face hyperprecarity—that is to say, those who are unable to use their bodies for production—face deeper marginalization in the capitalist mode of production. Marx calls those who are framed as unemployable, vagrant, diseased, or homeless the lumpenproletariat, which is a categorical distinction from the industrial reserve army of labor. Some of this exclusion echoes the experience of refugees; but again, refugees do not fit neatly into this conception. Without a doubt, they are not a relative surplus population insofar that they are easily accessible and easily situated back into the business cycle in times of economic expansion. However, refugees are not among the first to become employed, even though many are able-bodied. What remains, then, is the ideological discipline of self-reliance—the neoliberal answer to refugee survival.

Racialization and the Relative Surplus Population

Adding to materialist debates of the relative surplus population (LeBaron and Roberts 2010; Yates 2011; Soederberg 2014; Bernards and Soederberg 2021), I also emphasize the position of race and racialization as it contributes to this notion of a deeper surplus and speaks to the embodied nature of disposability. Here, gender and sexuality accompany the intersectional terrain of exclusion and redundancy and further deepen the embodiment of disposability. For instance, Melissa Wright's (2013) fundamental work on disposable women frames working bodies as an extension of machines with arms and legs as moving parts that are useful only as long as they continue to facilitate the extraction of surplus value. For Wright, disposability ties exploited workers to their utility and eventual redundancy vis-à-vis Marx's conception of variable capital, where the worker's wage is compared with the surplus value he or she produces. In Wright's work, it is women who take on the position of excessive marginality, where "the value of a Mexican woman's labor power declines over time even as her labour provides value to the firm. . . . This deterioration produces its own kind of value as she furnishes a necessary flow of temporary labor. . . . The Mexican woman personifies waste-in-the-making, as the materials of her body gain shape through the discourses that explain how she is untrainable, unskillable, and always a temporary worker. Meanwhile, her antithesis—the masculine subject—emerges as the emblem of that other kind of variable capital whose value appreciates over time" (72–73).

Marx's oppositional conception of the relative surplus population is apparent in Wright's work, where it is the inherent disposability of Mexican women that makes them employable and then, after a set amount of time, renders them as bodies that have been wasted and used—a gendered and dehumanizing feature of the maquiladora production. Viewed in the framing of fantasy, Mexican women are useful not only as low-wage workers producing surplus value but also in their inevitable redundancy, thereby facilitating a fresh source of unused and unskilled women who can be exploited as speedier producers in the factory. While refugees are often not formally employed, the notion of bodies wasted by capitalism remains relevant to the critique of disposability expanded on here. In particular, Wright allows us to question which bodies are being wasted. The gendered and raced implications of her work further highlight the fact that marginality is intersectional.

Disposability is thus seen as a by-product of the capitalist mode of production where scholars such as Bauman (2004) and Yates (2011) refer to certain workers as wasted. For instance, Bauman argues that "the three camps of Dadaab . . . show no signs of imminent closure yet till this very day they do not appear on the map of the country. . . . The future inmates are stripped of every single element of their identities except one: that of stateless, placeless, functionless people. . . . Out of place, refugees are an obstacle and a trouble inside that place they are forgotten" (2004, 128–139).

As I write this, however, Dadaab's camps are constantly under threat of closing, and the population of Somalis in these camps has been halved precisely because particular refugees are racialized and presented as a threat to the state.

While it is conceivable that the world has in fact forgotten the refugees in Kenya as media attention has pivoted to the EU, hindsight necessitates that Bauman's claims require some more nuance. In actuality, the presence of refugees in Dadaab is continually used as a political tool for more aid money. The Government of Kenya along with the UNHCR has managed to shut down parts of Dadaab and repatriate some refugees despite the fact that refugees continue to arrive in Dadaab even as of 2023. By all accounts, life in the refugee camp is one of extreme marginality with rampant sexual and other forms of violence, hunger, and generational trauma; but this does not mean that the camp is not infiltrated by global actors in capitalism. Disposability and what Elizabeth Povinelli (2011) refers to as abandonment are evident in the refugee camp. Refugees are disposable because of their ambivalent relationship with the capitalist mode of production—tethered to the market but never fully included and governed by extant logics of work and entrepreneurialism without these opportunities *actually* being available (at least in a sustained fashion) in their lived reality.

Racial logics of migration governance are present in recent works theorizing migrant labor (Davis 2006; Arnold and Pickles 2011; Pratt et al. 2017). For instance, Merrill (2011) explores how migrant labor is dehumanized through the ideological and material features embedded in the neoliberal state. This dehumanization diminishes the social mobility of migrants, thereby placing them on the fringes of capitalist society through peripheral and sometimes unpaid or extremely low-paid work. Merrill's Italian case shows us how racial governance is ever shifting—Southern Italians that were racialized as categorically different from lighter-skinned Northerners now enjoy a higher social position with the influx of many African migrants, thereby positioning Blackness as inferior to an emerging homogenous and national Italian white identity (2011, 1543). Unsurprisingly, Matteo Salvini, Italy's deputy prime minister in 2019, gained populist support and also managed to push through a bill that fines migrant-carrying vessels that seek to dock on Italian shores.[6] Merrill argues that "racial thinking is a relatively autonomous social phenomenon that in Italy emerged with Italian colonial expansion in Africa and nation-state formation. Racial logic began to circumscribe social relationships when southern Italian and African populations were socially and scientifically classified with atavistic traits linked with criminal behaviour" (1543). Merrill's conception of racial thinking provides a crucial link between disposability and racialization that can be adapted to various socioeconomic contexts. While much of the scholarly work on racism focuses on whiteness in Western contexts, the treatment of refugees in Kenya shows us how racialization occurs in postcolonial nations as well. Whiteness—and the colonial logics that it accompanies—has imprinted on colonized societies, and racism does not always require the white oppressor to exist.

Race, work, and the logics of disposability have always been part and parcel of how the great lever of the relative surplus population has operated. I am reminded of Robinson's analysis of the Irish worker, an example that illustrates how race played a role in exclusion at the onset of the Industrial Revolution: "The Irish worker having descended from an inferior race, so his English employers believed, the cheap market value of his labour was but its most rational form . . . the negations resultant from capitalist modes of production, relations of production and ideology did not manifest themselves as an eradication of oppositions among the working classes. Instead, the dialectic of proletarianization disciplined the working classes to the importance of distinctions: between ethnic, and nationalities; between skilled and unskilled workers, and . . . between races" (1983, 40–42).

The violence endured by Irish workers is illustrative of the central role that race has played in the process of surplus value extraction. Indeed, Wolfe (2001) further reminds us that race—an incoherent and slippery category of analysis—was used as justification for death, enslavement, indentured servitude, and marginalization of various racialized people. Without a doubt, thinking around race has material impacts. In effect, racialized people facilitate capital accumulation through their labor while simultaneously being disciplined through intense violence (Singh 2017). As described in chapter 2, preventing the theft of enjoyment from the nation underpins a central logic of refugee governance hinged on exclusion. In terms of disposability, refugees are thus always marginal because they are no longer biocultural kin in their country of origin or in their various places of relocation.

In his framing of refugees, Rajaram (2017) applies Marx's understanding of the relative surplus population: "a population of greater extent than suffices for the average needs of the self-expansion of capital" (Marx [1887] 1992, 435). I agree with Rajaram's assertion that refugees are unable to valorize their labor power in the capitalist system, where laborers have nothing but their bodies to sell for survival (2017, 633). For Rajaram, capitalism creates racialized pauperism, where the front stage of the system (between free laborer and capitalist, where the former gives up their body power in exchange for a wage) and the backstage (where those who cannot valorize their labor are exploited as surplus populations) are in constant tension (628). In Rajaram's words, "The surplus is not simply excluded but included through their exclusion as cheaply exploitable and dispensable labour" (628). This reasoning not only is reminiscent of Wright's gendered disposability but also points out an inherent ambivalent tension in refugee governance. If refugees are meant to be value-generating laborers in capitalism, they can only occupy the backstage, where they are mostly unable to find long-term work and shelter. In effect, refugees are not considered a reliable workforce, particularly in the face of rampant xenophobia; however, they are included (through exclusion) in capitalism insofar as they provide that extra kick of surplus value extraction. They are disposable because they are a population outside the purview of state-led welfare but are a stagnant force that can be squeezed for just that extra level of accumulation.

Importantly, theorizing refugees as part of this racialized surplus population is still limited. Unlike the Irish worker, for instance, the refugee is still not fully considered a worker in the global political economy of migration. It is not entirely sufficient to say that refugees are part of the relative surplus population, because they extend beyond this to the realm of the unwanted and the undeserving and the rarely, if ever, fitting in.

In the backstage of capitalism, Bhattacharyya's (2018) notion of the edge comes to mind. Refugees are populations on the edge relative to the needs and logics of capital where waged, nonwaged, and hybrid workers occupy spaces of noncapitalism or almost-capitalism (9). This reflects what Sanyal's influential piece referred to as the capital-noncapital complex, where "bereft of any direct access to means of labour the dispossessed are left only with labour power but their exclusion from the space of commodity production does not allow them to turn their labour power into a commodity. They are condemned to the world of the excluded, the redundant, the dispensable, having nothing to lose, not even the chains of wage-slavery" (2007, 53). This space of redundancy is where I situate urban refugees in Paris and Nairobi as those who exist on the edges. Spaces of non- or almost-capitalism are features also rendered most visible at the urban scale. For instance, in my analysis of refugee loan programs in Kenya, I found that many female refugees were relying on people in their own community for small sums of money just to pay for food, water, and shelter. Many attempted to work, but in Nairobi this was nearly impossible. On the streets of Paris, refugees cycled through various forms of assistance. In my participant observation with one refugee clinic, a paralegal told a refugee to "try and get arrested so you can have somewhere to sleep."[7] When arrest, detention, and potential deportation is the solution to survival, refugees truly embody the edge. They are thus disposable to the needs of capital.

This disposability has a longer history in capitalism, as Shilliam (2018) reminds us in *Race and the Undeserving Poor*. Particularly with regard to welfare, Shilliam argues, "the distinction that renders some deserving of social security and welfare and others not is racialized so as to classify collectives in order to judge individuals" (171). The deserving/undeserving poor binary is grounded in histories of racialism and colonialism. For example, the enslaved were undeserving because they did not embody Anglo-Saxon virtues of industriousness, patriarchy, and the like. Freed Black laborers were undeserving because they could not rid themselves of the essence of slavery. In the era of the welfare state, and in echoing Robinson's claim that racialism always divided up the fantasies of class consciousness, white working-class people were always privileged over racialized workers. Refugees on the edge of capitalism face similar structural, epistemic, and institutional forms of violence where they do not belong and are not considered deserving of survival or even the ability to make up the basic relative surplus population. Refugees' lives are governed by the wider fantasies of the Left and Right, and their racialized positions make them undeserving of welfare and assistance in a system already disciplined by logics of austerity and accumulation.

The exceptions are few and far between. In France, Malian refugee Mamoudou Gassama, despite living illegally in the country, was granted honorary citizenship after he scaled a building to save a child. He was also lauded as a hero and presented with a medal by President Macron. Gassama transformed himself from undeserving to deserving refugee, but the fact remains that many Black Africans from former French colonies live in substandard housing without job security. As Seale writes, "Most Africans in France who are, as we say, '*sans papiers*' must be proud of Mamoudou Gassama but they must also feel excluded from his victory. They must wonder who is there to save them, if they don't save one of us first."[8] Disposability refers to the backstage, the undeserving, and the unabsorbable people of capitalism. Thus, the emphasis of survival is placed on the refugees themselves. Sometimes they must commit feats of heroism to be noticed, or to a lesser degree, start their own businesses and show that they too can become ideal citizens. This fantasy has limits as well, and for many the story is one of redundancy, ongoing displacement, and various forms of institutional and epistemic violence from country of origin to city of relocation.

Disposability as Liminality

By way of conclusion, I want to go even further beyond the material realm of the relative surplus population to emphasize the liminal position of the refugee subject. My aim is to queer the refugee experience and, in turn, point to the ways in which refugees can deepen our understanding of dis/belonging. Like all queer subjects, refugees are in a constant state of dis/belonging that extends beyond the analysis of the relative surplus population and its accompanied racial violence. Framing disposability, in the backstage of capitalism, as liminality requires taking Butler's (2004) claim about a critique of identity seriously. According to Butler, "More important than any presupposition about the plasticity of identity or indeed its retrograde status is queer theory's claim to the opposed to the unwanted legislation of identity" (7). This section thus responds to Oswin's (2008) call to arms of queer theory going beyond a critique of heteronormativity to truly become subjectless and destabilize understandings of what it means to be queer and the spaces in which all sorts of incongruent identities exist. As Smith notes, a subjectless critique strips away the insistence of a proper object or subject and thus allows for a wider field in which a queer analysis can point to all sorts of social violence (2010, 44).

While many queer theorists (especially in International Relations and human geography) trace back to Foucault's *History of Sexuality* (1976), I instead position a Lacanian reading of queerness in its application to refugees through *jouissance* (pleasure-pain) or enjoyment, which I discussed briefly in chapter 2. I do this because a focus on pleasure-pain situates both corporeal experiences of survival and the wider fantasies of the nation and society, who see their enjoyment being stolen away by unwanted others. Take, for instance, Tim Dean's analysis of the AIDS crisis and the naming of it as a gay disease that framed gay men as "plague-spreading sexual deviants, along with junkies and non-white immigrant groups" (2003, 246). The public health discourse at the time focused on preventing the spread of the disease to the general population, implying that there was a disposable population that *deserved* to die because they were responsible for the disease in the first place. Those excluded from the general population (i.e., the heterosexual population) included gay men but also those of various other sexual and gender identities, races, classes, and nationalities that, for lack of better words, committed the theft of enjoyment. I raise this because the queer experience is one of exclusion, and those who are queered are often misfits and blamed for extant issues in society—masking social realities of death and despair.

Whoever the demonized "other" is in a historical moment (e.g., the so-called savage Irish, AIDS-spreading gay men, terrorist Arabs, job-stealing Mexicans, Somali Islamists, or irregular/terrorist refugees) is a queer subject, and the violence they face points to the "subjective incompleteness" that somebody else is doing better than the general population (Dean 2003, 249). As Žižek ([1989] 2009) argues, other racial and ethnic groups are fantasized as being oppositional to the general society. Antisemites imagine that Jews have stolen their riches, white supremacists fantasize that the country is overrun by immigrants who steal their resources, and the same logic can be applied to LGBTQ people framed as those involved in excessive and indecent pleasure (due in part to the actual deaths from and public health failures of the AIDS crisis). Whoever the queer demonized group is, in fact, masks the existing social realities of inequality and crisis, and instead the general population sees a theft of their enjoyment by the "other" instead of the more existential threat to their own existence in contemporary capitalism.

Rereading *Refugees from Amerika: A Gay Manifesto*, by Carl Wittman, shows a literal connection between the diasporic identity of a refugee and the alienation of gay men. Wittman opens with "San Francisco is a refugee camp for homosexuals. We have fled here from every part of the nation, and like refugees elsewhere, we came not because it is so great here, but because it was so bad there."[9] Wesling provides a clear link between the refugee and the queer subject by arguing that "the nation, through structural arrangements of citizenship, marriage law, and immigration regulation, always and unconditionally privileges heterosexuality. . . . Queerness challenges not just the nation's familiar metaphor of belonging but disrupts national coherence itself" (2008, 33).

Bhabha's foreword once again points to the relevance of Fanon (who was often criticized for his take on homosexuality) as it pertains to many colonial others. Bhabha writes, "In occupying two places at once . . . the depersonalized, dislocated colonial subject can become an incalculable object, quite literally difficult to place" (Fanon [1986] 2011, xii). This quotation reflects not only on Fanon's colonial subject—partly in / partly out—but also on the refugee who in dislocation is rendered liminal and thus queer.

So, what exactly is queer about refugees? First, as the empirical sections will show, I do not wish to present my findings in this book as though they are blind to sexuality and sexual politics. While a queer approach to refugees is a viable one for the reasons listed above, my entry into the field in both Paris and Nairobi involved contact with LGBTQ refugee organizations. My initial foray into examining refugee survival in capitalism started with a project involving LGBTQ refugees in South Africa (Bhagat 2017, 2018). I am hoping this book will indeed speak to multiple dimensions of queer identity—what I name, in the most concise possible way, as incongruence with the general population. Second, in responding to queer theory as a subjectless critique, I parallel experiences of exclusion and violence in non-mutually exclusive refugee and LGBTQ people. This is because, regardless of variegated societal acceptance, the queer experience is largely distinguished by some form of othering. Refugees, too, even with the heroics of Mamoudou Gassama, always approach a limit (in the mathematical sense) to acceptance but ultimately struggle to find political belonging. Third, refugees are queer in a much simpler sense as they are forced away from their families and their homes, face various sorts of conflict that result in trauma, and are often removed from their kin. Even Engels in *The Origin of the Family, Private Property, and the State* ([1942] 2010), where he contends that the sexual division of labor is rooted in the capitalist mode of production, takes for granted the family unit—a unit that a queer analysis names as heteronormative and that refugees cannot easily access.

To borrow from Edelman (2004), I assert that refugees—as liminal subjects—have "no future" in their various sites of relocation. In Edelman's *No Future*, queerness is portrayed as oppositional to the image of the child, what he calls reproductive futurism or the ability of societies to reproduce and enact various forms of violence under the guise of protecting the nation's children and, in turn, the nation's future. Lauren Berlant's (1997, 1) argument that "a nation made for adult citizens has been replaced by one imagined for fetuses and children" is buttressed by Edelman, who suggests that while many LGBTQ people fight for various rights such as marriage, adoption, and military service, their fights are always undone by reproductive futurism. Not only are queer refugees undone by this desire for the nation to protect the children, but refugee life in general is propped up by the image of the child. Ultimately, the refugee as a host of single Brown and Black men, either in camps in various states in East Africa or on the streets of Paris and other major European cities, is denied a future.

Through Alan Kurdi—a Syrian child who drowned in the Mediterranean Sea—the image of the child took center stage in 2016 and in many ways symbolized the European refugee crisis. This image of the violence that children face drew mainstream media attention to the plight of refugees who were otherwise mere Black and Brown adults from violence-prone nations. Despite the fact that refugees are accepted in part because of the notion of "saving the children," many refugees, whether in acceptance or denial, have no material future, particularly in relation to their long-term survival through political belonging, shelter, or income. Beyond the material features of survival, refugees are imagined only as passive victims of aid in various frontier states and borderlands. They face an erasure upon relocation, where they are lumped with the rest of the relative surplus population despite facing unnamed and unaccounted-for violence.

As mentioned in chapter 2, it is ideologies embedded in neoliberalism that weave together various tensions in the governance of refugees, and I return to this concept briefly as it pertains to the subject. As Hennessy (2000) argues, the hidden kernel of capitalism is the basic inequality found in the wage relation between capitalist and worker. To resolve this tension, ideology emerges as a way to organize various social differences. She writes, "Ideology naturalizes differences (between men and women, whites and blacks, straight and gay, able and disabled, rich and poor, etc.) and so legitimizes human relations of exploitation and domination. . . . Ideology offers individuals an imaginary relationship to the material inequities they live, a relationship that has material consequences in that it shapes desires and actions" (19).

Refugees, in their existence between many spaces (nations, worlds), embody multiple fantasies as potential workers or passive victims of aid, or destabilizing terrorists, or even people taking away material resources from French and Kenyan people. Ideology, analyzed within the Marxist-psychoanalytical framing popularized by Althusser, allows refugees to occupy these types of static positions upon relocation. Queering refugees thus allows us to frame them as populations that go against the grain of the general population because of a variety of intersecting and affronting identities; this type of queering challenges their framing as part and parcel of the relative surplus population in scholarly debates too. Refugees experience a deep liminality because they are sometimes lumped together with other backstage actors in capitalism, but they often do not fit neatly into extant Marxist categories of wasted labor, lumpenproletariat, and so on. Refugees are recognized as their sheer size is posed as a threat to the stability of nation-states; but upon relocation, their struggles for material survival are disappeared. The threat of the refugee is permanent, but the urban scale of refugee survival is ignored—a key aspect of the refugee crisis trope.

Marx's relative surplus population provided a launchpad for my framing of disposability in this chapter. Along with processes of racialization, the framing of refugees as disposable populations in the backstage of capitalism or as the undeserving poor in various spaces of relocation points to the various inequalities in capitalism. Adding to this, the reading of refugees as queer subjects further theorizes disposability as a liminal experience in capitalism. Refugees are of many worlds but are also afforded no tangible future regardless of piecemeal humanitarianism or abject rejection. Despite this, the refugee experience illustrates a central aspect of queerness as critique—namely, their struggles for survival are inherently stories of resistance.

4

THE REFUGEE FANTASY AND THE
EUROPEAN FRONTIER

Europe has been portrayed as a region in perpetual crisis (eurozone, refugee, COVID-19, climate), and thus this chapter examines EU-wide governance strategies of dealing with the so-called crisis of refugees. When the detriments and contradictions of capital arrive at Europe's doorstep, the knee-jerk reaction of states and financial institutions is to use the terminology of a crisis as opposed to questioning what drives these perpetual crises in the first place. A crisis is an acute situation that can be solved by economists, politicians, and technocrats; however, global displacement is not caused by heightened tensions in geographically distant places but should actually be understood as a continuous feature of contemporary capitalism. I present the European case first, because Europe seems to be utterly ignorant of the fact that many countries in the global South are contending with chronic refugee management issues. Europe has dominated media discourse around global displacement, and I hope that by giving the European case center stage, we can blur the boundaries between the global North and South while also pointing to the contradictions of humanitarianism in a region that prides itself on its human rights and refugee acceptance record.

At once, Europe appears humanitarian while also concealing its goals of border securitization through various commitments to human rights. For example, irregular migration must be stopped because it encourages human trafficking. In tandem with chapter 5, this chapter sets the stage for an examination of refugee survival in the Paris case. My key exploration here is to understand the refugee fantasy and the trope of the refugee crisis through the Common European Asylum System (CEAS). The CEAS offers many contradictions under the guise of human dignity where the system appears neutral, progressive, liberal, and concerned with the rights of refugees. Ultimately, this chapter illustrates the ways in which refugees are rendered disposable at the level of the EU as they attempt to enter member states—in contradiction to the rights-based rhetoric of the CEAS. The European frontier, by which I mean border sites and the countries that the EU pays to warehouse refugees, represents a prevention strategy to keep refugees out of the EU.

A political gap emerges with regard to refugee welfare, and thus I also highlight the built-in tensions surrounding income and shelter across the twenty-seven member states (EU-27). Systemic issues concerning refugee welfare point us to the authoritarian turn in neoliberalism where, instead of a coherent agenda for shelter and long-term work, many states focus on border security and the naming (and framing) of refugees as threats to the economy and cultural coherence of the EU.

In the aftershocks of the 2008 Great Recession, frontier states—the first states of arrival for asylum seekers in the EU—such as Italy and Greece dealt with multiple rounds of austerity. For example, Greece's unemployment rate hit 26.5 percent and Italy's 12.7 percent in 2014,[1] right before the initial spike in migrants from Syria. With these extant structural issues in mind, it is unsurprising that EU policies intensified the need for border securitization. As Pradella and Cillo (2015) highlight, the global financial crisis resulted in intensified austerity that attacked workers' rights and trade unions, resulting in high levels of unemployment, increased precarity for immigrant workers, and the heightening of anti-immigration policies and practices. It goes without saying that austerity and increased migration have dovetailed to create a xenophobic atmosphere in Europe, which, in turn, distracts from the realities of everyday survival for those who have faced the most harm in the aftermath of 2008. This is a recurrent theme throughout the book because refugee governance disguises inequalities endemic to capitalism where refugee crises are removed from the material social realities of relocation. What unfolds in this chapter, then, is a series of examples that are illustrative of the refugee fantasy and its incongruence with social reality. Again, the refugee subject is a liminal one—simultaneously in Europe but belonging nowhere while always present as an existential and haunting threat to the EU-27.

The Refugee Crisis Trope

In 2015, the shutdown of camps in Macedonia, Calais, and Lesbos invigorated xenophobia in the EU and strengthened right-wing politics through images of the so-called refugee crisis where racialized refugees were portrayed in dehumanizing ways. This crisis cut across multiple scales and discursively framed refugees as "swarming, flooding, and marauding," as Shariatmadari helpfully calls out in his *Guardian* piece.[2] At Europe's frontiers, an endless mass of refugees threatens Greece and Italy. In Calais, refugees have set up makeshift camps that are continually destroyed by authorities only to pop back up weeks later. In cities such as Berlin and Gdansk, images of refugees on the streets challenged the EU's position as an advanced and developed region in the world. The crisis is a trope because it blames refugees even though an organization such as Abbe-Pierre in its annual *Overview of Housing Exclusion in Europe* (2015–2021) has highlighted that homelessness/rough sleeping has risen over 70 percent in Europe since 2010.[3] Refugees may exacerbate these issues, pointing to various gaps in the welfare commitments of states, but issues surrounding housing and work are also part and parcel of neoliberal regulation. Solutions to these crises appear in the form of capitalizing on the potential labor power of refugees. As the codirector of migration, displacement, and humanitarian policy at the Center for Global Development says, "Europe should invest in creating skills among potential migrants in Africa—specific skills the EU needs. This is a long-term investment, alongside (not instead of) more traditional short-term measures" (Clemens 2018).

The answers to refugee poverty surround an investment in skills building. While enhancing the skills of refugees is potentially useful, it does not address systemic issues that make it very difficult for refugees to "belong" in cities of relocation in the first place. European refugee governance is ambivalent in the following ways. On the one hand, refugee camps illustrate the failures of EU member state national policies of relocation where refugees are detained or moved around. This dehumanization drums up right-wing fervor as racialized refugees are portrayed as invaders who will stop at nothing to reach Europe, and this in turn provides the justification for the strengthening of borders and national antimigrant policies. On the other hand, liberal governments that do accept refugees (France, Germany, Sweden[4]) struggle to integrate refugees and rely on the potential (fantasy) of refugee labor power.[5]

How does this play out in the CEAS? Well, the isolation of refugees on remote islands and makeshift camps at frontier states have been central to EU policy. The carceral logics of refugee governance (LeBaron and Roberts 2010; Wacquant 2010) are apparent in various refugee camps. These policies are hinged on asylum seekers staying in place (detention) or a quick deportation. Since December 2018, the European Commission has made an additional €289 million available to Greece and €5.3 million to Italy in a disbursed fund that already includes €578.6 million and €358.6 million, respectively, for each country.[6] The camps, like prisons, are sites of intense surveillance, and countries are funded in order to keep refugees from entering and settling in major cities such as Paris. Since EU strategies focus on prevention, many refugees feel as though they have no choice but to pay smugglers and enter the EU through other means—outside processing centers in the Greek islands, for example. In 2016, *The Guardian* reported that over ten thousand trafficked children were being sold for sex work and other forms of labor for €4,000–€8,000 per child.[7] The rise in trafficking—an unnamed consequence of EU policy—has resulted in upcoming EU-UNHCR legislation concerning the UN Protocol to Prevent, Suppress, and Punish Trafficking in Persons, Especially Women and Children. In March 2020, the EU home affairs commissioner, in agreement with the national-level government of Greece, offered to pay migrants around €2,000 to return to their country of origin. Reading EU policy through the lens of the fantasy shows us oppositional tensions where the EU does not want to take in any refugees (and is literally willing to pay them to go away) and is also committed to human rights issues such as antitrafficking.

Refugee prevention as a strategy operates in a twofold manner: First, the EU intends to fund refugee-producing and refugee-managing states to keep refugees out of the EU territory; this is evident in Turkey and Libya, where refugees often face detention and other forms of violence, human trafficking, and forced labor.[8] Second, if refugees arrive in the EU, they are left without appropriate welfare assistance. At the same time, in acceptance, refugees represent potential utility on two fronts: (1) refugees are *potential* labor and future labor, and (2) the refugee figure strengthens liberal conceptions of humanitarianism—a state can flex its humanitarian muscle by illustrating its human rights commitments through refugee acceptance. In turn, this type of human rights flexing is also centered on determining the authenticity of the refugee subject. The images and discourses of refugees fleeing conflict and washing up on Europe's shore as dominant conceptions of who is deserving of aid and of Europe in general also allow many more people with valid refugee claims to be framed as irregular. Refugees also present some utility in being rejected in two important ways: (1) in the state of detention, a new avenue for tech-based surveillance is being rolled out particularly as states are increasingly attempting to track refugees through the capture of biometric data; (2) the discursive framing of refugees as economic opportunists and job stealers bolsters the political platforms of right-wing politicians.

To reduce the numbers of asylum claimants at frontier states such as Greece, Italy, and Hungary, the EU has struck deals with authoritarian leaders such as Turkey's president Recep Tayyip Erdogan. For the sixth consecutive year, Turkey has hosted the most refugees in the world (UNHCR 2020), with more than three million refugees, mostly of Syrian, Afghan, or Iraqi descent.

The landmark EU-Turkey deal of €6 billion is intended to keep refugees out of Europe under the false pretenses that Turkey is a safe country for asylum seekers who are reframed as guest workers. Through this deal, Greece has fast-tracked many claims, turning welcome reception centers into de facto detention centers (Amnesty International 2017). In their transformation from asylum seekers to guests, many refugees do not have legal claims to settle in Turkey; thus, in major Turkish cities such as Istanbul and Ankara, they face ongoing criminalization and deportation back to their countries of origin (Chehayeb and Hunaidi 2019). At the same time, Erdogan is able to threaten the EU with the release of refugees because the EU has lagged on its promise to allow Turkish citizens access to the EU for the purposes of visa-free travel (Baboulias 2019). This speaks to the looming and ever-present threat of this fantastical refugee figure—a problem exacerbated by the fact that the EU cannot absorb refugees into housing or work.

A similar deal was struck with the Libyan government for €237 million under the premise that Libya would prevent human trafficking and irregular migration into the EU. The Libyan coast guard is meant to intercept migrant vessels crossing into the EU, coinciding with EU commitments to break the business model of smugglers. However, a redacted document released by the EU (Limite EU) illustrates that detention centers in Libya (along with the coast guard) are mistreating refugees, forcing them into labor, exposing them to sexual and gender-based violence, and sending illegal smuggling vessels into the EU anyway (Council of the European Union 2019).

The inherent contradictions of refugee management in the EU and the operant fantasy of the refugee as simultaneously useful for capital and unwanted appear in an interview I conducted with a representative from an EU-funded humanitarian aid organization. Interestingly, I met the director in the organization's Kenya office. To paraphrase our conversation, he said that the EU was directly involved in investing in Africa to prevent future migration, especially in refugee-producing nations like Libya, Somalia, and South Sudan. Development or so-called positive initiatives (he rolled his eyes here) are to secure the EU's borders (Interview 35).

The director's statement reflects the key mission of EU development organizations in Africa. While they might be well meaning in order to spur development projects in various informal settlements and border sites, the hidden agenda is to invest in Africa in order to prevent refugees who are decidedly unwanted in Europe. That said, these investments are still based on entrepreneurial interventions—transforming refugees into businesspeople—and this strategy, as I will show in subsequent chapters, is piecemeal and ineffective for alleviating poverty.

The EU deals with Turkey and Libya—and the presence of EU-Aid in sub-Saharan Africa—illustrate the overarching foreign policy of containment, prevention, and detention. These are of course external to the EU region, and so I now turn to a more sustained analysis of the CEAS that is more focused on the actions of the EU-27. Although refugees present specific policy challenges, in naming the crisis as a trope I shed light on the ways in which refugee governance is an actual issue related to contemporary capitalism. Policies surrounding social housing, work, immigration, and the like are not separate from global displacement.

Contradictions in the CEAS

While I have so far focused on EU actions at the frontier, it is important to flesh out the various policies that prop up the CEAS. There are five key organizations in terms of political and legal refugee management: European Parliament, European Council on Refugees and Exile (ECRE), European Commission, European Asylum Support Office (EASO), and Frontex (see table 4.1). In addition, there are three policies that form the backbone of the CEAS: Dublin III, Eurodac, and the recast EU standards of Refugee Reception.

Except for ECRE, the key governance organizations in the EU are committed to strengthening border security, stopping human trafficking, and identifying authentic versus irregular refugees. As the budget increases for refugee management in Greece and Italy show, the overall spending on refugee governance has

TABLE 4.1 Summary of governance organizations in the EU

ORGANIZATION	ROLE
European Parliament	Passes legislation through consultation with other governance organizations. Politically and economically motivated and focuses on managing tensions between refugee acceptance and international human rights laws.
European Commission	Proposes, implements, and upholds EU treaties. It influences parliamentary laws and is the central overseeing body managing refugee governance in the territory. Political cohesiveness and economic growth are tenets of its key competencies. Explicit focus on strong borders underpins asylum policy.
European Asylum Support Office (EASO)	Center of expertise on asylum (practitioners and legal advocacy). Assists member states in cooperation, aids in fulfilling international commitments, and provides technical and practical support. Influences policy through evidence-based research.
European Council on Refugees and Exile (ECRE)	Protects and advances the rights of refugees through research, advocacy, and communication. Provides legal support for refugees and advises on migration policy in the European Parliament and European Commission.
Frontex	Promotes, coordinates, and develops EU border management. Focuses heavily on strengthening and guarding borders, especially in frontier states. Conducts risk analysis and monitors influxes of migrants.

increased. In 2016, the EU-wide Asylum Migration and Integration Fund (AMIF) was introduced to support EASO and the newly mandated Frontex coast guard and border security agency. The budget for migration and integration nearly doubled, with the European Commission allocating €9.2 billion for expenditures within and outside the EU.[9] This figure is expanded in the EU budget proposal to €34.9 billion between 2021 and 2027. While this expansion in funding seems to contradict the dimensions of EU-wide austerity, a closer look at the spending proposal reveals that €15 billion is dedicated to Frontex and border management. The rest is unevenly divided between integrated border management and euLISA—the agency for large-scale IT systems in the Area of Freedom, Security, and Justice—which happens to be another technological solution for border control. The smallest chunk is allocated to EASO for actual refugee integration.[10]

A key issue highlighted by all the EU organizations interviewed for this book is the varying degrees of refugee acceptance per member state. The exclusionary impetus of the CEAS is apparent in the EU Commission's review: "The large-scale, uncontrolled arrival of migrants and asylum seekers since early 2015 has put a strain on many Member States, asylum systems and on the CEAS as a whole. The EU now needs to put in place the tools to better manage migration flows in the medium and long term."[11] The terminology of managing migratory flows is a thinly veiled policy-based metaphor for exclusion particularly of racialized people from Africa and the Middle East. The tools concern a prevention-based approach that bars racialized migrants in the context of region-wide instability and inequality.

The Dublin III Regulation is central to the coherency of the CEAS. While even representatives from EU states suggest that Dublin III is an imperfect system, the EU is hesitant to abandon it entirely. In brief, Dublin III applies to all EU-27 states, Iceland, Norway, Liechtenstein, and Switzerland. The central tenet of the regulation allows member states to quickly determine responsibility in terms of asylum claimants. Through this regulation, member states can return asylum seekers to the country of entry. This has resulted in countries such as Italy and Greece contending that they have been overburdened with asylum claims.[12]

The current iteration of the Dublin Regulation has a few main elements and results. First, it aims to prevent the shuffling of asylum seekers between various states and only seeks to place them at the country of first entry. Second, it prevents an individual from launching multiple asylum claims. Third, it prevents asylum shopping—refugees should remain at the port of entry. Fourth, it determines a hierarchy of responsibility if the refugee happens to move from the port of entry to countries such as France and Germany.[13] Systemic refugee governance, set up by the Treaty of Amsterdam and Treaty of Lisbon and evidenced in the Dublin III Regulation, seeks to promote EU stability as opposed to refugee welfare.

The monitoring and border securitization aspects of Dublin III go hand in hand with the Eurodac Regulation. Eurodac seeks to establish a database of fingerprints that will allow Dublin III to be applied. According to the European Parliament, "By comparing fingerprints, EU countries can determine whether an asylum applicant or a foreign national found illegally present within an EU country has previously claimed asylum in another EU country or whether an asylum applicant entered the Union territory unlawfully."[14] Importantly, both Eurodac and Dublin III are used in tandem to exclude refugees from entering the territory.

A landmark study commissioned by the EU Parliament Policy Department for Citizen's Rights and Constitutional Affairs (EU Parliament 2016) concerning the implementation of the CEAS emphasizes the changing nature of EU-wide refugee governance. The public debate in many member states reflected a high degree of support for refugee governance for Syrian refugees in early 2015. However, since the recent media coverage of alleged refugee-related stabbings and sexual assaults—symptomatic of the influence of alt-Right perspectives in Europe—the discourse has shifted from *welcoming* refugees to framing them as *economic opportunists* and *illegal* or *irregular* migrants. This change in rhetoric indicates that the moment of acceptance has been replaced by calls for more intense scrutiny. Indeed, the term *refugee* itself is only afforded to those who are deemed authentic, while the term *migrant* is derogatory and indicative of a more slippery and insidious claimant.

Thus, the Dublin III and Eurodac Regulations are being weaponized to accommodate this change in perspective. However, three major contradictions arise from how these regulations are implemented. First, the distinction between economic migrants and those deserving of status is arbitrary and left to the judgment of the particular member state. In effect, the aims of a unified and just CEAS are empty rhetoric as the decision-making power comes from national-level member states. The CEAS works to absolve EU actors (and EU-wide legislative direction) of the responsibility of refugee survival—a risk that is passed along to national- and urban-level states. Second, in prioritizing a hierarchy of responsibility, the Dublin Regulation makes it difficult to adjudicate asylum claims in a responsible and humane manner. The camp, or site of entry, is taken for granted as a safe place for refugees, and the EU has lauded the efforts of Frontex in managing the crisis. However, a report by Human Rights Watch found that "Greek security forces and unidentified armed men at the Greece-Turkey land border have detained, assaulted, sexually assaulted, robbed, and stripped asylum seekers and migrants, then forced them back to Turkey."[15] If member states return asylum seekers to camps, they are returning them to a situation of intense violence. Third, because the Dublin and Eurodac Regulations potentially harm more refugees than they save, they are inevitably inefficient at meeting their own goals. Asylum seekers can avoid fingerprinting at frontier states as policing and other administrative procedures and systems are weak. Member states such as Italy and Greece may also avoid fingerprinting refugees because they do not want to be overburdened with returns from other EU countries. In trying to avoid the Eurodac, asylum seekers choose riskier travel routes to get to safer countries like Germany, Austria, France, and Sweden.

Policy directions of migrant flow reduction and border strengthening are also reflected in many of the interviews and other correspondence I conducted during field research where Dublin III took center stage. For example, email correspondence with the European Commission explicitly highlights the organization's focus on reducing flows, protecting borders, and providing aid abroad as the three key competencies of its agenda in Europe (Email correspondence 1). The commission's focus on reducing migratory flows dovetails with its emphasis on policies that save migrant lives. President Jean-Claude Juncker's State of the Union address (2017) is reflective of this contradictory mindset of protecting the border—Italy was seen by Juncker as protecting the EU's honor in the Mediterranean for instance—while also saving refugees who deserve EU assistance.[16] Regarding border protection, the commission further highlights that more than fifteen hundred members of the coast guard are deployed to support frontier states and over one hundred thousand border guards are patrolling member states with a high influx of migrants.[17] It is important to highlight the doublespeak here where refugee life is saved through intense policing. This implies that intense surveillance is part of the commission and Europe's humanitarian duty under the guise of antitrafficking. The ideological elements of these variant stances fuse together. With the refugee fantasy in mind, the refugee needs saving, and the only way to save and care for them is through policing—another feature of the carceral logic of refugee governance.

Seemingly in contrast, ECRE has leveled concerns against Dublin III and takes a more humanitarian stance on refugee acceptance, focusing on the EU Charter of Fundamental Rights, EU Commission of Human Rights, and the Geneva Convention. For instance, a representative from ECRE's public relations noted the following in an interview:

> A large bulk of the work in Dublin is at the frontier states and substantive rights have been procedurally denied through the system and the use of Dublin by member states. Many applicants who use our help contend that the conditions in frontier states [Greece and Italy] do not

meet EU charter requirements. . . . At the moment, Greece and Italy do not have the capacity to house migrants properly. . . . There is not a standardized set of good quality reception conditions and using Dublin to return migrants to their first country of arrival does not give migrants an opportunity to enjoy a life of dignity. (Interview 3)

Dignity can be a slippery word, depending on how it is used. Arguably, a bed and access to basic facilities in detention centers can be a form of dignity. That being said, ECRE is pushing for important changes; however, the guise of humanitarianism has a way of minimizing the plight of refugees while also denying them the ability to even arrive in major urban centers. The push for more humane detention also avoids the fact that most refugees live in urban settlements, and so solving reception or detention conditions does not speak to the *actually existing* issues of relocation—namely, that most refugees are barred from entry.

My informant went on to highlight that Dublin III allows for far more flexibility in terms of refugee acceptance than is currently practiced. For example, the condition for family unity, while emphasized in EU-level policy, is not adequately implemented. Individuals have high evidential burdens to prove family linkages, and most are sent back to frontier states. In short, Dublin III is largely understood as a problematic and ineffective system of refugee governance, even by NGOs and policymakers, but it continues to be upheld as it supports Europe's ideological commitments to humanitarianism while also allowing for the rejection and circuitous displacement of many refugees. Nevertheless, there have been internal pressures to alter Dublin III with a Dublin IV Regulation proposal put out on May 4, 2016 (legislation still pending).

In correspondence with European Parliament, the email exchange suggested a move toward a more comprehensive and centralized asylum system that is based on national quotas:

The Member of the European Parliament (MEPs) also called for a centralised EU system for asylum claims which could include a quota for each EU Member State, as outlined in the Parliament's press release on 12 April 2016. MEPs say a new system is needed to ensure fairness and shared responsibility, solidarity, and swift processing of applications. The Dublin Regulation establishes the Member State responsible for the examination of the asylum application. The European Commission presented proposals to reform this Common European Asylum System, which are detailed in the Commission's press release as of 4 May 2016. MEPs discussed the proposals in a plenary debate on 11 May 2016. . . . [In terms of the EU-wide hotspots approach] The European Commission's "hotspot approach" aims to allow the Union agencies to work on the ground in affected EU Member States to swiftly identify, register, and fingerprint arriving migrants and to assist in investigating and dismantling migrant smuggling networks. (Email correspondence 2)

The Dublin IV proposal doubles down on the security gaps that emerged from Dublin III. It aims to enhance the system's capacity for determining responsibility, ensure fair sharing of responsibility through the quota-based allocation system, discourage abuses and prevent secondary movements through procedural and material consequences in case of noncompliance, and protect asylum seekers' best interests through stronger guarantees for unaccompanied minors. The concession of Dublin IV involves extending the definition of family members to assist in reunification.[18] On balance, however, Dublin IV seeks to expand the security apparatus of the CEAS and harden punishments for refugees who asylum shop.

In updating the coherency of the CEAS and with the potential of a recast Dublin regulation, EASO has expanded its role as a support agency to become a full-fledged organization that member states can call on for operational and procedural support. EASO notes that its resources provide training, data analysis, and country-of-origin reports that influence the adjudication of asylum claims. EASO has plans to transform itself into the European Union Agency for Asylum, but at the time of writing this full transformation has yet to occur.

According to an informant at EASO,

> The main issue with Dublin is that it has created a lot of political divisions among several EU countries. . . . At EASO we prefer the term migration as opposed to crisis. Crisis seems to refer to a sudden rise of migrants; however, this is the reality for Europe. No, we need a system where a Nigerian who applies for asylum in France gets the same treatment in Sweden or in any other member state. The new Dublin seeks to create an automatic system where a certain number of asylum seekers are relocated from Greece and Italy. Let's say if a hundred migrants land in Greece, five would be sent to France, seven to Germany etc. The goal is more even distribution. We need to get rid of the system that puts too much pressure on Greece and Italy and instead have a system that is streamlined and coherent. (Interview 7)

While EASO's definition of crisis is more progressive than the stance of the European Commission or European Parliament, the implicit aims of border protection are hidden under the guise of streamlining. The Nigerian referred to in the excerpt would actually have a much weaker chance of securing asylum status under the Dublin IV proposal.

The EASO employee went on to say,

> Currently, asylum seekers do the utmost to avoid fingerprinting. . . . If he is fingerprinted in Italy and moves to France then the French will send him back to Italy. . . . The reason we have camps on remote islands is to prevent irregular migration. This is not only to secure borders but for the protection of refugees themselves. Sometimes they are smuggled from islands and many of them are harmed or exploited by professional human traffickers. If the new asylum system is to work, we need to have increased border control to minimize and eliminate irregular migration. . . . Not all irregular migration is illegal; only economic migration is. (Interview 7)

The ambivalence of humanitarianism is evident in this excerpt by the employee of EASO—perhaps the EU's most progressive organization in terms of upholding refugee rights. The statement seems to blame the victim for leaving the camp and enlisting the aid of human smugglers instead of pointing to the root causes that facilitate this ongoing displacement in Europe. While the representative noted that the AMIF funded state-of-the-art camps, it is not entirely convincing that refugees are satisfied with the limited mobility associated with in situ camps that are disconnected from urban centers. Further, the increase in border security is framed as a benefit for refugees themselves. For EASO, an increase in border security would allow asylum seekers to be fingerprinted with ease and rigor.

The central aim of the Eurodac is, of course, to determine which migrants are economic and which are authentic/deserving. Border security is buttressed by the operational and procedural support provided by Frontex, via the deployment of coast guard and border patrol personnel to any member states. The public relations representative from Frontex said, "Through an increased management we are able to conduct rapid intervention where we are able to airdrop around fifteen hundred security personnel within five days" (Interview 1). When asked what this security deployment entails, the representative suggested that they aid in fingerprinting and guarding the border, thereby preventing migrants from overwhelming coast guards in the member states of arrival. The representative further said, "We are able to airdrop fifteen hundred security personnel within five days. . . . I do not want to suggest that Frontex is evil or a big bad wolf organization. . . . That is how we have been portrayed in the media. . . . Okay we are just doing our job; we follow what the EU legislation tells us to do. If we are not present to secure borders, then there will be utter chaos. . . . We need border security to make sure the right people get into the region" (Interview 1).

Another element of Frontex's core competencies involves risk management, where Frontex monitors potential flows of migrants from Africa and the Middle

East to preempt and intercept potential large influxes of migrants before they arrive in the EU. As the security arm of the EU, Frontex coordinated the return of
14,189 third-country nationals (key indicators of success for the organization) to
the country of origin. Frontex's risk analysis unit received expanded funding and
responsibility in 2016 and provided data on migrant activity to EUROPOL Law
Enforcement.

As previously mentioned, border security is the top priority in terms of creating stability in the CEAS, and refugees are implicitly racialized as criminals. The
message that only "the right people" should be allowed in implies that there are
all sorts of wrong people that are illegal, that they should return to their countries
of origin, and that the violence they face is justified. Economic hardships that cast
many racialized people as economic migrants should be overcome at the country
of origin through hard work—either way, it is the refugee who is considered defi-
cient through rejection at the frontier or through ongoing self-reliance even with
status upon relocation. The root causes of systemic violence in racial capitalism
are of course missing in these fantasy-based deployments of border security.

Political Belonging, Labor, and Shelter Issues in the EU

Although the EU has committed €3 billion to migrant integration, EU president Antonio Tajani said, "Migration is our biggest challenge. It is putting at risk
the future of the European Union."[19] This sentiment is echoed by European
Council president Donald Tusk, who said, "It is the job of every political authority to enforce the law, to protect its territory and the border."[20] This statement is
an example of the thinly veiled racism directed toward migrants. Both the president of the EU and the president of the European Commission (at the height of
the crisis) were equating regional instability with irregular migration. These positions carve out who belongs and who does not in the EU. Undoubtedly,
political belonging goes beyond the quest for refugee status—and this is central
in the following chapter, which takes up the Paris case. However, it is important
to empirically show that despite EU-wide claims of humanitarianism, many
more refugees are rejected.

Positive media coverage of states such as Germany, in its acceptance of Syrian migrants in particular, is contrasted with rates of rejection that tell a different story. The top six refugee-accepting countries in 2017 were Germany, France,
Italy, Sweden, Austria, and Greece. As illustrated in table 4.2, Germany rejects
the least number of refugee claims, which is still over half. France, the country
with the second highest number of positive decisions, rejects 73 percent of its

TABLE 4.2   Rates of acceptance, temporary protection, and rejection in the EU

COUNTRY (TOTAL DECISIONS)	RATE OF REJECTION (%)	REFUGEE STATUS GRANTED (%)	TEMPORARY PROTECTION (%)
Germany (90,905)	52	23	18
France (30,480)	73	15	12
Italy (18,590)	60	7	7
Sweden (15,105)	56	22	21
Austria (14,730)	49	37	13
Greece (6,780)	57	38	5

Source: *Asylum Quarterly Report*, 2017 edition. All the reports can be found here: https://ec.europa.eu
/eurostat/statistics-explained/index.php/Asylum_quarterly_report.

claims and has given only 15 percent of claimants full refugee status, with 12 percent receiving subsidiary (temporary) protection.[21]

The racial dimensions of neoliberal refugee management are evident when considering the country of origin of asylum seekers. Syria, Afghanistan, Iraq, Nigeria, Pakistan, and Iran are the top six countries of origin of asylum seekers in the EU. Of these, Syrians have a rejection rate of 7 percent; Afghans, 52 percent; and Iraqis, 45 percent. Nigerians and Pakistanis had rejection rates of 77 percent and 88 percent, respectively (table 4.3). Syrian refugees have received preferential treatment in Europe and are unequivocally considered the most vulnerable group of refugees. Apart from Eritrean migrants (93% acceptance), refugees from African countries such as Gambia (3%), Somalia (57%), and Guinea (17%) face lower rates of acceptance than do Syrian refugees. Black Africans, particularly those from the Libyan coast, are more likely to be considered economic migrants; this is despite regional instability in terms of conflict, climate change, and other forms of violence.

Further evidence that the EU sees Black migrants from Africa as unwanted (thereby indicating their lack of political belonging at the very onset of their asylum journey) comes from the EU-initiated Emergency Trust Fund for Africa. By 2019, the fund had spent €3.59 billion and divided this among the Horn of Africa (€1286.6 million), North Africa (€582.2 million), Sahel/Lake Tchad (€172.1 million), and a crosscutting program funded for €167.1 million. Within this allocation the EU has targeted Ethiopia, North African states, and the Gambia as key sites of irregular migration—that is to say, migrants from these regions are threatening to the EU. For example, the Stemming Irregular Migration in Northern and Central Ethiopia Project aims to address issues such as economic opportunities, job training, and income-generating activities in an effort to prevent migrants from leaving the Horn region.[22]

TABLE 4.3 Acceptance rates by country of origin

COUNTRY OF ORIGIN (TOTAL DECISIONS)	REJECTIONS (%)	SUBSIDIARY PROTECTION (%)	RATE OF ACCEPTANCE (%)
Syria (29,620)	7	47	45
Afghanistan (29,140)	52	18	18
Iraq (17,446)	45	32	20
Nigeria (9,185)	77	2	7
Pakistan (8,430)	88	2	5
Iran (8,210)	46	2	51

Source: *Asylum Quarterly Report*, 2017 edition.

While the EU is committed to keeping refugees outside its borders through job creation, the recast Reception Conditions Directive (RCD), which pertains to refugee survival upon relocation, is an important feature of the CEAS. With regard to labor, the RCD proposes to reduce the wait time for refugees to access the labor market from twelve to nine months. The European Parliament and European Commission even proposed a six-month period of labor integration to the European Council and many member states, but the states wished to retain the twelve-month restriction (RCD 2013). In light of the new guidelines, member states have found loopholes in which they prevent refugees from accessing the labor market by limiting them to certain sectors of employment. According to ECRE, even in the most generous circumstances, such as Germany's pilot program that allowed refugees to enter the job market in three months, refugees were unable to secure sustainable employment.

The ambivalence inherent in the fantasy of the refugee subject points us to a central issue in EU policy that emphasizes a swift integration of refugees into labor markets in member states of relocation but also offers little financial or political support. An article in *The Economist* reflects the disposability of refugees by suggesting that "European countries should make it easier for refugees to work. . . . It eases the fiscal burden without hurting locals' prospects" (2018, 1). Despite the difficulties of refugee integration, the International Monetary Fund (IMF) reifies self-reliance as a key priority, stating, "Europe's population is forecast to age rapidly over the next few decades, reflected by several decades of low birth rates and rising longevity. . . . In the absence of migration this will lower potential [economic] growth and likely place a large burden on public finances" (IMF 2016, 26).

My interview with a representative from ECRE further showed the lack of available resources for refugees. My informant noted that there are no plans for any sort of long-term integration of refugees. "The crisis is being dealt with as though it is going to be a short-term issue; however, refugees are here to stay" (Interview 3). As we have seen in countries like Denmark, some EU member states have taken decidedly anti-integration stances.[23] Sweden's turn toward the right—and its acceptance of fewer refugees[24]—further illustrates EU commitments to prevention at the national scale of refugee governance.

In contrast to what national states are enacting in terms of their own refugee policies, the European Commission (2016a, 8) has highlighted that employment is usually the single most important determinant of third country nationals' overall net fiscal contribution. In short, the commission is making a business case for refugee acceptance. In 2016, the EU employment rate of foreign-born migrants was 66 percent compared with 71.8 percent for the native-born population. The unemployment rate for migrants born outside the EU is 8.4 percent higher than that of the nonmigrant population. Additionally, migrants who enter the workforce are increasingly in part-time or temporary employment. While the rise of part-time or flexible employment is endemic to neoliberalism, these trends establish that migrants, when employed, are less likely to find long-term sustainable employment than their native-born counterparts.[25]

Despite the lack of available data on refugees, the European Commission, noting that refugees face increased barriers to accessible labor markets, has devised an EU-wide refugee labor integration program. The *Action Plan on the Integration of Third Country Nationals* indicates that refugees make a positive fiscal net contribution if they are well integrated in a timely manner vis-à-vis language instruction, job training, and political acceptance into the labor market in respective member states (European Commission 2016b).

Much EU-led research makes a solid case for refugee integration in terms of economic growth; however, the burden of finding work and surviving is placed on refugees themselves—a key element of refugee governance within the context of welfare retrenchment. The *Action Plan*'s reasoning for refugee poverty suggests that the barriers stem from refugees' own poor language skills and inappropriate work-related qualifications, but systemic issues of low-wage labor, racist discrimination, and labor flexibilization are hidden. Refugees are disposable populations because system-wide issues of xenophobia and extant crises of capitalism surrounding work and shelter are unaddressed. The calls for refugees as valuable laborers are empty because they reflect ideological positions of hard work and self-reliance embedded in neoliberalism while being disconnected from the social reality of joblessness and homelessness—another unaddressed issue of integration in the CEAS.

Work and shelter are inextricably linked indicators of disposability, and I argue that refugees—as queered and liminal subjects—exist on the very fringes of capitalist inclusion in relation to what Bhattacharyya (2018) calls edge populations. In many ways, the refugee survival experience is distinguished by racialized exclusion. This process begins at the frontier for people who are placed in detention and continues—regardless of whether an individual has formal status—at various member states of relocation. An OECD report (2017)[26] states that the average cost of refugee integration in the EU is around €10,000 per person. The European Commission (2016a, 3) indicates that most member states face short-term budgetary costs related to displacement and that social housing spending is one of the costliest aspects of refugee acceptance. The commission's report on macroeconomic justifications for refugee integration further suggests that poorly funded social housing schemes limit the chances of refugee integration, and the longer a refugee is held in an asylum accommodation center, the less likely he or she will be able to integrate into the host society's labor market.

While the statistics for refugees remain uncollected on a macro level, some insight can be gleaned from trends in homeownership with regard to overall migrants. Across the EU, 70.5 percent of nationals ages twenty to sixty-four live in owner-occupied dwellings compared with only 32.1 percent of foreign nationals. Only one-third of EU citizens are tenants, whereas two-thirds of foreign-born populations live in rental housing. The quality of accommodations for foreign-born nationals is much lower than that for native-born populations as 22.2 percent of foreign-born nationals live in overcrowded dwellings with one room per household, often with the entire family (including children) sharing a single bedroom. Migrants are also overburdened with housing costs,[27] and there is a crucial link between unemployment/underemployment and poor housing quality. In 2016, 12.4 percent of all migrants were part of households in which the adults worked less than 20 percent of their total work potential. This is further evidence that migrant workers are employed on a flexible or part-time basis—another indicator of their racialized disposability upon relocation to member states.[28]

As the president of Housing Europe stated, house prices, along with unprecedented energy costs and the influx of refugees from Ukraine, are putting pressure on already underfunded social housing in the EU.[29] Homelessness is on the rise and is a clear indicator of the failures of neoliberal housing policy, which has created systemic shocks across the region (Housing Europe 2017). In 2005, public funding of social housing projects hovered around 47 percent of the overall capital expenditure on housing related costs, and this percentage has decreased year over year to the point where only 25 percent of the housing budget was publicly funded by 2015.[30]

While owner occupation remains the most common type of housing, there has been a remarkable decrease in homeownership across all member states; among low-income groups, renting is more common, pointing to the importance of the rental housing question as regards refugee survival. Housing construction, for both social and private shelter forms, has been slow to recover from the financial crisis. According to the European Construction Sector Observatory (ECSO), slow construction has contributed to the problem of housing insecurity. Housing shortages are also emerging in large cities with increased migrant populations, and as ECSO notes, these migrants are placing increased pressure on already tight housing markets (Eurofound 2016). Since housing shortages and housing prices are inextricably linked, refugees are unable to find permanent housing in major EU cities and are further displaced to peripheral areas or bounced out of the region entirely. In general, social housing provisions have been ravaged by cuts to public funding, and even countries like France, which has a tradition of social renting, have seen a reduction in the stock of social housing.

Interrelated conditions such as a decrease in homeownership, housing shortages, an increase in rental prices, and a decrease in social housing stock (and funding) have resulted in a widening affordability gap in the rental section. According to the Organisation for Economic Co-operation and Development (OECD) (2016) and Habitat for Humanity (2015), unaffordable rental housing is resulting in homelessness, evictions, and overcrowding in crisis-ridden countries such as Greece. Countries with high numbers of migrants, such as Germany, Sweden, and France, have seen increased poverty in the ongoing aftermath of the global financial crisis. For example, in France, the number of people registered for social housing increased from 1.2 million in 2010 to 1.9 million in 2016 (Habitat for Humanity 2015; OECD 2016; Housing Europe 2017).

Homelessness in the EU has also risen dramatically since 2005. According to a report by the European Federation of National Organisations Working with the Homeless (FEANTSA 2018), France, Germany, Greece, and Austria have seen increases in homelessness, especially with regard to the current migration event, since 2015. France has seen the greatest rise in homelessness with a 50 percent increase in the numbers since 2006. Germany's homeless population has risen by 35 percent since 2015 (what is widely recognized as the onset of the Syrian refugee crisis). Greece, crippled by severe austerity cuts and its placement at the forefront of the migration crisis, has seen its homeless population increase by 71 percent since 2011 (FEANTSA 2018, 10). Undoubtedly these statistics illustrate the conditions in which the refugee crisis trope—an ideological feature disconnected from housing insecurity—is embedded. The statistics also reveal the implicit racial dimensions of shelter access.

With regard to refugee housing, the European Parliament released a briefing that calls for further research into shelter access, noting, "The incentives for irregular migration have become one of the main objectives of both external and internal dimensions of EU migration policy."[31] In preventing irregular migration, the European Parliament suggests that in-kind assistance in terms of housing is far more useful than cash incentivization schemes. In general, housing accommodations that consider the needs of refugees are more durable than shuffling refugees around the country, as is common in France. These scant suggestions do not result in robust relocation assistance. Again, the prevention of (loosely defined) irregular migration implicitly suggests that refugees discovered within member states without appropriate documentation could, and should, be returned to their countries of origin and denied access.

While the European Parliament and European Commission are focused on the quelling of irregular migrants, EASO has provided a more robust set of guidelines for states. The three key elements are housing, infrastructure, and security. Although member states are free to choose from different types of housing strategies, they must ensure "effective geographic access to relevant services, such as public services, schools, social and legal assistance, a shop for daily needs, laundry, and leisure activities" (EASO 2016, 10). But as I show in the next chapter, these guidelines are not followed in France, and many shelters (or makeshift camps) are far from the city's core, indicating that refugees face barriers to essential services. EASO also outlines such infrastructure requirements as sufficient furniture, one room per person in the family, and sanitary living conditions. However, these guidelines are disconnected from the social realities of overcrowding at various stages of refugee shelter survival.

ECRE, in particular, is critical for the EU guidelines for reception, as evident in the following statement:

> The Receptions Conditions Directive allows for sufficient reception needs but provides only hazy definitions which means that member states can get around it by not providing decent regulations. We at ECRE advocate for refugee rights and use the Charter Rights for Human Dignity as a cushion for our claims. So many countries have not met their objectives. . . . Most will provide some reception accommodation but many of these are makeshift. . . . In Belgium, for example, it is a former army barracks with bars on the windows. This does not show that refugee lives are valued. . . . Is it another form of detention? Not really, but it does indicate that refugees are perhaps unwelcome. Asylum applicants can't just be left on the street or in poverty or in destitution . . . but this is just as the EU level as well [in response to whether the charter is a useful tool in the migration crisis]. The Charter implies more than just a standard; it is binding. . . . A person's life must be dignified! (Interview 4)

This excerpt shows the disconnect between EU-wide regulation and its urban implementations. In fact, it points to the inherent ambivalence of states that are humanitarian in a general sense but whose actions do not match their rhetoric. Beyond dignity, it is clear that EU-level laws (such as the charter) are not binding and do not reflect the social practices of refugee management. Although the laws seem to afford many benefits to refugees, they also give member states sufficient control over their service provisions. This is partly so that a country like Hungary does not have to provide the same quality of services as a country like Germany; however, the RCD also allows member states to get away with minimal provisions. As mentioned throughout this chapter, many of the EU organizations interviewed for this book emphasize border security and the necessity of sorting authentic and irregular claims. Missing in the CEAS is an acknowledgment that the lack of appropriate services in many member states might push refugees to seek better accommodations in countries such as Germany and France. So-called irregular migration is clearly motivated by the need for good-quality housing and sustainable income, neither of which is provided through detention at the frontier or upon relocation to major urban areas.

In this chapter, I sought to introduce the refugee fantasy as an element of EU refugee governance. In so doing, I showed that refugee governance is underpinned by concerns of border security and propped up by ideological commitments to humanitarianism while excluding many refugees from Europe's frontier. The legal instruments of the CEAS also work to buttress this preoccupation with security that implicitly racializes refugees and renders them disposable. These legal directives are matched with shelter- and work-related insecurity in the EU-27, pointing to extant and unaddressed issues of neoliberal capitalism. Upon relocation, the fantasy of the refugee as one that is quickly employed appears simultaneously with issues of homelessness and joblessness. I argue throughout the book that refugees survive on the edge of these spaces in urban capitalism, and in the next chapter I take a closer look at what happens upon relocation in Paris.

5

DISPOSABILITY AND SURVIVAL
IN PARIS

When I arrived in Paris in 2017 to conduct my fieldwork, France was undergoing a resurgence of alt-Right populism—a rise in white nationalist social movements and political tactics coinciding with the US presidential election in 2016—crystallized in the candidacy of Marine Le Pen. These issues have not disappeared. For instance, Louis Aliot of the National Rally Party has been elected mayor in one of the poorest cities (Perpignan) in France. For those who watched the pre-pandemic election of Boris Johnson in the UK, it is no surprise that former left-wing strongholds have given way to antiliberal, Far Right pressures centering on economic insecurity. Emmanuel Macron has repeatedly courted the Right, particularly on issues of the border and the perennial Muslim/Arab threat amid the quest to restore France's glory. Central to alt-Right platforms (globally) is antimigrant xenophobia—or to echo Shilliam (2018) the prevention of the undeserving (nonwhite) poor taking away resources from the deserving (white) poor. A platform of antiglobalism means that pro-migrant, pro-gay, pro-Black, pro-Muslim, pro-trans, and pro feminist liberal discourses are seen to contribute to the theft of national enjoyment. In turn, these discourses, while important for a just society, do not target the everyday existing material inequalities that people face. Since neither liberals nor conservatives address issues of class the alt-Right has captured the political base of the white working class through the fantasy of the migrant. This chapter thus focuses on the disposability of migrants upon relocation owing to crosscutting tensions of race and neoliberalism in Paris (and in France more widely).

9

In this chapter, I aim to show how EU concerns over border security that characterize many of the issues surrounding refugee policy in chapter 4 are embodied. Here, France and Paris—and the refugees who struggle to relocate there—embody the violence of security threat, race, and the so-called preservation of European (white) identity. The EU, France, and Paris are chain-linked scales of the CEAS, and this framework undoubtedly structures the governance of refugees on the urban level. But it is important to highlight that the CEAS offers very little regulatory guidance as it pertains to urban resettlement. Thus, an exploration of the Paris case is important in unearthing the everyday dimensions of violence in racial capitalism. The French case is in turn undergirded by racial logics of neoliberal governance, as exemplified by then French prime minister Valls, who said, "Europe cannot afford any more refugees."[1] The framing of refugees as costly to France and other member states justifies their arbitrary detention.

Statements such as the one made by Prime Minister Valls mask the fact that refugees arrive in a country where some ten million people live in substandard accommodations without secure and affordable rental tenure and around four million people do not have adequate housing (Abbe Pierre Foundation 2018). In Paris, homelessness has increased by a staggering 84 percent since 2005 owing to cuts in social service expenditure and the devolving of poverty management to cities and civil society organizations. Although France has one of the highest rates of refugee application rejections in western Europe, Paris remains a hotspot for displaced people who are fleeing improper treatment elsewhere in the EU (Abbe Pierre Foundation 2018).

The French case of disposability is further illustrated through the closure of the colloquially titled "refugee jungle" in Calais. Davies, Isakjee, and Dhesi (2017) highlight how the migrants in Calais are a concentrated symbol of the separation of racialized migrant others and European citizens who live in adequate housing. Calais, following Achille Mbembe's necropolitics, is framed as a morbid spectacle of death-in-life or where refugees are kept alive in a state of injury.[2] The CEAS presents itself as a banal exercise through what Davies, Isakjee, and Dhesi name as discourses of subtle power through cooperation, partnership, best practice, and technical know-how (2017, 1267). Through the lens of disposability, I add to these conceptions of governance by expanding on the treatment of refugees in Paris through the analysis of material issues in capitalism, particularly those surrounding shelter, income, and political belonging. Key to this argumentation is the creation of the migrant fantasy that renders the often violent spectacles of refugee management acceptable. These fantasies are buttressed by illogical ideological commitments of neoliberalism surrounding accumulation and self-reliance. In the face of widespread material insecurity, the pure dream of ideology supports the unstable system. With Fanon in mind, refugees must

translate their humanity in Europe in order to survive. They must speak the colonial tongue, they must embody the disciplined neoliberal worker, and, if they
require some sort of assistance, they should quickly shed this assistance and integrate without a fuss.

Historical Displacement and Racism in Paris

Despite the scapegoating and violent removal of refugees from Paris, the city
holds the majority of asylum seekers in France; estimates range from eighteen
thousand to thirty thousand individuals. The French government estimates that
the country has received between six thousand and ten thousand refugees per
year since 2015. There are no hard and fast numbers. Most refugees arrive on
the streets of Paris and are unhoused and unaccounted for. Soederberg's (2018)
conception of erasure as it pertains to homeless populations can also apply to
refugees who become disposable and erased as they struggle to survive. In addition to the large number of migrants in the city, Paris has a burgeoning homeless population of approximately 29,000 in the metropolitan area, and France
has 141,500—an increase of 50 percent from the recorded numbers in 2001.[3] Indeed, the "crisis" of managing refugees cannot be divorced from deepening
neoliberalization in France and its resultant effects on the racialized poor, or as
Marx might refer to them, the relative surplus population.

Structural violence toward homeless people or the racialized poor is not new,
and as Wacquant (2008) shows us, Paris has a long history of expelling the poor
from wealthy arrondissements in the city's core. Refugees, facing similar pressures
of expulsion through policing, surveillance, and the lack of affordable housing,
end up in lower-rent arrondissements. These former working-class neighborhoods
are also undergoing gentrification, making Paris one of the most expensive cities
in Europe in which to rent a home.

The expulsion of migrants and the urban poor can be traced back to the era
of Baron Haussmann, who is often credited with transforming Paris into the City
of Light. The aim of the Haussmann project was to turn Paris into a city of modern boulevards, fashion, and culture—a decidedly upper-class plan that required working-class labor. In the aftermath of the revolution of 1848, Napoleon
Bonaparte appointed Baron Haussmann to this undertaking in order to address
issues of surplus capital and unemployment. Parking this capital in the built
environment would allow Napoleon to maintain political power. As Harvey
(2008) suggests, these crises were only temporarily resolved as Haussmann's re-
development strategy relied on financial (debt) institutions—Credit Mobilier

and Immobilier. In so doing, Paris absorbed massive quantities of labor and capital and suppressed any worker dissent. In addition, a vast number of laborers from elsewhere in France arrived in Paris, creating a reserve army of labor. Haussmann abandoned common citywide policies of the eighteenth century that fed the poor and instead argued that the city's only role was to provide jobs. The poor were blamed for their inability to survive. This story repeats itself for refugees as it pertains to the now neoliberal trope of self-reliance—perhaps one that is endemic to capitalism itself.

Workers were necessary to build the new wide boulevards of the city but presented a crack in the fantasy of the new Paris as a center of commerce and culture: the poor did not belong here. Haussmann envisioned a city of consumption, cafés, and fashion, and the working class was not part of this bourgeois project. To expel these individuals, Haussmann pushed industry—viewed as noxious and unwanted—from the city center, thereby diminishing any working-class power and placing the burden of employment on workers themselves (Harvey 2003, 158). Haussmann's credit-reliant system, which repurposed surplus capital through consumption for higher classes in Paris, worked well for fifteen years—until the financial market crashed in 1868. Haussmann's policies overextended the speculative financial system, and the city's debt rose from 163 million francs to more than 2,500 million, making up more than 40 percent of the city's budget (140).

The lacuna left by the financial crisis and the sudden shock to the labor market from the large reserve army of labor led to the formation of the Paris Commune. While the historical significance of the commune extends beyond my purpose here, it is important to note its legacy and the possibilities it presented for future working-class solidarity and resistance. It also illustrates the arm of the state that used military power to crush anticapitalist solidarity. In the end, twenty thousand insurrectionists were killed, thirty-eight thousand were arrested, and seven thousand were deported (Ross 2015), revealing that violent expulsion has always been in the realm of possibility. In the context of authoritarian neoliberalism, state violence—not welfare—is always an option. Informal refugee shelters are continually dismantled. Refugees face police violence, arrest, and eventual deportation.

The class divides present in the Haussmann era prevailed in the nineteenth and twentieth centuries as well with the arrival of eighty-eight thousand internal Breton migrants, and later with the arrival of Italian and Polish migrants. I raise this here because Paris has a long history of treating migrants poorly; the racialized other was ever-present. The Bretons were mistreated and cast as the other of France while still fulfilling low-wage labor requirements. As Moch (2012, 182) writes, "Breton culture was central to stereotypes held by Parisians. First and foremost, the religiosity of Bretons was held against them, particularly at the turn of the century when the battle to create a secular state and secular schools was at its most intense." This is reminiscent of Paris's current Muslim other, who are also portrayed as inassimilable because of their religious values. The racialization of Islam homogenizes Muslims from vast socioeconomic, ethnic, and cultural backgrounds—the fantasy of the other has always been the bedrock of low-wage extraction.

After the Second World War, France received another influx of migrants from its soon-to-be former colonies and other regions within the protectorate. The racialization that the Bretons faced was extended to African migrants, who were seen as unwanted labor. Economic stagnation in the former colonies and in parts of Africa more widely pushed many migrants to seek a livelihood in France. This created a divide between "good Black French citizens" and "unwanted African others" that parallels the CEAS's focus on sorting authentic and inauthentic refugees. Some African and Caribbean migrants were granted French citizenship, whereas others faced intense scrutiny by the police and were often deported as illegal immigrants in the 1960s and '70s (Germain 2014, 2016).

African migrants faced an entirely different set of rules than Jews and other Europeans arriving in France after the Second World War. Migrants from former French colonies were given French nationality but were barred from French citizenship. Racialized immigrants lived in shantytowns on the outskirts of Paris and were considered the noncitizen workforce. By 1961, the Algerian War for independence from France was in its seventh year, with over 180,000 Algerian migrants settled in informal housing (racialized and ghettoized spaces) in the Parisian outskirts. Algerians in Paris faced extraordinary amounts of police violence—an extension of colonial repression. The French state's violent disposition toward the racialized poor led to the Paris massacre of 1961, in which the Parisian police beat, imprisoned, and killed many Algerians in order to suppress anticolonial protests in the city. Despite being considered French citizens, Algerians clearly did not fit into wider Parisian society—a hangover from Haussmann's bourgeois social planning. They faced constant surveillance, persecution, inadequate housing, and higher rents, all while filling the lowest wage jobs in the city (House and Macmaster 2006).

The parallels between the Algerians and refugees in this current moment will become more obvious as this chapter progresses, but it is worth noting that this racialized violence and its intimacies with extractive labor have not disappeared. Disposability keeps shifting, but the tensions between potential utility for the purposes of accumulation (even as an abstract and illogical force) and the imaginary that racialized people are thieves of enjoyment are not new.

Despite racial violence toward colonial migrants, France pursued policies of open immigration to fulfill the labor requirements of the growing French industrial sector. Immigration was an indicator of an economic boom but also revealed a housing problem—racialized workers could not live in or afford the city but remained necessary to industrial manpower. This catch-22 echoes the tensions of Haussmann's urban development scheme. The racialized poor challenge the modern imaginary of Paris but also require a confrontation with the real of capitalist accumulation—the thing that cannot be avoided or symbolized, to use the Lacanian framework. To have modernity, one must extract low-wage employment and at the same time transform low-wage workers into bourgeois consumers. It is this impossibility that creates ongoing displacement in Paris. The solution to housing the poor arose through the formation of banlieue suburbs that further entrenched racialized dimensions of working-class expulsion from the city. While the brutalist suburban developments provided a solution to the shantytowns, the eventual decline of welfare spending resulted in ghettoized communities with widespread unemployment and social alienation in the neoliberal era (Angelil and Siress 2012).

Neoliberal restructuring affected the banlieues directly and intensely. For example, the suburb of Asinieres termed the slum areas around it as "insalubrious zones" that needed to be cleared of the North African migrants who lived there (Byrnes 2013). As Sassen (2005) suggests, the effects of neoliberalism in Parisian suburbs vis-à-vis the rolling back of essential state services echo tensions between the core and the periphery on a global scale. Beginning in the 1990s, the banlieues were characterized by the presence of dark-skinned others who required strong-arm interventions—an extension of what Haussmann named *les classes dangereuses* in reference to the unwanted poor. Despite the presence of banlieue housing as an alleged solution to eradicate shantytowns, over seventy-five thousand people in France continued to live in informal settlements outside the city of Paris (Bernadot 1999).

In contemporary times, French citizens whose parents emigrated from non-European countries are twice as likely (24.2%) to face unemployment, and 40.5 percent of those without a diploma will likely be unemployed compared with the average rate of unemployment of 10 percent for French citizens without immigrant parents (Barou 2014). The ghettoization of the racialized working poor has not disappeared despite middle-class gentrification. The Charlie Hebdo attacks in 2015 reinvigorated discourses of spatial evil (banlieues) and good (city of Paris). Again, dark-skinned men were blamed in conjunction with their upbringing in banlieues, spaces that were demonized as breeding grounds for violence (Hancock 2017). Meanwhile, Paris's need for cheap labor has not vanished. As Enright (2013) points out, the city developed a mass transit system that sought to create a more accessible and unified Île-de-France region that boosted financial, industrial, and cultural clusters. The market-based rationality of this development project failed to highlight the further displacement of the urban poor owing to increased property values in areas that were better connected to Grand Paris.

Antimigrant sentiment is evident in policy despite humanitarian rhetoric of acceptance. On the France-Italy border, over 35,000 asylum seekers were arrested. Over 70,000 refugee claims were rejected, and out of 97,300 applications, only 37 percent obtained French protection. Fifty-five percent of foreigners or foreign-born people are homeless (INSEE 2017a; OFPRA 2018). These pressures constitute the intense regulation that refugees face on the urban scale. According to a 2018 report by the French Office for the Protection of Refugees and Stateless Persons (OFPRA), France has 36,533. The majority come from Sudan, Afghanistan, Haiti, Albania, and Syria (OFPRA 2018, 45–66). Refugees from sub-Saharan Africa face an admission rate of 25.5 percent, whereas 49.4 percent of Asian refugees (including the Middle East) are admitted. Syrian refugees are admitted at a rate of 97.7 percent, Afghanis at 80.9 percent, and North Sudanese and refugees from the Democratic Republic of Congo at 42.3 percent and 18 percent, respectively. Île-de-France territory receives the greatest number of refugees, and Paris receives the greatest numbers out of any city or town in the country, with 10,151 refugees in 2016 (OFPRA 2018, 100).[4] Urban refugees, who are insufficiently housed, are unable to work, and have poor language skills training and psychological trauma, face ongoing expulsion upon relocation to Paris, due to their class and race positions within the logics of neoliberal accumulation, austerity, and racialism.

French (Racial) Neoliberalism

The neoliberal fantasy of accumulation and the potential utility of migrants deserves exploration in terms of its French particularities. France's experience with the neoliberal process is tied to its colonial history of integration and assimilation. National policy models interlace French nationhood and neoliberalism as a means of discriminatory integration (Bonjour and Lettinga 2012). French neoliberalism has followed a different trajectory than the United States or Britain and is referred to by Fourcade-Gourinchas and Babb (2002) as pragmatic neoliberalism. Indeed, the French state privatized its industries and deregulated its labor and financial markets, but unlike the United States or Britain, it maintained high taxation in its welfare and industrial policy.[5]

Instead of removing state regulations, the French state continues to intervene for the sake of capital accumulation while maintaining some of the welfare rights of French citizens. Thus, French neoliberalism is referred to by Dikec (2006b) as "state-enhanced" neoliberalism. What we see in the characteristically French neoliberal turn is an increased commitment to the strengthening of French nationalism that is intolerant of social and cultural diversity.

The neoliberal experience in France, at least in the mid to late 1980s and 1990s, was defined through the exclusion of racialized others. This is in contrast to that of the United States and Britain, which focused on a more explicit dismantling of the welfare state amid deregulation. French neoliberalism is often considered a contradiction because the policies of dirigisme before 1983 were championed by the Right rather than the Left. At the height of the so-called refugee crisis, France underwent five rounds of austerity measures through a combination of tax increases and public spending reductions, placing a heavy burden on households. Austerity measures have undoubtedly led to greater poverty, with over seven million French citizens being considered poor. Inequality has widened, and unemployment has remained steady at around 9–10 percent since 2013 (INSEE 2017b). The commitments to racial exclusion under the guise of nationalism and nation-building return us to Shilliam's divide between the undeserving poor and the deserving poor. The former are seen as stealing away the collective enjoyment of the nation, but this theft works to solidify the nation itself. It is only in accusing "the other" of stealing enjoyment—an enjoyment that is unearned and undeserved—that the nation's myth and the unachievable impossibility of citizenship emerge. Even when racialized people are granted citizenship, they are French only on paper and cannot rid themselves of their liminal positionality. Refugees fulfill these commitments to exclusion. Welfare is intended for those who are appropriately French and thus compose the "deserving" poor in France. Refugees, owing to their liminal positions, are permanently undeserving. The debates over who gets welfare and who does not indicate political belonging—that is, who makes up the nation and who does not.

Despite deepening neoliberalism owing to economic integration with the EU, the French state has maintained a sense of social welfare, and social housing is one such aspect of the French welfare state. A prominent French housing scholar interviewed for this book said, "There is nothing neoliberal about *logements sociaux* [social housing] in France . . . because everyone is guaranteed, under the law, some form of shelter" (Interview 8). What this claim ignores is the poverty in urban centers that have been dismantled by neoliberalism. The informant misses the fact that despite the guarantee of housing for everyone in France, about 1.8 million people are still waiting for social housing in the country. Homelessness is on the rise in every EU member state, and housing issues cannot be divorced from the inequalities driven by neoliberal capitalism.

As some French scholars argue, universal social housing programs render poverty invisible by favoring middle-class interests and reducing the number of social housing units under the guise that *everyone* (not just the needy) requires social housing. This is predominantly through social-mix policies, which are intended as a tool for class-based integration. In universalizing social housing policies, discrimination based on race or ethnic indicators is unrecognized by the state. The same scholar interviewed on social housing had this tongue-in-cheek response to my question about race and discrimination: "The French do not believe in racism; it does not exist in France [*smiles*]. . . . It is in our colonial history. If everyone is a French citizen then how can race exist? It is a contradiction that hides discrimination based on race" (Interview 8). French scholars have pointed to obvious cases of discrimination based on ethnicity (Balibar and Wallerstein 1991; Kirszbaum and Simon 2001), and as Hancock (2017) further suggests, French constructions of race, gender, citizenship, and nationhood within universalized social housing policies renew tensions surrounding barriers to access in urban space instead of reversing this trend (see also Sala-Pala 2010). Despite the promise of social-mix strategies to alleviate issues of ghettoization and increase interracial solidarity, racialized minorities are excluded from the urban life of Paris because race and class are intertwined.

The proliferation of universalized social housing and neoliberalism occurred simultaneously in France. This could be read as a potential contradiction in the era of rollback neoliberalism committed to cutting social spending. Recalling France's commitment to citizenry and republicanism is important here. The Besson Law of 1990 defined housing as a right for the entire nation. While the banlieues were built in the 1960s and 1970s, the exclusion and marginalization through underfunding and hypersurveillance led to mass-scale violence in urban peripheries all over France (Jazouli 1992; Blatt 2013). These developments placed immigration issues and racial tensions on the map, at least in terms of neoliberal social housing development initiatives.

The Besson Law led to another urban housing policy in 1991 named *Loi d'orientation pour la ville* (LOV), known colloquially as the anti-ghetto law. The purpose of this law was to mandate social mixing: areas with populations larger than 200,000 should have 20 percent of their housing designated as social housing units (Paris still falls short of this goal). The LOV was followed by the *pacte de reliance pour la ville* (PRV) in 1996, which targeted the racialized banlieues for deeper economic integration through tax concessions and public subsidies. The LOV and PRV are both features of French neoliberalism disguised as welfare. The social mix law arises in order to mitigate racial violence in banlieues and prevent communal solidarity along racial/ethnic lines. In turn, banlieues are further stripped of welfare resources as every urban neighborhood needs to be stratified via an income-based mix. The PRV strategy served to deepen neoliberalism by offering tax concessions to areas that can better integrate the urban poor through employment. Workfarist logics are prevalent here as the solution to poverty involves placing the poor in low-wage employment (Dikec 2006, 2011).

While social mixing seeks to diversify the poor population in various arrondissements in Paris, only four out of twenty arrondissements hold on to any viable numbers of social housing stock. The poor can barely afford the rapidly gentrifying 10th, 18th, and 19th districts, which form the outskirts of the city's core. The racialized urban poor continue to be displaced as buildings that formerly housed the working class are demolished for the sake of private interest within ongoing gentrification. As Kipfer (2016) notes, bourgeois interest in social housing stock in Paris forces the working and nonworking poor into banlieues. The average rent per square meter of social housing in Metropolitan France is €5.30, while Paris's rent per square meter averages €7.70. Not only is social housing difficult to attain, owing to long wait times and the overall housing shortage, but it is also far more expensive in Paris than in other French cities. On average, rent, even in the cheaper arrondissements, hovers around €1,000 per month, making private rental housing unaffordable for most refugees. In general, finding social housing in Paris takes at least three years and, depending on family size, can take up to seven to ten years.

I interviewed another expert on social housing in France, who stated that "social-mix strategies are an example of abject racism." He told me that while previous socialist governments had done a good job of raising housing stock, there was just not enough social housing to go around. Two-thirds of the people in France could have a viable claim to social housing. For him, social mixing masks tensions of racism on the grounds that buildings should have a proportional number of white people. He found that the policies are in fact designed for assimilation under the premise of "housing for all" (Interview 10). Social housing provides a new avenue for assimilation under universal principles of social mixing. Indeed, race and class operate at once in a way to discriminate against the wider racialized poor in Paris.

The spatial terrain of social housing governance in Paris further places refugees in precarious positions. Although the statistical data is sparse, it is important to note that refugees in Paris live in makeshift shelters in the 18th, 19th, and 10th arrondissements, which are home to areas such as Porte de la Chapelle and the metro stations Juarez and Stalingrad. Since emergency shelter services are backlogged in the city, refugees and the extant homeless are forced to seek shelter in highly policed and contested spaces such as subway stations in order to survive.

While race might be a social taboo that challenges French nationalism, Hazan's *The Invention of Paris* opens with the following statement: "Town planners, speculators, and police never stopped pressing the poor . . . further from the centre of the city" (2010, xii). This quote highlights the formation of the banlieues and emphasizes how the city of Paris keeps its poor at a distance, because the poor always present a challenge to the fantasy where Paris aims to maintain its image of benevolence, wealth, and diversity even against social realities of homelessness, joblessness, and austerity.

Disposable and Abandoned Refugees in Paris

I have provided the context within which refugees are governed in Paris and described how this context is influenced by the French particularities of neoliberalism on the national scale. As mentioned in chapter 1, the framing of the refugee crisis treats migration as though it is an ahistorical event removed from capitalism; however, the Paris case shows us how the exclusion of racialized others is built into the very fabric of Paris through its treatment of the racialized poor even before 2015.

The fantasy of refugee governance renders refugees liminal as they attempt to access shelter and income while quite clearly being framed as oppositional to idealized conceptions of French citizenry. Recall that Mamoudou Gassama was granted citizenship only after putting his own life in danger by scaling a building to save a French child; many other migrants and refugees, meanwhile, continue to be left in limbo. With regard to work, the goal of assimilation requires refugees to become French citizens virtually overnight and find employment so as not to overburden the state's welfare capacities. Again, the fantasy operates in a way such that refugees are permanently undeserving and are not part of the French nation. The same could be said of Muslims in France in recent times, with the targeting of hijabs under the fantasy of secularism. The push for refugee self-reliance is argued here as fueling disposability because it presents refugees with unsurmountable pressures of survival while rendering their struggles invisible.

Since the implicit goal of refugee integration rests on self-reliance, many of the NGOs and IOs operating within Paris focus on work skills, entrepreneurship, and integration in order to receive government tenders and funding. Urban refugees in Paris face intense regulation as most are prevented from accessing state services including social housing and, relatedly, other forms of income generation. If we take seriously the political economy claim that shelter is a key aspect of survival in capitalism (Aalbers and Christophers 2014; Soederberg 2018), then refugees in Paris are left out. They make up what Bhattacharyya (2018) refers to as populations on the edge. Refugees have no choice but to become self-reliant—a key aspect of disposability that emerges in Nairobi too.

TABLE 5.1 Acceptance of refugees by country of origin

COUNTRY OF ORIGIN/CONTINENT	TOTAL PRIMARY DEMANDS OF ASYLUM IN FRANCE	PERCENTAGE ACCEPTED
Sudan	5,897	42.3
Afghanistan	4,058	80.9
Haiti	4,927	3.4
Albania	4,601	11.4
Syria	3,615	97.3
Democratic Republic of Congo (DRC)	2,551	15.6
Guinea	2,336	28.6
Bangladesh	2,276	7.1
Africa	29,060	26.5
Asia/Middle East	21,221	49.4

Source: Adapted from INSEE 2017a.

To show this argument empirically, I explore the various emergency, short-term, and longer-term forms of shelter access and highlight that shelter survival depends on both political belonging and income in Paris. Three aspects of ongoing displacement are highlighted as follows: (1) the expulsion of refugees from France and Paris through the use of EU law, (2) the contradictions in government assistance in which shelter is provided only if refugees agree to relocation, (3) the devolving of welfare responsibility from the national to the urban scale, through community service organizations, NGOs, and the like. Disposability captures the compromise between the alt-Right and the liberal Left where refugees are never truly accepted but are seen as potential sources of labor and future labor (the relative surplus population). Self-reliance absolves the state of its own responsibilities but allows the French state to maintain its ideological commitments to empty humanitarianism (the fantasy of a benevolent France and Europe).

To reiterate, the terrain of refugee governance in France-Paris is fraught with contradictions. Over 70,000 refugee claims were rejected, and out of the 97,300 applications in 2016, only 27 percent obtained French protection. Fifty-five percent of foreigners or foreign-born people are homeless. Meanwhile, the Greater Paris Area built over 10,000 new housing units for asylum seekers (these are called CADA,[6] short for Centre d'accueil pour demandeur d'asile) in 2016, but only half (45,247) of the asylum seekers received these units (INSEE 2017a; OFPRA 2018).

As table 5.1 illustrates, the refugees who are accepted are from the Middle East, with Syrian claims receiving the most favor. Syrian refugees are deemed the most authentic, while African refugees are more often considered irregular. The imagery of Alan Kurdi's body washing up on the Mediterranean shore came up many times in my interviews as a rallying point for refugee acceptance (re-call that the European migration crisis was first referred to as the Syrian migra-tion crisis), captivating French officials and private citizens alike. The shifting discourse on refugee acceptance dovetailed with Marine Le Pen's presidential bid and the globalization of Trumpism.

Regardless of their country of origin, all refugees must apply for asylum in the following way: First, upon entering the city, refugees must apply for a per-mit at the prefecture that is sent to the OFPRA. Second, and simultaneously, they must apply for assistance at the Office of Integration and Immigration (OFII) for housing and welfare payment. Third, as these applications are being pro-cessed, they must try to find housing—a nearly impossible task considering the overcrowding in the city's emergency shelters and lack of CADA availability. If refugees are lucky enough to receive status, they must leave their emergency housing as soon as possible and look for private accommodations and employ-ment, with little assistance from the local government (Interview 14).

Central to refugee management in France-Paris is the Dublin III treaty, dis-cussed in chapter 4, which allows officials to return asylum claimants to their port of entry. Despite claims of violence and incarceration in Hungary, Italy, and Greece, OFPRA returns many people to these countries, citing the Dublin treaty. Out of the 66,000 asylum applications in 2014, for example, 16 percent of refu-gee applicants were approved on their first attempt, and only 27 percent of ap-pealed claims were approved, meaning that the rest were relocated either to their country of origin or to their port of entry in the EU (OFPRA 2016).

A recurrent theme during my fieldwork surrounded this exact concept of be-ing *dublined*, where asylum claimants were forcibly removed from France through the EU legislation. I interviewed one official who works in one of the relevant migration and refugee departments who stated, "Many people in [department hidden] are racist French nationalists. . . . They do not want refu-gees in the country and 'Dublin' as many people as they can" (Interview 15). This was an interesting encounter because the official felt immense guilt for the way his own department was treating refugees. The interview illustrates the violence of bureaucracy where abject discrimination has a legal facade. Claiming asylum in France-Paris is difficult; claimants make an application at the prefecture that decides whether a claim is legitimate. While certain policies must be followed according to national and international regulations, the prefectures lean left or right politically, thereby denying or accepting claims on the basis of political in-clinations (Interview 15). Legal fantasies of justice and fairness under the law boil down to personal politics. Bureaucracy is thus both banal and evil. It is wrapped in the gauze of justice and humanitarianism while ignoring the actu-ally existing violence that refugees face on the ground.

I draw the link between dublining and disposability as a form of circuitous displacement—an exhausting and seemingly never-ending process that denies refugees political agency and belonging. Through an interview with a cis male South Sudanese refugee named Abdul,[7] I gathered that the prefecture decisions regarding Dublin are firm and that evading this decision would result in arrest and deportation. In Abdul's situation, his caseworker told him that he had to return to the country of origin, where he was fingerprinted upon entering Europe (Italy in Abdul's case). Abdul said that the conditions in Italy were brutal and that he wants to stay in Paris; however, his caseworker informed him that under Dublin this was an impossibility (Interview 16). Reflecting on Abdul's journey to the streets of Paris is important to illustrate the ongoing nature of displacement in the EU. Like Abdul, many refugees enter the EU in Italy or Greece and manage to escape to various third countries—most often Germany and France. While in France, they struggle to survive in homeless or refugee shelters before being dublined back to their port of entry. Abdul clearly does not want to return to the brutalities of potential detention in Italy, and yet this system of constant displacement works exactly as it was designed. The urban, national, and regional scales of displacement are linked.

On the same day, I sat in on a caseworker's conversation with two cis male Syrian refugees who were fingerprinted in Germany but fled to Paris because of poor economic circumstances and lack of close kinship ties. They, too, were told to return to their port of entry. They understood that they arrived in Paris illegally but were hoping for their Dublin period to expire so that they could seek asylum from the prefecture in Paris. The caseworker told them that their only option was to evade arrest. She said, "If you get arrested, they will send you back!" (Interview 17; Participant observation 1). In their handling of cases of homeless asylum seekers who wanted housing assistance, some of the caseworkers suggested to the individuals that they should get arrested because this would give them emergency shelter. While this is in direct opposition to the advice given to asylum seekers who had no choice but to live in Paris illegally, the case workers' advice rested on kinship ties, class position, and the particular situation of the asylum seeker. The police wanted refugees off the street and out of the city center of Paris, and so these individuals were often placed in shelters. This suggestion may seem brutal, but the caseworker explained to me that this in fact ensured them a bed (not necessarily jail time) and was a better situation than spending nights on the streets.

Before the increase in migration in 2015, many refugees congregated at camps at metro stations in the historically working-class arrondissements of the city. Metros Juarez and Stalingrad were popular locations, as they are close to emergency, health, and education services. These camps are characterized by donated tents and blankets from local NGOs. Fuel, food, and emergency health care were also donated by private citizens. At the start of the Syrian event, the city provided migrants with free Wi-Fi and electricity during the cold winter months. Despite the presence of these camps, many refugees were (and continue to be) in a precarious situation as there were not enough emergency resources to serve this population (Interview 15). Metro stations and bridge covers hardly qualify as secure housing; however, they provide temporary shelter for a large number of people. By the summer of 2015, the residents of the 18th and 19th arrondissements had grown discontented with the refugees in their area, and as mayoral election season approached, the city decided to "clean up" the metros.

By July, the police had shut down the makeshift refugee camps near Juarez and Stalingrad, closing off the area with barbed wire and large stones in order to prevent new migrants from squatting. Refugees staying in these shelters were rounded up and sent to rural and remote CADA housing in France, illustrating yet another example of expulsion of the racialized poor in Paris—the first within the European migration event (Interview 15; Interview 18). The camps, despite being repeatedly shut down by national police, keep popping up, telling a story of urban resistance as well as necessity. In 2017, the camps returned to Porte de la Chapelle, reigniting the tussle between police and refugees because the latter have nowhere else to stay. During the pandemic, there were several news reports of police cracking down on makeshift tent communities. Refugees are seen as health hazards—another wrinkle in the never-ending story of surveillance and ongoing displacement.[8]

During my time in Paris, the city created the first emergency shelter (or urban refugee camp) in France. The Bubble, located in the 19th arrondissement and funded entirely by the city of Paris, is both a processing facility and an emergency shelter. A city official told me, "The city sees itself as pro-refugee, it is a triumph for us that we have opened the Bubble in 2016 so we can provide emergency housing" (Interview 13). Two additional housing shelters with about four hundred total beds and serving both men and women were also opened. The city official assured me that the municipal government was still bound by the Dublin obligations but that it was doing everything it could to help refugees.

I asked him about the ongoing evictions and closure of makeshift camps. He told me that the police, who are controlled by the national government and not by the city, were responsible for these actions. Contradicting this testimony, a prominent refugee rights NGO told me that while the police are complicit, the city is also to blame, in its protection of the interests of affluent and white French citizens. There was a big push to clean up the city and expel refugees, forcing them to the banlieues or poorer areas of the city. The logic of Haussmann seems to prevail.

I visited the Bubble a few times, and while this might have been a useful site for recording and processing incoming asylum claimants, its potential for emergency housing was largely overblown. The Bubble was crowded then, so it is unsurprising that the problem of refugee homelessness remains. The city and the police continue to dismantle makeshift slums/camps, but to no avail. At the site of the Bubble, I found that many refugees were living on the street. Some people were using cardboard boxes as shelter. One informant told me that he comes to the site every day to check whether there is any room or assistance for housing. Eventually, when refugees are processed at the Bubble, they are allowed to stay a maximum of fourteen days before either returning to the street (while they await social housing and the processing of their claims) or finding housing outside the city. At this stage, refugees await a decision from OFII and an interview from OFPRA. If they cannot find emergency housing in Paris, they end up leaving the city and sometimes go to rural areas, where informal work is easier to find.

Although Paris has some streams of emergency housing, the rising number of both homeless and displaced people results in an insurmountable task for NGOs and city shelters. I interviewed two people who were organizers at a homelessness prevention NGO who told me that refugees have no other option but to call the 115 number to see if they can find a room. They also told me that most refugees sleep on the streets, under subways, or in hospital waiting rooms, which they referred to as the harsh reality of Paris today (Interview 19).

Emergency housing shelters in the city are poorly maintained and underfunded. A cis male Somali refugee I interviewed said, "My hostel is dirty . . . people are stealing my things . . . there is always a threat of violence and people are fighting all the time" (Interview 20). Unfortunately, these shelters are among the better options for refugees who are waiting for CADA allocations.

Refugees also receive an allowance, called the ADA, for rent and daily expenses. The ADA amounts to about €7 per day or €190 per month (for a single person). Initially, refugees were given a card similar to a debit or cash withdrawal card,[9] but this has been replaced by a payment-only card that can be used at authorized vendors. Without the ability to withdraw cash, asylum seekers are placed in an even more precarious situation, as they could often use their ADA payment for rent in (often overcrowded) lodging. The ADA was initially introduced to subvert the CADA backlog—a refugee cannot hold a CADA unit and receive ADA at the same time.

I interviewed the director of a renowned LGBTQ minority rights advocacy organization and was told that the housing shortage for refugees and homeless people is so chronic that OFII has no choice but to break the law. He informed me that affordable housing and emergency shelters were chronically underfunded. "Where do you think people will go . . . first CADA is full, so then refugees go to homeless shelters. . . . Okay so then those shelters are full so then they go to the streets" (Interview 21).

The informant went on to tell me the following story of one of the queer refugees his organization was helping:

> This whole system is a trap for many vulnerable people. Say you are a gay Congolese refugee and you finally arrived in Paris. You have nowhere to go so you stay with an acquaintance that houses many other Congolese. You have to again hide your sexuality because things could become violent. Say you are HIV positive then you have to hide your medication and you also have to hide that you are seeking asylum on the grounds of sexual orientation. Even if all this does not happen, many of the refugee houses know that you are receiving ADA so then you might get charged €240 a month plus another €60 for expenditures. . . . Many relatives and friends of friends arbitrarily extort them [LGBTQ refugees] for money because they know they are receiving ADA leaving less than €50 for personal expenditure per month. (Interview 21)

The plight of queer refugees illustrates the liminality of the refugee subject in general. Queer refugees often face deeper marginalization owing to intersectional vulnerabilities of race, class, sexuality, and gender identity. Many flee their countries of origin for this reason and face ongoing harassment—an invisibilized reality in a city like Paris (Bhagat 2018). Moreover, refugees rely on ties to kinship networks to access shelter and on their ADA supplements to survive.

This involves what another prominent LGBT rights NGO in Paris calls "going back into the closet." According to the informant,

> They [refugees] must hide their sexuality because they are not often out to their relatives back home. They also fear violence from their landlords or friends or relatives here because sexuality is still a taboo in Middle Eastern or African countries. Many of them are ashamed of their sexuality and it even prevents them from gaining refugee status because they hide their sexuality. . . . In some ways it makes sense for them not to disclose their status—look many of them have not had a stable home for a long time, so when they finally get a place that seems safe and secure they rather just stay in the closet. (Interview 22)

Disposability speaks to the multiple invisibilized spheres of violence. While most refugees use their ADA payments to live outside the city, the refugees who are able to live in Paris face extreme housing inadequacy. In the 19th arrondissement, informants working at a refugee housing NGO told me that "it can take eight to ten years to get an adequate enough space within the city especially if they [refugees] have bigger families . . . whether they want to or not, eventually, many are forced out of the city" (Interview 18). The informants were working closely with a family of seven that had been living in a twenty square meter apartment since the migration crisis and had been waiting for social housing ever since they were given status. This overcrowding is sometimes long term.

While the ADA provides some refugees with short-term sustenance, it also facilitates continuous displacement and expulsion. Through ADA, the pressure on CADA housing is somewhat eased as refugees find Paris unaffordable and thus move to areas outside the city or region. Even when they remain in the city, housing precarity, coupled with unemployment/underemployment, constrains survival. It is thus important to reflect on the various ideological tensions and fantasies that obfuscate the lived social realities of refugee housing in Paris. On the one hand, housing is deemed an unequivocal right according to the legal infrastructure in France and for refugees according to the OFII and the recast refugee conditions directive. On the other hand, the quality, durability, and timeliness of housing access are constrained within dual logics of austerity and accumulation. Disposability and abandonment appear on multiple scales of refugee survival governance from port of entry to constant relocation. The particularities of the Paris case show us how refugees—like many other racialized people before them—are incongruent with the fantasies of both the political Right and Left and of capitalism in general. These ambivalent tensions overlay the refugee experience and are ultimately empty (yet pacifying to the wider citizenry) in guaranteeing the long-term survival of refugees.

Although the city of Paris prides itself on being humanitarian and progressive, what we are in fact seeing echoes what I discussed as organized abandonment in chapter 3. There are multiple set pieces that organize refugee life in the city, and they are often designed to destroy the capacity of social reproduction for many people. While NGOs and other activist groups have attempted to assist refugees, the overall system remains one of abandonment—the dominant mode of refugee governance rests on prevention (i.e., keeping refugees from accessing major urban centers vis-à-vis exclusion in the realm of housing and work) and circuitous displacement.

Liminality and Refugee Life

In concluding this chapter, I draw attention to disciplinary logics of self-reliance in neoliberal Paris. I assert that refugees are liminal subjects because they are somehow overexposed yet invisible in terms of urban capitalism. The threat of the refugee as a thief of enjoyment speaks to the historical and material roots of racism in Paris. Refugees are not treated as viable actors in capitalism—their survival does not appear in any coherent fashion as part of an integration agenda. However, the ideal refugee subject is a worker or an entrepreneur who does not need state resources. An interview with a Parisian official revealed the following tension: "Refugees in this current moment are impossible to integrate. . . . We are trying but there are very many" (Interview 13). While this might appear callous, it reflects the lived reality of refugee survival in urban Paris. Simply put, there are not enough jobs and not enough houses, and the city lacks the infrastructural capacity to contend with the refugees who arrive on its streets. This is not the fault of the refugees. In fact, it is a crisis of capitalism that is exacerbated by a new, disposable population. Thus, many of the organizations I interviewed focused on aspects of refugee integration and were preoccupied with employment skills because of the underpinning logic of putting refugees to work and triaging state welfare responsibility.

The fantasy elements of the refugee "crisis" on the left and the right obscure social reality. The Right is convinced that refugees are using too many resources, and the Left is convinced that they are providing resources as adequately as possible. For example, UNHCR commended the city of Paris for creating an innovative integration program through piecemeal interventions like the refugee chef's food festival, which allowed refugees to showcase their culinary skills. Heartwarming, but ultimately this ignores the fact that the majority of refugees are unemployed. Chronic circumstances of unemployment and inadequate housing are not newsworthy—the refugee disappears upon arriving in Paris, and the struggles for survival are rendered invisible and disjointed from contemporary capitalism.

Statistics regarding refugee employment are not collected, and many refugees work in the informal sector. While many NGOs highlighted unemployment due to language barriers and low skills/training, the antimigrant and xenophobic societal-level barriers were often muted. Tensions surrounding French (white) homelessness and poverty were drummed up by Le Pen's presidential bid, in which she questioned why refugees and immigrants were allowed to come to France when the state did not take care of its own. While refugees are argued as a key population experiencing the highest degrees of marginalization in Europe, the category itself is fuzzy. In fact, the distinction between refugee and economic migrant is only useful in understanding the treatment these officially divided groups receive. On the urban scale, there is very little difference among racialized immigrants or otherwise unhoused people, or refugees who are awaiting status.

A clandestine focus group conducted by an organization under the cover of language training emphasized the need for housing support and work as key indicators for long-term refugee survival (in opposition to narratives that high-light citizenship/refugee status).[10] The director of the program said,

> Okay it is one thing for them [refugees] to get citizenship status—in fact in some cases it is a big deal, if they get the appropriate documentation then they can potentially apply for housing and work etc. But sometimes even when they get documentation it is not enough for them to pull themselves out of poverty or even get a house in Paris. So here we try to teach them at least a bit of French so that they can use it for employment. . . . Even still, people do not want to hire refugees because of some racial sentiments. . . . Okay sometimes they see a Syrian opening a restaurant; they see some people working in shops etc. but most refugees struggle to find a job here. (Interview 23)

With work being difficult to find, it is unsurprising that many refugees—particularly queer and other vulnerable minorities—turn to sex work. As another national LGBTQ rights NGO observed,

> Some of our clients are sex workers because they have no other choice. Many of them do not use protection and sometimes they are uneducated about it. . . . Sometimes their client will say okay if you don't use a condom then I will pay you more so HIV and STI risk is a big part of our program. . . . They get clients through Grindr[11] or they go to particular areas and many times they do not even want money they just want to stay for a night so they exchange sex for shelter. . . . Sometimes it is positive. For example, one of our refugee clients was referred by a guy he met on Grindr he said that the man came to ask for a place to stay . . . [refugee] immediately started taking off his clothes and he [the host] stopped him. . . . He realised the situation was desperate so he referred him [the refugee] to us. (Interview 22)

Looking at the urban scale reveals multiform incongruencies and uncomfortable realities of survival (both as a struggle and as a form of resistance). The LGBTQ rights organization who I interviewed in this excerpt provides housing to refugees on a needs basis but can fund only six refugees at a time. When asked why the number was so low, they noted that each organization in France has a very particular mandate and gets funding only for their stated role (Interview 22). This is of course another version of austerity that affects refugee housing and survival. As it stands, NGOs and other organizations like church groups are only able to help refugees in a haphazard, uneven, and nonholistic way. The central responsibility for refugee integration and welfare was given to France Terre

D'Asile (FTDA)—an organization that focuses on refugee housing and swift integration into the labor market.

FTDA has adopted the functions formerly assigned to OFII and is part of the government's devolution of responsibility to the NGO sector. The government's role is budgetary monitoring and evaluation, but the state still takes little part in the day-to-day management of refugees. FTDA receives about €20 for each client it serves, and it is the sole organization responsible for refugee life once refugees receive citizenship status. Since most refugees cannot afford social housing, and those that can wait for a long time, they are placed in an FTDA apartment that seeks to slowly discipline them through rental tenure. Refugees are charged 25 percent of their basic income to familiarize them with paying rent. Most refugees only earn around €500 a month, making this a sizable contribution.

I interviewed a worker from FTDA who said,

> The basic income percentage is actually unfair because the quality of houses they live in are characteristically overcrowded and dilapidated at times.... We're charging them too much for what the house is worth.... There is also a paradox, first of all OFII knows there is a shortage of housing for refugees even on our end so they try and reject as many people as they can. The ones they accept they put into homeless shelters, but those are also full. So, when they come to us, they have no choice but to take a house outside Paris and that's exactly what they want. Paris is for the rich not the "poor and lazy."... So our goal is to integrate them through some skills and hopefully one day they can find a job. (Interview 24)

As the interview suggests, FTDA housing also exists outside the city, so placing refugees in these units is also a form of expulsion. This is where the tensions of austerity and racialization overlap: refugees are cast as disposable populations, and most of them are rejected. The ones that are accepted are meant to live outside the city, and even the organization that is funded to house them ends up charging them rent that is often unaffordable. The goal of integration seems at odds with disposability; however, it implies that refugees are worthwhile citizens only by contributing to society by finding a job—the same society that prevents job access because of racial and xenophobic mind-sets and other systemic barriers to entry.

Another state-funded organization that operates on a smaller scale than FTDA also houses refugees who receive official status. Touted as the "Airbnb for refugees," CALM connects private French citizens with refugees who share common interests. Over eight hundred people hosted refugees in 2015, and the number of hosts continues to rise. Syrian and Afghan refugees are seen to be of most need. French citizens host refugees for free. The central goal of the organization is to integrate refugees into French society, connect them with meaningful employment, and help them become "productive members of society" (Interview 25).

The employee at CALM said that 44 percent of refugees found meaningful employment through the pilot program, while 27 percent continued their education. The program is designed to offer job training and increase refugee employability while also priming them for integration (Interview 25). It has been successful in accomplishing its mandated task; however, the implicit logics of integration through employable skills, productivity, and language learning indicate that refugees must become productive members of society. Some of them are success stories, and organizations like CALM are only able to get government funding if they can speak to these ideological dimensions of productivity that underpin the metalogic of capital accumulation even for NGOs.

The France-Paris case illustrates the various issues of survival, particularly in the context of a state with a history of social welfare. Despite this socialist commitment, refugees face ongoing displacement and a lack of access to basic services in their attempt to navigate various systems that are backlogged in a country that cannot provide for them. They face deep exclusion amid instances of ideological humanitarianism in Europe, France, and Paris, making them impossible, incongruent, and liminal subjects. Refugees in Paris are global actors that appear as a constant threat in the psyche of French citizenry but are also invisible in everyday life. Their makeshift settlements are actively erased, and they are physically moved away—a process of historical salience in Paris.

REFUGEE GOVERNANCE AND ENCAMPMENT FANTASIES IN KENYA

The discursive construction of refugees as actors that drive political, economic, and cultural crises in Europe also implies refugee movement as sudden, rapid, and thus ahistorical and unpredictable. As I have shown, refugee governance and survival cannot be separated from ideological and material tensions in capitalism. The Kenyan case—particularly at the national level—is discussed here as a way to historicize the management of refugees as a long-standing process rather than a response to an unannounced crisis. By centering Kenya in this discussion, the temporal focus shifts to the chronic violence of forced displacement in the developing world and also serves to deepen our conception of state-driven violence at the refugee camp. The world—including the global aid industry—is ambivalent to the plight of refugees in Kenya (and in sub-Saharan Africa in general). The camp is a global fantasy where racialized refugees are managed away from cities and in a space of limbo. Refugees are twinned with the image of the camp because they are seen solely as humanitarian subjects—passive recipients of aid who are grateful for some safety as they are fleeing unnamed war-torn regions "somewhere in Africa." In reality, refugees in camps struggle to survive. They live off ever-decreasing aid and face tremendous violence. Take, for example, Kenya's Dadaab camp or Melkadida refugee camp in Ethiopia, both of which have been ravaged by funding shortages, particularly the slashing of rations provided by the World Food Programme. Refugees in these camps are on the brink of starvation and must rely on informal markets and kinship ties to avoid harm.

As I showed in chapter 4, the EU provides an apparatus for refugee management across its member states, and despite its inherent contradictions, the Common

European Asylum System (CEAS)—buttressed by economic and political leverage vis-à-vis the rollout of security-based measures for policing refugees—provides a loose framework to understand the regional dimensions of refugee governance in the EU. This is not the case in the East African Community (EAC), which includes Kenya, Rwanda, South Sudan, Tanzania, and Uganda, despite calls for greater co-ordination of refugee management among the member countries. Thus, focusing on Kenya not only captures regional variation in refugee management but also shows us how international actors such as the UNHCR interact with the national-level state.

In so doing, I decenter the conventional narrative that refugee management is globally regulated through the Geneva Conventions. Yes, Kenya is a signatory, but the social reality of refugee governance is far more disordered, especially keeping in mind the role of race and exclusion. As one refugee interviewed for this book in Nairobi said, "We refugees are our own ethnic group. . . . It doesn't matter if you are Somali or Congolese or Ethiopian if you are hungry, you are hungry, if you need health care, education, anything it is all the same, we refugees are different than Kenyans" (Interview 26). Indeed, the refugee becomes a racialized subject in the face of widespread poverty for Kenya's deserving poor, thus becoming the target of xenophobic violence.

As the Refugee Consortium of Kenya (RCK) emphasizes, Kenya has hosted refugees since its independence in 1963. The country receives refugees because of various migratory movements and conflicts in Uganda, Sudan, and Ethiopia, and this has resulted in the formation of the refugee status determination pol-icy. In the late 1960s and 1970s, the Immigration Act allowed refugees to obtain a Class M work permit, a de facto integration strategy where refugees could en-gage in an occupation, trade, or business. The legal landscape shifted with the mass displacement of Somalis and Ethiopians. The Kenyan state became over-whelmed with its management responsibilities as more than two hundred thou-sand asylum seekers entered the country between 1990 and 1992 (RCK 2019).

At the onset of heightened Somali migration, Somali refugees were given prima facie[1] status, which was revoked in 2016. The 1990s represented the first era of encampment, and as a key informant from RCK said, "Look at where Dadaab is placed. They put them there on purpose. . . . Refugees are always seen as temporary in Kenya. . . . The reason that Kenya accepts refugees is for money" (Interview 28). This statement is corroborated by Jaji (2012), who names the en-campment of refugees in Dadaab as a social technology of control for contain-ing the threat of the refugee other: keep them in place and far away from major urban centers.

The beginning of Somali migration to Kenya in the 1990s mirrors the fantasy of refugee governance in the EU—that is to say, the tension between liberals and the Right. By accepting refugees, Kenya can show its commitment to humanitarianism while also preventing integration in any meaningful way. The materiality of encampment is illustrated by the fact that Kenya received $475 million (USD) in 1990 and continues to receive among the highest amounts of Official Development Assistance, totaling $2,665 million in 2016 (*New York Times* 1991; OECD 2016). The refugee encapsulates both disdain and economic opportunity, pointing to the ambivalent nature of refugee governance through encampment.

Aid flows to Kenya have slowed down since the 1990s and spiked only with the advent of another cycle of displacement from Somalia in 2012 (roughly $3.3 billion). Meanwhile, Al-Shabaab's attacks on Garissa University, Westgate Mall, and the DusitD2 complex have resulted in renewed calls for the closure of Dadaab. The Government of Kenya (GOK) has shut down refugee camps but still relies on refugee aid, which has indeed fallen since 2012 with other EAC countries receiving a comparative increase in funds. Refugees in Dadaab are the ultimate scapegoat, even though they are kept separate from major urban centers in Kenya. The refugee is a phantom figure existing in the imaginaries of state actors who must simultaneously contend with extant issues of poverty and widespread inequality in Kenya.

A key informant from a prominent NGO in Kenya told me, "The government always calls for ending refugee hosting and blames terrorist groups, but this is just scapegoating. . . . On one hand they want to send Somalis back [to pacify public interest and statewide xenophobia] on the other hand they want the aid money" (Interview 29).This statement further attests to the material operations of the refugee fantasy at the national-level state—one that is constrained by international pressures and promises of aid money and assistance while also needing to placate societal xenophobia. Like the refugees in Europe, refugees in Kenya offer potential increases in aid funding. Countries such as Turkey, Libya, Italy, and Greece are often funded to process more refugees or detain them in various encampments. Kenya is no different in its want for global aid and refugee management funding as the EU has expanded its funding in Africa and the Middle East to prevent refugees from arriving at its own shores.

Meanwhile, xenophobia toward Somalis, coupled with reductions in aid flows, has altered prima facie policies, stripping Somalis of their de facto status. As an informant from RCK said, "If they [GOK] admit that there is an ongoing problem in Somalia then they have to accept more refugees. . . . They are being smart, they do not want to acknowledge that Somalia is unstable because then repatriation is violating international law" (Interview 28). Prima facie status was revoked in 2016, and by 2017 the number of Somalis in Kenya had been reduced by about 35 percent. Kenya hosted about 413,000 Somali refugees in 2016 but had retained only 284,000 people by the end of 2017. Despite this drop in Somali refugees—a type of targeted ethnoracial discrimination—refugees coming from the Democratic Republic of the Congo and South Sudan have seen higher rates of acceptance. South Sudanese refugees now receive prima facie status, and the majority of non-Somali refugees are relocated to the Kakuma refugee camp.

As of December 2018, the Dadaab refugee camp hosted 208,633 people, a drop from the earlier figure of ~400,000. A total of 187,349 refugees reside in Kakuma, and there are around 75,000 refugees in urban settlements, with the majority residing in Nairobi—although there could be many unaccounted-for urban refugees (UNHCR 2018b, 2020). Of these numbers, Somalis still make up the majority of the refugee population at 54 percent, followed by South Sudanese (24%), Congolese (9%), and Ethiopian (6%) refugees (UNHCR 2018b, 2020). The overall trend toward rejection and reduction is prominent in both France and Kenya as is the separation between inauthentic and authentic refugees. Once considered worthy of assistance, Somalis are now rejected (UNHCR Kenya 2015), whereas South Sudanese refugees, owing to their prima facie status, are seen as deserving the most assistance. In late 2022, about 80,000 people in Dadaab were forced to return to Somalia because of drought and conflict in these camps.[2] The structural conditions of organized abandonment seem to be evident on multiple scales, and these conditions are what govern refugee life. Kenya has committed to an integration policy alongside the slow decay of camps. While the effects of this turn toward integration vis-à-vis job permits are yet to be seen, early evidence points to this type of legal commitment to integration as another face of self-reliance and abandonment.

Key Policies and Actors

Keeping in mind the various incongruities concerning refugee management among the EAC, global aid, and the GOK presented above, I look at the Kenyan Refugee Act of 2006 and the Tripartite Agreement among the GOK, the government of Somalia, and the UNHCR. I also highlight some key organizations that assist in refugee governance; however, unlike the EU, Kenya relies on a variety of international organizations (IOs) to govern refugees, such as the International Rescue Committee (IRC), the International Organization for Migration (IOM), and various UN agencies. Table 6.1 focuses on a few key organizations and the type of work they undertake, but it is important to note that countless international, national, and local organizations could be included in the Kenyan case.

As illustrated by table 6.1, the two main actors responsible for refugee governance in Kenya are the UNHCR and the GOK, which is split into various departments and agencies. Many of the informants interviewed for this study highlighted the tension between the GOK and the UNHCR. Although Kenya

TABLE 6.1 Summary of key refugee governance organizations operating in Kenya

ORGANIZATION	ROLE
United Nations High Commissioner for Refugees (UNHCR)	The key organization responsible for refugee governance in Kenyan refugee camps and in Nairobi. The UNHCR is politically and economically motivated, bridging international expectations with those on the national level. The UNHCR is the de facto state in refugee camps and is also responsible for coordinating aid and other IOs and NGOs that assist refugees. It is also a key actor in facilitating voluntary repatriation for Somali refugees to return to Somalia and is paying them between $200 and $500 (USD) to return.
Government of Kenya (GOK)	The GOK is the progenitor of the Refugee Act and the key actor that determines whether to accept refugees or return them to their country of origin. In 2016, the GOK disbanded the Department of Refugee Affairs and replaced it with the Refugee Affairs Secretariat. Before this, the UNHCR was responsible for most of the processing of refugee claims in Kenya, but now it is committed to leaving refugee processing duties to the GOK.
Refugee Consortium of Kenya (RCK)	RCK is a national-level NGO that is critical of the GOK and the UNHCR and has repeatedly challenged court decisions to end refugee encampment and repatriate refugees back to Somalia. RCK aids in the transfer of refugees from urban areas to camps and vice versa and protects refugee rights from a legal and constitutional perspective. It places Kenyan law in the international context—the basis for its legal challenges.
International Organization for Migration (IOM)	IOM is responsible for the orderly and humane management of migration. Its key role is to provide humanitarian assistance in Kenya (in camps and urban settlements) and, since the Tripartite Agreement, relocation in Somalia. It ensures the safe movement of migrants from country of origin to relocation and vice versa.
International Rescue Committee (IRC)	IRC seeks to aid refugees and host communities in conflict and disaster zones. It provides women's protection, human rights, and education services and works with the GOK and UNHCR, especially in Dadaab and Kakuma. It also provides emergency health care and supplies and advocates for refugee rights.
Refugee councils of various European countries	During my fieldwork I liaised with various refugee organizations that were funded by European countries, such as the Danish Refugee Council and the Norwegian Refugee Council. These organizations hire Kenyan workers to oversee both urban and camp-based refugee issues and mandate small grants as well as job-training activities.
Local NGOs, religious organizations, privately funded organizations	Many church groups, neighborhood/area-based organizations, and privately funded charities help particular kinds of refugees or have incidentally assisted refugees outside their own mandates.

has been a signatory of the Geneva Convention since 1966 and of the African Union's Convention Governing the Specific Aspects of Refugee Problems in Africa since 1969, the Kenyan Refugee Act (2006) continues to be the most important legal document that directs refugee policy in the country.

The first tension between the GOK and the UNHCR stems from the deployment of prima facie status. According to my informant from the UNHCR, "The status determination process is severely backlogged which is why South Sudanese people received prima facie status in the first place. . . . We are trying our best to process them in camps, but those in Nairobi are more difficult because they are scared to be sent to the camps" (Interview 32). Although prima facie status expedites asylum claims, it also creates uneven access to refugee status for those who relocate to Kenya. The UNHCR has granted refugee status to many South Sudanese refugees, whereas refugee claims from other countries remain in limbo.

Before mass Somali migration in 1990, the GOK was open to refugee integration in urban areas as the country hosted only about twenty thousand people (Nanima 2017). Although refugees can still apply for a Class M work permit, their claims are often rejected, because according to the Refugee Act, "Every refugee and member of his family in Kenya shall, in respect of wage-earning employment, be subject to the same restrictions as are imposed on persons who are not citizens of Kenya" (2006 2 (16)). This work-related restriction is lifted in France and most of the EU within twelve months of asylum application, but it is never lifted in Kenya. The illegality of gainful formal employment—which seems to be shifting with Kenya's new integration-based commitment—is a type of racialized strategy that targets refugees in particular and forms the key justification for encampment as a temporary process. The new language in the act states, "Subject to the laws applicable, and taking into special consideration the special circumstances of refugees, a refugee recognized under this Act shall have the right to engage individually or in a group, in gainful employment or enterprise or to practice a profession or trade where he holds qualifications recognized by competent authorities in Kenya" (2021 28 (5)). Kenya appears to be practicing both encampment and integration at the same time. Although there seems to be some movement toward job-based integration, the legal dimensions do not provide any guidance on how refugees would find jobs in a constrained and informal labor market.

The encampment or designated areas policy, which requires refugees to reside in a specific location, remains part of the 2021 Refugees Act. The policy has three main issues: First, refugees are prevented from fully integrating into the Kenyan economy, and so they must become self-reliant in order to survive in the context of diminished humanitarian assistance and lack of welfare support from the GOK. The clause fails to deal with the social reality of urban refugees, who face undue marginalization simply because they are de facto illegal in cities like Nairobi. The question of what a designated area is and for whom remains. During the time of my fieldwork, refugees were often targeted by the police regardless of their refugee status and as the policy directive remains ambiguous it is imaginable that refugees still face undue targeting by the police. Second, refugees are divided along the lines of deserving/undeserving poor, with Dadaab holding mostly Somali refugees close to the border of Somalia, while Kakuma hosts acceptable South Sudanese and other refugees in Turkana County—the poorest region in Kenya. Third, the GOK does not get involved in any form of refugee assistance and leaves this responsibility to various IOs. As a representative from RCK said, "Why would the Kenyan government care if refugees go? Sure, they want aid money, but they do not involve themselves with refugee camps they believe it is not their responsibility" (Interview 28). This sentiment was echoed by a UNHCR employee, who added, "We are trying to get the government more involved in the management of refugees because ultimately it is their responsibility" (Interview 32).

The UNHCR, of course, is not an innocent actor in all this. Encampment was international protocol during the 1990s, and it is only in the shrinking of the UNHCR's operational budgets that policies of self-reliance and integration have been championed. In 2017, for example, the UNHCR requested $231 million in aid funds but received only $66 million (UNHCR 2018b). Organizations such as the World Food Programme (WFP 2017) have reduced their food rations in Kenya by 30 percent, further illustrating global ambivalence toward refugee survival. With diminished funds, and politically tense situations motivated by xenophobia, some refugee lives are more valued than others, as shown by the current framing of Somalis as security threats despite ongoing instability in Somalia. Refugees entering both France and Kenya are treated differently based on ideas of race and ethnicity.

The targeting of Somali refugees is particularly evident in the Tripartite Agreement among the GOK, the government of Somalia, and the UNHCR. The preamble of the document reads, "Considering that voluntary repatriation constitutes a durable solution for the *problems* of refugees and the attainment of this solution requires that refugees will voluntarily return to their country of origin in conditions of safety and dignity" (Government of Kenya, UNHCR, and Government of Somalia 2013, d; emphasis added). The preamble also acknowledges Kenya's hospitality (as opposed to responsibility) and the huge economic, environmental, and social burden (g–h). The language in the agreement is transparent about framing refugees as costs and burdens, and thus the only solution to chronic displacement is return—a push for the Somali state to get its act together.

Although the agreement was drafted in 2013, it is not until the ending of prima facie refugee status for Somalis that voluntary repatriation starts to occur. The GOK is responsible for security escorts, repatriation convoys, joint registration, and documentation in terms of legal status; it also has a loose commitment to provide assistance to all refugees until durable solutions are found (Government of Kenya, UNHCR, and Government of Somalia 2013, Article 24). Regardless of this named legal responsibility, it is the UNHCR that coordinates the transition of refugees back to Somalia. An operations strategy report for 2015–2019 published by the UNHCR reads, "UNHCR provides return assistance comprising pre-paid transportation, a cash grant of $120 per individual ($150 for persons with special needs) to refugees traveling by road or $60 per individual ($75 for persons with special needs) to those traveling by road from Dadaab and Kakuma" (2015, 13). These cash transfers are opportune in that they provide relief to extremely indebted refugees in Dadaab.

The tensions are well detailed by Sieff (2017), who examines the role of cash transfers in facilitating both debt relief and displacement—a type of constrained choice. Refugees, unable to buy food or raise enough capital for their microenterprises, turn to shopkeepers and other middlemen who give them a loan for consumption-based survival, or what Taylor (2012) refers to as consumption smoothing. As a refugee cited in Sieff's piece says, "I just want this debt to be over" (2017, 2). The case grant of $150 allows refugees to pay back these middlemen, and thus, in taking the grant, they have no choice but to return to Somalia.

My interview with the UNHCR sheds further light on the voluntary nature of refugees' return to Somalia. The informant said, "Yes, Somalia is not the safest place, but we are doing our best to place refugees where they want to go and also returning them to traditional lands." The informant went on to state that "Dadaab has left these people with no skills and no assets. . . . It is not sustainable from a financial point of view, it is not sustainable because you maintain people in a state of dependence for too long, you do not maintain their potential they do not have opportunity to use their talent" (Interview 32). Self-reliance is implicit in this statement amid neoliberal wordplay such as *opportunity, talent*, and Dadaab as *unsustainable*. The neoliberal emptiness of this directive is supported by political and economic instability in Somalia—the notion of self-reliance conquers social reality by placing the burden on individuals to help themselves despite being returned to a failed state.

An employee of the IRC, who was critical of the UNHCR, told me, "Voluntary repatriation occurs when UNHCR says they send people back but actually they are paying people to leave. . . . There is increased support for Somali dreamers—to use the American term if you are familiar with DACA—that have been in Kenya for more than three decades. The UNHCR money is used to survive, almost because they have no choice, so the voluntary part of voluntary repatriation does not exist" (Interview 33). In a more candid interview, an informant from IOM, which has sole responsibility for the safe transition of refugees from

Kenya to Somalia, said, "Repatriation is a key issue for us because the government cracks down on refugees. . . . Come on! The Kenyan state is bankrupt. They are looking for scapegoats so they show up at refugees' houses and just make arrests and deportations out of our control" (Interview 34). Paying refugees to leave is not a new phenomenon—recall that the EU offered to pay migrants in Greece €2,000 to go home in March 2020.[3] The position of both IOs is revelatory of the insidious nature of voluntary repatriation that appears humanitarian but ultimately facilitates mass displacement and the return of many Somalis who accept these terms only out of constrained choice and poor survival outcomes in Dadaab.

The informant from RCK further pointed to the complexity of voluntary repatriation, saying, "Yes, there is debt, they want to pay back their loans, but you know some of them come back. . . . The government does not want to recognize this but there is nothing left for them in Somalia, so they go and come back" (Interview 28). The UNHCR's meager cash incentive dries up, and although reductions in global aid have resulted in Dadaab's chronic underfunding, the situation in Somalia is even worse—hence, cyclical displacement.

The Refugee Act and the Tripartite Agreement reflect the structural impediments that facilitate ambivalent refugee governance in Kenya, where the humanitarian rhetoric of refugee acceptance is incorporated into the legal jargon of both the UNHCR and the GOK. Through this empty humanitarianism for refugees, who are meant to live a life of dignity, all sorts of policies are justified. Voluntary repatriation is framed as an opportunity for refugees to develop their skills and hone their talents, even though Somalia is in no shape to provide any sort of assistance to those who return. Meanwhile, some refugees accept repatriation only to return later. The ending of prima facie status thereby makes these returning refugees illegal or irregular (to use the EU terminology) because voluntary repatriation can be justified only if the country of origin is deemed safe for refugees to return.

Kenya's commitment to integration in the renewed Refugee Act of 2021 remains a bit suspicious. On the one hand, the new language in the act allows refugees to get jobs; on the other hand, there is still an emphasis on refugees remaining in designated areas—a vague and ill-defined term. The act also commits to a new refugee identity card, allowing some degree of freedom of movement. But as a study from Refugees International (2021)[4] highlights, refugees often struggle to access identity documents because of corruption and discrimination; this in turn makes it difficult for them to integrate or start businesses. Despite a discursive shift toward integration, refugees still remain disposable to the needs of state and society. One might question whether these commitments to integration reflect another feature of organized abandonment.

Dual Fantasies of Encampment

Refugees in Dadaab and Kakuma are not treated the same, and I seek to examine two fantasies of refugees in encampment that operate at once. As I mentioned earlier in the chapter, refugees in Dadaab are of Somali origin (97% of people in Dadaab), and Kakuma's population of 171,085 is ethnically composed of South Sudanese (55%), Sudanese (5.6%), Ethiopian (5.8%), Congolese (5.9%), Burundian (4.4%), and a sizable population of Somalis (22.1%), who also face voluntary repatriation (UNHCR 2017b). The key working document for refugee governance in Kenya, agreed upon by a variety of IOs and NGOs, is the Kenyan Comprehensive Refugee Program (KCRP),[5] which lays out a set of policies that are ideologically motivated by self-reliance.

The 2016 iteration of the KCRP is of particular relevance because it reflects a shift in refugee policy from encampment to integration. As the document states, the refugee program will see a reorientation from traditional care and maintenance in the camps to "truly solutions-oriented programming" (UNHCR Kenya 2016a, 1; UNHCR Kenya 2019–2020). This programming refers explicitly to self-reliance in terms of refugees' food, shelter, and work-related needs. Self-reliance is framed as *the* long-term solution for refugee assistance—a neoliberal turn from aid-related welfare to providing the tools for refugees to become entrepreneurs. This approach is justified in the document, which further states that $199 million was allocated to the UNHCR and partners for protection services; however, there is a discrepancy between the allocated amount and the actual amount on hand. A total of $110.2 million is required for food aid, of which only 43.1 percent has been secured. Since 2015, funds received for operational costs have declined by 10 percent and those received for overall assistance costs by 21 percent, and the bulk of this decline has been recorded in the resources pooled from international donors (UNHCR Kenya 2016a, 3).

These funding constraints are due in part to the pivot of the world's attention from Africa to Europe. An informant who works with a prominent EU agency operating in Kenya said, "The Syrian refugee crisis has made it difficult for us to market more long-term situations like those we see in Kenya. . . . It is what we call donor fatigue; people are tired of seeing the same images and it is hard for agencies to raise money" (Interview 35). The images of dark-skinned bodies are seen as tiresome—an ambivalence on a global scale—and the plight of refugees in Kenya is secondary to those in Europe. Indeed, it is the imaginary of Europe itself that is humanizing, while refugees in camps in Kenya fit within the imagery of African poverty in general. Mittelman and Neilson (2011) refer to the images of dark-skinned bodies of poverty in Africa as development porn, thereby desensitizing donors and deprioritizing refugee life in Africa on a global scale. Recall Bauman's (2004) conception of the refugee camp as a site of permanence and the refugees who live there as a forgotten population.

The material consequences of defunding are evidenced in the Dadaab refugee camp as its budget has seen a steep decline with the GOK and UNHCR's closing of many of the encampments. In 2011, the received funds for operational costs were $96.3 million (or 80 percent of the requested budget). In 2015, this number fell to $40 million and covered only 44 percent of the required budget for operational costs (UNHCR Kenya 2016a, 11).

With these operational costs and population declines in mind, the GOK and UNHCR have agreed to roll out biometric identifiers and a countrywide database to track migrants. This is similar to the Eurodac policy, discussed earlier, in which refugees are tracked by EU actors for their irregular status and returned to their port of entry. The GOK and UNHCR, in their bid to consolidate refugee services in the name of efficiency and surveillance, intend to conduct fingerprinting and retinal scans and place refugees in a national database called proGres (UNHCR Kenya 2016b, 12). This database will play a part in the Integrated Population Registration System, which records the identities of Kenyan citizens and the number of foreign-born people currently residing in Kenya. While the UNHCR highlights the benefits of these tech-driven refugee management tools under the old neoliberal adages of transparency and accountability amid making the refugee management system more robust, the key perceived benefits are cost reduction and the prevention of irregular migrants entering Kenya. The racial exclusion of refugee management is buttressed by neoliberal logics of efficiency and austerity. Tech-based surveillance assists in preventing asylum claims under the guise of fairness—it racially excludes and targets Somalis in particular. Somali refugees in Dadaab face one angle of disposability—abject exclusion. Even when they follow the rules of self-reliance in the doctrine of refugee management by attempting to start businesses and work informally, they still face debt, violence, and relocation. To use Roy's (2017) notion of racial banishment, Somalis in Dadaab are in fact beyond displaced—they cannot return to the camp or the country and are permanently excluded even from selling their labor power or existing on the fringes of Kenyan society.

The ongoing dismantling of Dadaab has highlighted the austere logics of refugee governance in Kenya. Kakuma, meanwhile, represents potential opportunity for profit making along the lines of a so-called untapped market of refugees waiting to be pulled out of poverty—the second operant fantasy in a geographically separate camp. The penetration of financial technology (fintech)—the creation of a financial ecosystem in which the poor are recipients of unregulated financial services through technology (Gabor and Brooks 2017)—has produced alternative strategies of service delivery to refugees in the context of neoliberal governance. Gabor and Brooks (2017) refer to this as the fintech-philanthropy-development (FPD) nexus, in which financialization is extended through rapid growth in digital innovation and incorporates the poor into capital accumulation vis-à-vis the digital economy. Kakuma represents another encounter between the poor-refugee and the FPD industry vis-à-vis financial inclusion.

In the first fintech project, initiated by the WFP and the UNHCR, refugees used cell phones to access cash-based transfers in digital e-wallets. This service was facilitated by Safaricom through M-PESA, a widely used e-currency system in Kenya that predates quick payment methods such as Apple Pay and other e-wallets. M-PESA played a huge role in allowing Kenya to become the foremost cashless economy in sub-Saharan Africa and also include smaller vendors in the formal economy. Safaricom charges 1 percent per transaction, and the UNHCR suggests that cash-based transfers allow refugees more freedom to choose their products and services outside of the general food ration that was provided before 2015 (UNHCR Kenya 2016a, 10–13). Through financial inclusion, as the UNHCR and Kenya's Comprehensive Refugee Response Framework report notes, "the cash-based transfer program contributes to raising the standard of food quality and safety in the camp markets, improved service levels, and increased livelihood opportunities for refugees and host communities" (UNHCR Kenya 2016a, 10).

The potential profit hidden in poverty is of course a central feature of Soederberg's (2014) debtfare. What Kakuma teaches us about this iteration of fintech-driven accumulation in the refugee camp is that refugees are open to experimenting with development strategies regardless of the lack of empirical evidence of the success of entrepreneurial or self-reliance-based strategies of poverty alleviation. Refugees become a population for experimentation through fintech because they are seen as stagnant yet untapped people in camps—an enclosed testing ground for FPD strategies that ultimately (win or lose for refugees) generate profits for companies like Vodafone.

This experimentation is further evidenced in the creation of the Kalobeyei settlement, a joint project of the GOK, UNHCR, and Turkana County (the poorest region in Kenya). The key purpose of this settlement—the first of its kind and a marked shift from encampment—is to integrate refugees with the Turkana people. Within the context of diminished aid funding, the Kalobeyei integrated settlement moves away from the "aid model" and pivots toward self-reliance (UNHCR 2017b). Foreign capital investment in fintech in Kakuma and Kalobeyei has allowed private capital to penetrate these settlements, co-opting informal and customary financial ecosystems and connecting refugees to the global North via the accumulation of capital through fees and data collection that enables the offering of financial products to refugees.

For instance, Tara Nathan, Mastercard's executive vice president of public-private partnerships, sees the building of financial ecosystems and the leveraging of the data collected through this infrastructure as the best way to effect development and humanitarian outcomes. Nathan envisions the future of development as occurring specifically through networks of private sector companies (private-private cooperation without state involvement).[6] Leveraging the refugee market, for example, requires empowering refugees through economic growth, providing value for host communities to incentivize integration, and stretching donor funding—key aspects that motivated the building of the Kalobeyei settlement. Underpinning ill-defined terms and lofty ideals of poverty alleviation are ideological commitments to neoliberal-led growth that mask potential revenue streams for companies like Mastercard.

In April 2018, the International Finance Corporation (IFC) released its extensive *Kakuma as a Marketplace* report. The report invited private investors to view the refugee camp as a space of potential investment under the pretense that the private sector would allow refugees to live "self-determined lives" (IFC 2018, 5). The report characterizes the camp as an informal economy built on entrepreneurship (Mastercard and Western Union 2017). In turn, Kakuma refugees are framed as employable and entrepreneurial, as well as consumers and producers. This stands in contrast to statements such as "[refugees] living in Kakuma for decades with little prospect of returning home, becoming a Kenyan citizen, or being resettled in a developed country" (IFC 2018, 5), which portray Kakuma as a wasteland without financial investment.

In the *Kakuma* report, the IFC identifies the camp as a new opportunity and challenge for the private sector. Thirty-nine percent of Kakuma's residents own businesses, and the goal of the IFC and other private sector actors is to extend financial services through fintech to these informal actors in a market that is valued at $56 million. As the IFC notes, credit is a key demand in this camp, as many rely on friends and family for support. The formal banking sector could fill this credit gap by using data from M-PESA to measure client risk in favor of collateral (IFC 2018).

Kakuma as a Marketplace reflects a partnership between Mastercard and Western Union and their collaboration on new digital infrastructures such as mobile money, digital vouchers for refugees, and card-based solutions intent on promoting self-reliance for refugees (Mastercard and Western Union 2017, 5). The model being implemented in Kakuma and Kalobeyei is meant to serve as a "scalable blueprint for underserved populations to access formal financial services" (3). It aims to eliminate or formalize informal money transfer organizations like hawala and eliminate the middleman. Refugees are urged to use Western Union and M-PESA (digital money transfer) to send remittances directly; however, the sender bears the transaction costs, absorbing 9.4 percent of the value of remittances sent to the East African region (World Bank 2018).

The goal of implementing financial technology is to accelerate the process of financial inclusion. Digital transactions generate data on customers (which include refugees as well as other poor people in countries like Kenya) that companies then use to evaluate their credit and offer targeted financial services (Roderick 2014). According to the head of customer relations management at Western Union, "Refugees across the world want to be empowered to break the chains of dependence and to rebuild their lives in meaningful ways" (Western Union 2017). The solution, in Kakuma and Kalobeyei, lies in the production of new digital infrastructures vis-à-vis the delivery of mobile money, digital vouchers, prepaid cards, and the tracking of refugee behavior. Violence, social stigmatization, and the threat of forced repatriation are avoided under the FPD nexus, where refugees become a test market for digital infrastructures in deeply marginalized spaces (Bhagat and Roderick 2020).

In the following chapter I return to some of these issues surrounding financial inclusion as it pertains to urban refugees in Nairobi. But for now it is worth emphasizing the false promises and ideological embedding of the FPD nexus as it relates to self-reliance and disposability. As this chapter has shown, refugees are either unwanted migrants who are sent back through the fiction of voluntary repatriation or a stagnant population that is worth caring for insofar that they provide potential revenue streams for various financial actors. With diminished funding, the self-reliant turn in refugee management policy rests on very little empirical validity. It is boosted by the pure dream of neoliberal ideology that puts the onus on refugees to pull themselves out of chronic poverty. This last-ditch effort of poverty alleviation—regardless of whether it works—benefits financial actors and fintech companies that are able to extend their tentacles to previously untapped markets such as refugee camps.

This is disposability. It explains why certain populations are prone to violence. Meanwhile, Dadaab is steadily underfunded and condensed, and the refugees who live there are debt-ridden, starving, and far away from economic hubs in Kenya. Mirroring those in the EU, refugees in Kenya are divided along the deserving and underserving lines of Kakuma and Dadaab, respectively. The rollout of biometric and surveillance technology under the guise of refugee security and the speedy evaluation of claims targets refugees along racial-ethnic lines. In Kakuma the introduction of fintech supported by corporate interest also frames Kalobeyei as a place of capital accumulation through the use of data capturing vis-à-vis financial service provisions for the poor. Challenging Bauman's (2004) concept of the camp as an isolated space of wasted bodies, I in fact show the opposite. Yes, refugees are disposable and their survival is de-prioritized, but the neoliberal governance of refugees in camps allows for multiform actors that see poverty as an economic opportunity.

Two refugee fantasies operate at once. Somalis in Dadaab are permanently undeserving—they threaten state security. Non-Somalis in Kakuma and the Kalobeyei settlement provide opportunity for experimentation. Both places render refugees disposable: on the one hand, through abject exclusion, and on the other, through an attempt to use fintech to alleviate poverty. The latter is an un-proven strategy but emerges as a key policy direction in neoliberal refugee management because the nexus of state-IO actors is unable to provide any sem-blance of welfare for ever-increasing numbers of refugees. The refugee fantasy remains crucial to my analysis here and is demarcated by those refugees who are seen as raced and unwanted others. Somalis in particular are viewed as thieves of enjoyment—undeserving of political belonging when so-called actual Kenyans are experiencing poverty too. If refugees are allowed to exist in Kenya, they can only do so by becoming self-reliant. Even when they do, recent news updates from Kenya point to the shutdown of Kakuma camp too on the basis of unaffordability.[7] The penultimate chapter of this book looks at urban refugees in Nairobi, who often flee from camps. But experiences of disposability do not disappear.

DISPOSABILITY AND ABANDONMENT IN NAIROBI

In developing this book, my initial (and I suppose still implicit) question was, Who do cities belong to? For me, the refugee subject captures the liminality of dis/belonging. The lives of urban refugees, in particular, are underexamined compared with refugees in camps; scholars and policymakers are captivated by the jarring images of depravation and violence in the latter. Understanding the urban dimensions of refugee liminality requires a confrontation with capitalism and its operations for those at the margins, particularly in the face of neoliberal defunding. With neoliberalism in mind, I return to the three prongs of survival and frame survival as a form of resistance. In a nutshell, refugees struggle for shelter, livelihood, and political belonging in a city that casts them out.

It is important to remember that race/racism/racialization is not something that happens "out there" in the Western world. Postcolonial societies like Kenya still field the aftereffects of white supremacy and colonial legacies of race-based violence. Racial logics of differentiation and the actual presence of expatriates that dominate the NGO sector show us how the imaginaries of race and coloniality have contextualized the current neoliberal moment. Refugees are a problem to be solved. An excerpt from Keguro Macharia in the book *The Fire Now* reiterates this point: "White guests continue to receive preferential treatment in Kenya's hotels and restaurants and general shopping spaces. Kenya is profoundly racialized. . . . In Kenya, colonial-era distinctions about abilities continue to dominate the Kenyan imaginations. But we have no political vernaculars—generally shared languages and strategies—for thinking about and discussing blackness in Kenya and how blackness in Kenya relates to blackness in the US and Europe and the Caribbean. . . . We might try to create ways to think about blackness and ethnicity as products of colonial modernity across different geo-histories" (Macharia 2018, 184). Thus, I am concerned with how these racial log-ics apply to refugees as outcasts in Nairobi.

In contrast to Paris, the Refugees Act in Kenya makes urban refugees illegal subjects in Nairobi. In the eyes of the state, refugees do not belong in the city. There is no gray area. The state/city surveillance apparatus does not have to lure refugees to more desolate parts of the country as they do in Paris with promises of housing. The camp or deportation suffices as threat. In effect, refugees are ig-nored and make up a forgotten fringe of the extant poor in the many informal settlements in and around Nairobi. Although the plight of urban refugees is not new (UNHCR 2009), the government of Kenya and the UNHCR has shifted toward integration as official policy only recently.

Seeing refugees as a globally racialized category foregrounds my theorizations of disposability and twins the Paris and Nairobi experiences of survival. Refugees as disposable people are framed in part through Marx's relative surplus popula-tion but also in combination with queer liminality in relation to the preexisting "surplus people" in cities of relocation. As I have maintained throughout the book, I am interested in the ways that refugees survive under capitalism. Through dis-posability we can understand refugee life in relation to humanitarian commit-ments. But when it comes down to it, refugee policies in both Nairobi and Paris that focus on self-reliance leave refugees with very few material capabilities to se-cure their long-term futures as they contend with expensive rental markets, un-deremployment/unemployment, and political erasure—issues of exclusion are endemic to the neoliberal moment of refugee governance.

Kenya's Neoliberal Turn

Kenya was among the first countries in the world to receive a structural adjust-ment loan in the early 1980s from the World Bank. Kenya was notoriously noncompliant—accepting the loan but failing to fully denationalize certain food-producing industries. The World Bank opined that those Kenyan industries "continued to be unofficially protected by their monopoly position, higher tar-iffs, and/or prohibitions on competing imports and ad hoc duty exemptions on raw materials" (1994, 15), leading it to call for more transparency and account-ability surrounding property rights and competition governance. I raise this front and center to break up the unidirectional narrative of structural adjust-ment; however, it is worth noting that Kenya's public sector continued to erode as more loan conditionalities were accepted.

In the 1980s, Kenya was experiencing poor growth and industry development, which led to a deterioration in its national economy and international trade relations. The IMF and the World Bank highlighted three objectives for Kenya's transformation: First, the GOK would denationalize and privatize state industries in a bid to transfer capital from the public to the private sector. Second, the GOK would attract foreign direct investment, thereby reducing various barriers to entry and committing to opening up the economy. Third, in line with neoclassical theories of comparative advantage, Kenya had to undergo a green revolution in its agricultural sector and devalue the Kenyan shilling (KSh) to make its agriculture more competitive on a global scale. The only way to accomplish these objectives was to transform the economy through a model of export-oriented growth, which resulted in diminished wages and eventually widened inequality in the country (World Bank 1999; Rono 2002).

Neoliberal policies were entrenched throughout the 1990s with more waves of privatization, downward wage pressures, currency devaluation, and indebtedness (Ndungu 2013). The 1990s also coincided with the first encampment of Somalis, in Garissa County. Encampment policies allowed the government to both assist and track refugees close to the Somalia border (Veney 2007a). Perhaps coincidentally, refugees—throughout the neoliberal era—were increasingly blamed for Kenya's economic woes. The neoliberal era further coincided with the emergence of the refugee as a perennial threat to Kenya's state security.

Since the 1990s, the GOK has emphatically supported encampment (or designated areas, as stated in the 2021 Refugees Act) because it absolves the state of welfare responsibilities for refugee integration. At the same time, although the UNHCR initially practiced encampment as a way to assist refugees, it has instead pushed the GOK (and all other refugee-hosting states for that matter) toward an integration approach amid an underfunded and neoliberal aid infrastructure. For example, the Comprehensive Refugee Program (2016) emphasizes that job creation, entrepreneurship, and integration should be extended to refugees in camps and cities—a plan that was actively contested by the GOK until at least 2021. According to the program, the costs of refugee assistance in the Kenyan operation have amounted to $1.5 billion between 2011 and 2016. Evidently, the logics of austerity override humanitarian commitments.

> Although integration seems like a moral victory over encampment (especially when camps are described as open-air prisons), the neoliberal logics of welfare retrenchment should not be ignored. The UNHCR has pushed to expand citizenship rights to refugees (through marriage or lawful residence), but the responsibility of welfare through integration and appropriate documentation (moral as these might seem) is placed

on the individual. A prominent academic and refugee governance expert in Kenya had this to say about citizenship rights: "What is pushing people to take these huge amounts of risk to leave their countries? Shelter, income, health care, education none of these things can be guaranteed in Somalia for example. So, if the root cause of refugeehood is actually a betterment of lives then where does citizenship fit in in all this? The Kenyan government threatens the closure of camps as a strategy basically telling UNHCR that if you want to integrate them then you provide the resources!" (Interview 36)

The UNHCR's push to grant refugees citizenship status relieves some of the costs of encampment, because once refugees become citizens, they no longer need to be kept in camps. The GOK does not want to accept the responsibility of refugee welfare, pointing to a tension between the UNHCR and the Kenyan national-level state that is inseparable from neoliberal restructuring in Kenya.

So far, I have addressed the consequences of structural adjustment for refugee governance on the national level; however, the transformation of Nairobi requires some analytical attention too. In Nairobi, land privatization occurred as international financial institutions pushed President Daniel arap Moi's regime to adopt these types of reforms on a municipal level. The Moi regime diverted the private funds to its own electoral campaign, illustrating the link between neoliberal reform and the benefit of the wealthy ruling class—loan money was essentially pilfered (Njeru 2013a).

Unsurprisingly, Kenya's neoliberal turn and the resultant widening of the wealth gap were never matched with a consistent affordable housing plan, and the state's commitment to housing the poor has always been weak. Thus, large-scale private landlordism is the most common form of low-income housing provision for many of Nairobi's poor. In Nairobi, 84.7 percent of households rent or lease their accommodations, and people who live in this area are disproportionately rent burdened—average monthly rent ranges between KSh 2,000 and 4,800, and many people are unemployed or informally employed. The Kenyan National Bureau of Statistics estimates that 53 percent of urban renters pay less than KSh 2,000 (less than $12), 26 percent between KSh 2,000 and 4000, 16 percent between KSh 4,000 and 10,000, and only 5.5 percent above KSh 10,000 (2016; CAHF 2019).

The colonial legacies of inadequate housing provisions are extended within the neoliberal era. This is evident in the works of Huchzermeyer (2007) and Amis's (1984) important study on landlordism and tenant exploitation. Indeed, the slum upgrading schemes of the World Bank caused housing speculation in slum areas, and this has not disappeared.

Ongoing displacement coupled with high rental rates and ethnic tensions appears in the stories of many of my interviewees. One of the refugees I interviewed told me that he was evicted because his neighbors learned that he was from Uganda and assumed he was gay—his neighbors told him that Kibera was for Kenyans only (Interview 38). As Benet-Gbaffou and Oldfield (2014) highlight, the state is able to bulldoze entire areas, leaving organizations such as Slum Dwellers International with no choice but to offer ad hoc solutions based on in situ upgrading and savings programs for people living in informal settlements. While ethnic cleavages often prevent access to shelter for refugees, some landlords rent to refugees at higher rates, knowing that their temporary or illegal status could allow for a rental premium. At the same time, many of the refugees I spoke with said they faced arbitrary eviction owing to the extant racial tensions in informal settlements.

While the Comprehensive Refugee Program is focused on integration via documentation, it has very little to say in terms of livelihood support and refugee welfare once the refugee is integrated. This is why I emphasize the notion of political belonging instead of citizenship, because having documents does not necessarily guarantee meaningful and sustainable work. UN organizations highlight events like the Artists for Refugees project or the inclusion of refugees in the Rio 2016 Olympic Games as a way to showcase the innovative spirit of refugees. While this is good public relations, the lived reality of urban refugees in Nairobi cannot be hinged to empty ideological or fantasy-related sentiments.

An employee of an IO for refugee assistance told me that the GOK did not want any IOs to be involved in the urban areas, in order to avoid the appearance of a commitment to urban integration. Thus, this organization focused on giving refugees access to loans and training entrepreneurs.

Self-reliance strategies overemphasize loans and allow IOs to subvert xenophobic GOK sentiments as these loans do not require state involvement and are funded by various donors. The GOK is also tacitly OK with an entrepreneurial strategy for refugee integration as they hand out business permits as long as refugees can afford them. However, the reliance on loans reflects a debtfare-style commitment to development assistance. Credit is the new welfare strategy, and the logic of capital accumulation persists for refugees too.

Disposability and abandonment are thus part and parcel of the Kenyan strategy of refugee governance. Whether it's self-reliance or encampment, Kenya's refugees face abandonment strategies from the camp to the city. On the one hand, refugees are prevented from accessing formal work, and the camps are continually under threat of being shut down. On the other hand, refugees are allowed to have documentation and the means of legal integration, but they must still rely on credit and debt to become entrepreneurs. Meanwhile, shelter- and work-related insecurity means that refugees are deprioritized and unable to be absorbed by capital amid a large population of surplus people. Despite a turn toward some form of legal integration, refugees continue to face shelter- and labor-based exclusion.

Sheltering Urban Refugees

Urban refugees in Nairobi, like those in Paris, are denied legal access to status, long-term housing, and formal employment. Refugee survival thus depends on a piecemeal network of NGO and community support. This also takes the form of cash grants and microfinance as well as merry-go-round loans[1] that are self-organized. Moreover, urban refugee survival cannot be divorced from decades of neoliberal restructuring of housing markets and real wages. The support of large-scale private landlordism over social housing demonstrates a lack of a viable welfare state—one that was dismantled before it was allowed to become robust. As a result, private property developers and elites purchased land in low-income and informal areas, driving up rents and poverty vis-à-vis housing inadequacy. Instead of addressing issues of inequality and poverty, the GOK has pursued a policy of persecution and scapegoating of refugees, often blaming them for security issues and economic struggles. Through racialization, refugees are characterized by their permanent disposability and face a deeper level of marginalization than that of the urban poor, who are already struggling to survive in Nairobi. The refugee is cast as the ultimate thief of enjoyment—one who consumes material resources daily and poses a danger to deserving Kenyans.

For example, out-casting occurred with Somalis in the wake of the Westgate Mall attacks in Nairobi (although state-led violence toward Somalis in particular occurred after the Garissa University and DusitD2 complex attacks too). The main area where Somalis live is Eastleigh, colloquially known as Little Mogadishu. Since there are many ethnic Somali Kenyans in the area, refugees of Somali origin become effectively integrated. Though many Somali refugees can find some form of work and shelter, cleavages exist between Somali citizens of Kenya and new migrants who have made Eastleigh their home owing to extant networks based on kinship.

A key event that some of my informants referred to was the roundup of Somalis after the Westgate Mall attacks. The police held Somalis, regardless of their refugee status, in Kasrani stadium and sent many people to camps. In a chaotic and knee-jerk display of jingoism against the so-called Somali threat, children were separated from their parents. According to my informant from RCK, the roundups were violent. Some people were beaten and bruised, and others were shot (Interview 31). These roundups reveal a xenophobic state that was reacting to a perceived threat against the nation.

Non-Somali refugees have an uneven experience of integration. Some live fruitful lives with little police persecution, while others are racialized as non-Kenyan citizens. I interviewed a refugee from the Democratic Republic of the Congo who said that he escaped the camp because of a lack of shelter, food, and employment opportunities. The Refugee Affairs Secretariat (RAS)—a government agency—continually tells people to return to camps, even though the camps are starved of funding (Interview 40).

In my observation of the interaction between the refugee informant and the RAS worker, I heard the worker ask the refugee the following questions: "How did you come to Nairobi?" "Why did you come here?" "Why don't you go back to Kakuma?" In my follow-up interview with the RAS worker who makes decisions on asylum claims, the worker said, "If the refugee wants to stay in Nairobi, then they can fend for themselves. The camps are equipped to care for them so if they are in Nairobi, it is by choice, and they ideally should have a transit permit from the government. Otherwise, they can be sent back to camps if they are caught by the police" (Interview 41).

It is worth noting that refugees are liminal subjects in urban spaces where the GOK treats them as illegal migrants, but the disposability of refugees often makes them invisible. Without a doubt, refugees are targeted by the police; but despite their illegality, many refugees continue to live (albeit precariously) in Nairobi. My observations at RAS illustrate a laissez-faire approach to the policing of refugees that once again shows the pervasiveness of self-reliance as a tool for survival. In short, the government agent suggested that refugees should get a permit; if they do not have one, they should avoid the police.

Self-reliance is the dominant ideological mind-set in regard to refugee housing. Many of my informants identified three main issues of shelter access. First and foremost, state persecution owing to citizenship status and arbitrary policing as evidenced through deportation or return to camps was a major concern for refugees. Second, finding a home and dealing with the associated rental debt was also a significant issue. Third, even when refugees were able to find housing, they faced arbitrary eviction and violence because of their ethnic identities and positionalities within informal settlements.

My interview with a local refugee housing-focused NGO suggested that urban refugees, because of their ethnic identities and lack of formal status, face the greatest challenges in accessing shelter. My interlocutor told me that while we might assume that Somalis from Dadaab will find secure shelter in Eastleigh, there are many tensions between the people who have lived in Eastleigh for decades. The core assumption that Eastleigh should or can shelter Somali refugees from Dadaab is a misunderstanding of social relations based on an oversimplification that national identities create social cohesion (Interview 42).

For most refugees arriving in Nairobi, slum living is the predominant type of housing.

Land tenure is contentious in Kenya. The government owns the land in Nairobi's largest slums, and while some people are able to afford units in these areas, the large-scale displacement of people continues to occur with the government's repurposing of slum land for residential and commercial zoning. These types of development activities in Kibera, for example, lead to forced evictions. In 2018, a new road was built in Kibera to help alleviate traffic congestion in central Nairobi. As a result, many people lost their homes, receiving neither any forewarning nor any compensation.[2] While Kenyan citizens can lodge complaints against the state, refugees, because of their temporary or precarious legal status, have nowhere to turn.

Refugees are often exploited in terms of rental debt, with many landlords charging a premium to house refugees once their status is discovered. A UNHCR (2012) report notes that rental costs are among the highest monthly expenditures for refugees in general and Nairobi is no different. Interestingly, the rental expenditures for the very poor and poor are not significantly different from those of the middle and upper classes. The very poor and poor pay around thirty to eighty US dollars a month, which averages to about 30–50 percent of average monthly income (UNHCR 2012, 35). In particular, data from Kayole, Kitengela, and Eastleigh—areas with various ethnic refugee enclaves—show variation in rental rates. The Eastleigh area, home to a majority of Somalis and a minority of Ethiopians, is among the areas charging the highest rent for refugees, among other costs. As the 2012 UNHCR report notes, refugees living in Eastleigh can cover only 70 percent of their survival costs. The survival threshold in Eastleigh is similar to that in Kayole and Kitengela at 65 percent. Importantly, the only way that refugees are able to survive is if they consume less than the World Health Organization's recommended daily caloric intake (UNHCR 2012, 36). Disposability has material costs, as does a lack of sustained attention to urban issues surrounding the basic necessities of survival.

Interestingly, racial differences and kinship ties are evident in areas such as Eastleigh. Somalis, for example, are able to find informal work and rely on kinship networks when they move from camps to, if they are lucky, relatively cheap rental arrangements. Ethiopians, however, do not have the same deep network and are thus more likely to struggle in finding employment and pay more for rent (UNHCR 2012, 18). My interview with an urban refugee department of an EU-funded NGO illustrates the experience for South Sudanese refugees attempting to access shelter in Nairobi. The informant had this to say: "Most Sudanese live in the Thika area of Nairobi, and many are spread far away from the city. South Sudanese refugees have good support systems mostly in estates which is just about where they feel safest. That is how they come and settle, because when you come to Nairobi it is not a designated camp. If they don't rely on their connections, then it becomes very difficult. . . . Rent is also cheaper; they can combine their incomes and we try to help them" (Interview 43).

The estate referred to by the informant is a type of safehouse designated for South Sudanese refugees in urban areas. Some refugees prefer a designated safehouse to struggling to find rental accommodations in informal settlements. This excerpt reflects the benefits of prima facie status and the differentiation it delivers on ethnoracial lines.

Living in informal settlements often involves interaction with the state and the police, even in terms of development policy. Thus, refugees who choose a safehouse may be protected from this everyday form of violence. The director of a local NGO operating in Karogocho made me rethink the ways in which refugees are affected by slum upgrading schemes that seem beneficial but have negative effects. He said,

> Karogocho has slum upgrading that started in the early 2000s. I know the nitty-gritty here. There is a congregation of Catholics working in Karogocho. They pushed the Italian government to have the debt cancellation with the Government of Kenya, the congregation comes from Italy, and it was easier for them to negotiate with the government. They worked in issues of infrastructure, they made some roads, and they were looking forward to work on the issues of housing which has its own challenges. Many people are scared that the government will repossess the housing and they will have to pay a certain amount at the end of every month. Part of this has been the creation of the hospital in Karogocho which has made the land go up in value. To make the matters worse, the refugee persons especially Muslims have nowhere to go. When government is improving the houses, you must produce an ID card and therefore it has been a big problem for refugees because they have nowhere to turn and where do they go so that their shelter is not being taken? They work hard to buy a house but then they do not have an ID card to guarantee what they have bought. (Interview 44)

Slum and infrastructure upgrading-based eviction is an untold story. The government only upgrades the houses of people who have legal property rights, and since only Kenyan citizens can own property, refugees are evicted, sent back to camps, or deported. This type of violence has led refugees to seek housing in precarious riverbed areas that are prone to excessive flooding. Refugees who live in these inadequate housing structures face cyclical destruction of their property and livelihood, as told by two refugees who lost their homes in 2017 (Interviews 46 and 47). Again, the name of the proverbial survival game is self-reliance. Those who do not survive are rendered disposable.

While the above excerpts refer to refugees who cannot make claims to their own homes, most other refugees rent or live in precarious housing in the back-yards of tenants or in unstable attachments that are prone to collapse. In a focus group I conducted with refugee women, many of them said they have lived in precarious housing without doors and feared that their possessions would get stolen or that they would face physical violence (Focus group B). Some refugees are able to buy a small shack, but because of their social precarity, they can lose their property if their neighbors decide to evict them. This happened to one of my participants, who said that he left his home unattended for a few hours and found his belongings on the street (Interview 45). Community leaders and gangs can also create problems for refugees along ethnonational lines.

Other issues concerning disposability in terms of housing access are tied to intersectional forms of exclusion. For example, an interview with a gay activist refugee from Uganda revealed the intensely violent persecution he faced when the residents of his community heard him speak Luganda. He told me that his neighbors assume all Ugandans are gay. He said, "How long can you expect someone to hide their identity?" He then told me that they used his perceived sexuality to evict him so that they could steal his property (Interview 48).

This type of eviction occurred in earlier fieldwork I conducted in South Af-rica (Bhagat 2017, 2018). Here, variant sexual practice combined with xenopho-bia resulted in a continuing cycle of forced displacement where queer refugees were unable to find a secure home. Queer refugee protection is covered in the mandates of a few NGO programs in Kenya and presents an intriguing inter-section of refugee assistance plans. On the one hand, the literature notes that LGBT refugees make up the most marginalized populations of migrants who relocate; as such, they deserve particular attention. On the other hand, Kenya does not recognize the rights of LGBT individuals. But as the above quotation shows, queer refugees from Uganda are accepted into Kenya thanks to interna-tional protocols on LGBT refugees.

Although it upholds a highly homophobic legal landscape, Kenya does not have hyper-regressive laws calling for the killing of homosexuals. A focus group conducted in Nairobi with predominantly queer refugees revealed that NGOs such as the Danish Refugee Council, RefugePoint, Hebrew Immigrant Aid So-ciety, and the Refugee Coalition of East Africa have created safehouses for vari-ous sexual minorities away from informal settlements.

An employee of one of these organizations noted the following as it pertains to safe-housing provisions for queer refugees: "Scattered safe housing is for LGBT populations and survivors of gender-based violence. We have trained refugees themselves and support these people. We support the family, give you money and take care of your basic needs. Homosexuality is illegal in Kenya, but they do not care as long as it is not in your face. As long as the community does not know that the person is gay then they do not care. They come to know because they see how LGBT people become known and communities evict LGBT people. Kenyans sometimes cause problems when they find out because of moral issues" (Interview 49).

The interlocutor displayed an implicit discomfort (in both speech and body language), particularly as she found it difficult to discuss "how LGBT people become known." This could be in reference to same-sex relationships or just queer expression. Nevertheless, the safehouse programs give refugees a safe and free place to live to protect them from any harm they might receive because of their sexual orientations/identities, despite Kenya's legal landscape for LGBT rights. As the informant emphasized, these safehouses are safe only if the people living there hide their identities (both as queer people and as refugees). Indeed, safehouses are also located in remote areas outside Nairobi. For instance, it took me about two and a half hours to drive to a safehouse in nonpeak traffic. Safehouses exist somewhere between living safely and creating an enclave of exiled queer poor. In terms of political belonging in Nairobi, LGBT refugees are cast out.

In the introduction to this book, I briefly discussed my experiences with queer refugees in a safehouse outside of Nairobi. Throughout my visit, I questioned who was being protected: was it queer refugees from homo/transphobic Kenya, or was it Kenya that needed protection from the so-called West and LGBTQ+ agenda? One of the people I interviewed here was a trans-identifying refugee who further revealed the issues that queer refugees face. They discussed their experiences in the safehouse as follows: "We are safe here. We can be gay.[3] I can wear lipstick and dresses and we can express ourselves. This is my home. I am also with other Ugandans, so we do not experience the real Nairobi. Sometimes I forget how it is because I am gay, and it is accepted inside these walls. Once we went to the town and they attacked my friend, so we have to still be careful. . . . It is safe here but not outside these walls" (Interview 50).

For my interlocutor, the safehouse represented a small part of the world where they could be free. While it does not challenge the overall structure of homo/trans/xenophobia in Kenya, the safehouse is a tiny spot of resistance—a small opening in an otherwise impenetrable heteronormative armor. Shelter survival illustrates the lived realities of liminality, and the experiences of queer refugees illustrate this in a literal way. Queer refugees are explicitly cast out of Nairobi, and in a homophobic political and social landscape, they find safety in safehouses. But this story is not one-note. The refugees who lived here also had desires for freedom.

Another person I interviewed talked about their life in Kenya and their potential future: "I am a gay now, I can do whatever I want . . . but in Kenya we are still not free. I love my community and my friends here, but I still want to go to America or maybe Canada with you! [He said this jokingly after we discussed where I was from.] I want a baby and a family."[4]

This tongue-in-cheek response to our play that I discussed in the introduction also illustrates a deep desire for belonging and acceptance. The safehouses provide this, but they are transient and cushion those who live there from the potential violence of Nairobi. In general, however, issues of housing illustrate disposability where housing tenure is often precarious and impermanent. Moreover, as even these various excerpts that cut across a vast array of refugee life show us, shelter access is uneven, ranging from camps to safehouses to ownership and rental arrangements in informal settlements.

Entrepreneurialism as Ideology

To reiterate, shelter and income are inseparable dimensions of survival when placing refugees in capitalism. They are features of political belonging that cannot be attained—piecemeal as that might be—without understanding the material contexts of survival at the level of the city and on the temporality of the day-to-day. I interviewed a Sudanese mother of five children (Lisa[5]) who illustrates this interconnectivity. Lisa told me that she had been living in an informal settlement in Nairobi for about fifteen years, and while she received support from her connections with fellow Sudanese refugees, she struggled with paying rent. She started a small handicrafts business and sometimes sold tomatoes at a roadside stand, but it was not enough to pay for her children's education. Being of South Sudanese origin allowed Lisa to gain a transit permit in Nairobi easily. Her nationality also allowed her to connect with other South Sudanese people in the city. Despite this, her income from her handicrafts—a gendered occupation—does not provide an adequate wage. She continues to rely on loans from NGOs to fulfill her day-to-day needs. While her story is one of survival amid various systemic oppressions, it also shows us the faults of self-reliance-based entrepreneurialism as a survival strategy.

A central issue surrounding income and the ascension of entrepreneurialism as a survival strategy for refugees involves work permits. Importantly, work permits, citizenship cards, and all other forms of documentation exist as a way to regulate people who are seen as undeserving and nonbelonging. I do not wish to fetishize the documents themselves, because they mask issues of xenophobia and inequality under the guise of legality. Work permits are given to very few refugees and are handled by the RAS. In contrast, business licenses are granted on the level of the county and act as a revenue stream for cash-strapped municipal-level governments that are not mandated to deal with immigration issues.

Entrepreneurship (as opposed to formal work, education, and skills-based training) is encouraged because a refugee who has what is referred to as an alien card can receive a business license relatively easily. Each application in Nairobi County costs KSh 200 (~$2), and each license costs between KSh 10,000 and 20,000 ($100–$200) per annum, depending on the size of the company. Even if refugees are unsuccessful in their application, the county still makes a small sum and secures a larger sum annually. The upfront costs of the licenses are sizable and either place refugees at the mercy of cash grants and loans from NGOs or drive them further into debt if they engage in microcredit loans.

For instance, I observed an interaction between a refugee from the Congo and a RAS worker regarding the refugee's request for a work permit. The official told the refugee that he was trying to get him a work permit but that it was very difficult to get one without appropriate documentation (an alien card in 2018 and a refugee identification card today). Such issues make it difficult for refugees to not only find formal work but also seek assistance from the government. The government does not wish to grant work permits under the overall framework of encampment, which is seen as a catch-all solution.

The director of a European NGO said this about work permits:

> I will use our own example; we requested the government to issue permits to our entrepreneurs but only received 10/13 which are required for all these people to legally work. But businesses are easier, [as a refugee] all I need is a business license and a pin number . . . say my refugee status is not been determined and I have children [to feed and care for] . . . [then I have no choice but to] start selling tomatoes to survive. But I am prone to arrest and confiscation of my own goods because I am not allowed in Nairobi. But the state is also mandated to protect through RAS and one of their roles is to provide ID cards and give recommendation letters if you want a class M work permit. RAS will write the letter, but practically most refugees do not get permits to work. (Interview 29)

Indeed, refugee livelihoods are precarious with or without work permits, but the turn to entrepreneurialism rests on the state's insistence to keep refugees out of urban areas in Kenya and keep them in camps. Selling tomatoes is neither an easy pathway out of poverty nor a long-term survival solution, but refugees must undertake these types of income-generating activities because of the state's antirefugee stance. Withholding status and continuing to arbitrarily arrest refugees and destroy their small-scale enterprises (even if they do have business permits) is an exertion of abject state violence—a form of targeted ethnoracial exclusion.

I interviewed many well-meaning NGOs, and most had some sort of business training and loan assistance program to stimulate an interest in entrepreneurship as a means of development assistance. It is worth remembering that the NGO sector flourished under neoliberalism as a way for governments to devolve welfare responsibilities to smaller organizations. An international NGO operating in Nairobi exemplifies this neoliberal commitment to entrepreneurship. A worker from this NGO told me that "refugees must first learn how to make a profit. . . . They are a flight risk you see." She went on to tell me that business loans were given only to those who passed a business skills training program and set up shop (Interview 29). It would be inaccurate for me to suggest that these loans have not provided a crucial lifeline to some refugees. Indeed, some people generate enough of a profit to run their households and send their children to school. But the metrics of judging refugee capacity for entrepreneurship, plus the management of organizational resources, means that this is not the most equitable or the most efficient way to assist urban refugees.

As the informant from the EU-funded organization pointed out, cash grants and entrepreneurial loans are only piecemeal forms of assistance. We cannot impart blame on the organizations themselves; rather, I situate these solutions (problems) within neoliberal processes of restructuring that are buttressed by ideological conceptions of self-reliance and hard work. I aim to illuminate the chronic violence of these logics.

In observing a microfinance small loan group, I learned that many of the refugees who received loans were unable to pay back the initial amounts. They asked for two-week extensions so that they could pay rent and take care of household expenses. The loan manager / NGO worker told me that these requests were common, and they tried not to be too harsh when refugees asked for extensions the first few times. Eventually, some of the claims were denied. Although no interest was charged on the loans in this particular group, refugees who could not repay their loans risked getting evicted from the group, thereby losing cash resources.

Since refugees are barred from accessing loans in formal banks, they often rely on one another in what the UNHCR calls merry-go-round groups. These groups, like the Congolese community microloan group I observed in Karagocho, were given a preset amount of cash by an NGO or IO. Members would then take a certain amount of money to start a business (and often to pay off expenses such as rent, education, and day-to-day living costs) and then return the money with a set amount of interest. If they were unable to repay the loan or pay back with interest, they were barred from participating in the group (Interview 29).

Another option available to refugees is the UNHCR-recommended Kiva microfinance loans.[6] While the company solicits specific donations from private supporters in the global North, it turns a profit through its various partnerships with Visa, Mastercard, PayPal, and the fieldworkers who act as loan managers on the ground. Kiva loans are zero interest, but they often lend to other microfinance agencies that hike up their interest rates for refugees and other poor people in Kenya. The UNHCR lauds the success of microcredit schemes such as Kiva, but the translation of these loans to poverty alleviation for a group as vulnerable as refugees is yet unproven. Refugees are sometimes charged interest rates of 15–30 percent to access the loan so that fieldworkers and associated agencies can stay afloat or make a profit within the Kiva model (MacFarquhar 2010).

Nairobi is often referred to as Africa's Silicon Valley. Ninety-nine percent of investment funding between 2010 and 2017—about $206.4 million—went to Kenyan fintech companies (Mwesigwa 2018). Fintech plays an important role in facilitating loan transactions—an indication of Kenya's neoliberalizing economy. Loans are still transferred from the global North to the global South, and KivaZip, for example, uses the M-PESA system[7] to provide these loans in the time range of 5 minutes to 24 hours (the range of time it takes for the money to arrive). M-PESA's history is an interesting one as it predates Apple Pay and South Africa's Snapscan and was initially devised by students at Jomo Kenyatta University in Kenya to bring financial inclusion to Kenya's poor. Safaricom and Vodafone's use of this knowledge could be read as a form of knowledge appropriation and a transfer of wealth from a technology developed in Kenya to a multinational that operates in the global North. Regardless of whether Kiva loans actually alleviate poverty, M-PESA makes money on each transaction on a sliding scale in which it earns about $1 for a $100 withdrawal (Jack and Suri 2011). The use of M-PESA as a digital innovation in terms of aid suffices to make a profit by taking an amount per transaction, illustrating the pervasiveness and power of fintech.

The issue of microcredit and loans arose in an interview with an established KivaZip partner and refugee NGO in Nairobi. The director was undoubtedly well meaning and cognizant of the various issues presented by microcredit but suggested that there was little else that refugees have access to: "In many ways NGOs like us have no choice but to rely on microcredit as our key solutions to refugee assistance. . . . Look there are many problems and it's neoliberal and all that, but what else can we do? The state doesn't want refugees; they don't want to protect them, there are no jobs, these people can't return to their countries and all the UN aid money has dried up. It's truly an awful situation!" (Interview 39).

The ideological power of entrepreneurship rests on the fact that there is no alternative, much like the informant suggests. Another example of this type of refugee assistance comes from the Women's Refugee Commission's Self-Reliance

Initiative. The aim of this program is to reach five million refugees with self-reliance programming in five years and usher in a paradigm shift in regard to refugee response. Self-reliance is hooked on the idea that "most refugees tell us that they want to 'stand on their own feet'—to take care of their own needs and those of their family" (RefugePoint 2018, 1). This notion of "standing on one's own feet" is a convenient narrative within the mythos of microfinance that is linked to the Global Compact on Refugees.

The key goals of the Global Compact rest on easing the pressure of hosting for countries like Kenya and enhancing refugee security through self-reliance while also supporting the development and stability of various refugee-producing nations (UNHCR Kenya 2016a, 1). Heeding this call, the Self-Reliance Initiative seeks to use microfinance to increase the savings of refugees and expand their access to credit. In particular, a report from the Refugee Coalition of East Africa 2017 revealed a multiorganization plan along with recommendations that fostered initiatives focused on refugee dignity through loans and rights. Most NGOs, despite touting the benefits of self-reliance, do not have a solid program or evidence to justify these policy directives.

Since urban refugees lack fixed assets such as land or homes, the need to develop nontraditional loans and microfinance products for refugees emerged. The report notes, "Due diligence is required from implementing partners to target households who are fully committed to the success of the enterprises and repaying loans as agreed" (UNHCR 2012, 58). In terms of targeting, the UNHCR seeks to facilitate business development with access to markets and finance for the poor and very poor and does so by contracting external technical assistance to facilitate access to finance (2012, 58–59). Despite these aims and a detailed survey of refugee households in various informal settlements (UNHCR 2012, 2017b), microfinance remains at an experimental stage for refugees because of the risk of lending to the poor and very poor. Indeed, the aims of microfinance lending are contradictory, representing a disconnect between perceived global solutions and the social reality for both refugees and private lenders.

Similarly, innovating lending through public-private partnerships is evident in the €5 million IKEA Foundation grant in partnership with the International Rescue Committee (IRC) to help refugees and young Kenyans in urban Nairobi. A press release from the foundation website further reiterates the dream-like nature of the refugee microfinance myth: "Refugees are often innovative and entrepreneurial; many run small businesses, whether in hairdressing, tailoring or running internet cafes, and sometimes they employ Kenyan nationals. But the challenge is that less than 10 percent have a bank account, and most cannot access loans" (IKEA Foundation 2018). There are some core assumptions that fuse with the ideology of self-reliance, such as refugees having an innovative or naturally entrepreneurial spirit as opposed to being forced into various forms of labor in order to survive. The foundation's goal is to seamlessly integrate refugees into their host communities by framing them as useful economic citizens; however, the core assumptions of entrepreneurialism as a neoliberal fantasy remain unchallenged.

An interview with a European NGO whose main purpose is the support of urban refugees in Nairobi reveals the director's commitment to self-reliance strategies. She said,

> Our work is to ensure how you fit into the urban fabric. . . . How do we support them towards self-reliance? Our biggest sector is the self-reliance sector our team now assists this capacity. . . . Do you need to go and continue your education? Do you need more skills? Professional training? Vocational training? Are these capacities useful for when you are in Kenya or when you return home? What kind of marketable skills can you bring back home? With all these in mind we offer start-up kits to start a salon, a barbershop . . . microenterprise. DRC [Danish Refugee Council] trains you on business skills. We take them through the market mix in Kenya and then they do their own research and provide a business plan. Only once that they can show they have a good plan then you will be given a small grant. (Interview 29)

It is evident that the organization's key role is to train refugees for starting a microenterprise. Another element implicit in this excerpt is the assessment of risk—that is to say, it is important to determine which refugees are at risk of defaulting on their loan payments. Therefore, the NGO evaluates each business plan and strategizes with the refugee to turn their loan into a profitable venture. I further probed the informant on what happens to the money if the client is unable to repay their debt. She said the following:

> After giving the grant we also monitor how you [refugees] utilize that grant in your business and how you keep your records. Being in a new area [relocating to a new country] means you are struggling with your *motivation* and struggling to meet your other kinds of bills. There are lots of shocks in the payment and repayment schedule. These are conditional grants. You must repay the grant after business starts. You are given a grace period of three months, but we tell them to repay 75 percent of the grant just to ensure that they, when they repay the amount, we give it to another person. It's a shared grant—without interest—it is their money and they can draw from it. In case donors withdraw the money, it is still self-sustainable. Yes, people do default, sickness, landlord has locked your house . . . what do you do? Keep the money and

sleep outside . . . no! It is important that they use the money for emergency needs we give them time to recover. Here, we are teaching them how to fish—so that they do not find themselves in Nairobi where they engage in negative coping mechanisms just to survive and entrepreneurship is one of the ways to survive. (Interview 29; emphasis added)

Although the loan is interest-free, the disciplinary logic of entrepreneurship persists. The NGO does not mean to make life difficult for refugees; however, the rhetoric of "teaching a man to fish" is part of a neoliberal fantasy where refugees can be trained to act as responsible and useful economic citizens. The entrepreneurial turn in development assistance is seen as providing a lifeline, but refugees are not able to pull themselves out of poverty as much of the literature on financial inclusion in the global South suggests (Soederberg 2014; Taylor 2016; Mader 2018). Instead, bootstrapping refugees is a form of ideological work that allows the state and the wider global system of development aid to further shirk its responsibility toward the poorest and most marginalized people.

I close this chapter with the words of a Ugandan refugee who spoke to me about life upon relocation to Nairobi:

When you are here in Nairobi there are privileges you cannot have that you get in refugee camps. You have to get on your own feet. Things like shelter, food, and protection you have to mark areas . . . you have to know places you cannot move at night because you are a refugee. There is some money they give you to start up life but after that money runs out you will continue on your own [charity-based start-up fund given to certain refugees by the Danish Refugee Council]. You need to look for a job to keep your life going on. Maybe you need to do other activities . . . anything you can to keep going. To live. You have to learn the time to come back home. You have to protect yourself. You cannot live like a citizen because you are a refugee and you have to be safe.

I am from Uganda; the first threat I have to avoid is by getting to be known by my fellow Ugandans. Because of my own issues . . . I am a LGBTI refugee you see. There are people who are going to spread the rumors. They can go back to my family in Uganda.

I again will talk about my citizenship. If you are looking for a house to rent, talking about your citizenship comes last. If they don't ask about it then you keep it. If they know you are Ugandan then they will think you will develop some bad habits because they think Ugandan is LGBTI so I chose an area to live with cheap rent where there are not many Ugandans.

In terms of work, I am still waiting for my alien ID card so maybe I can find work after this, but I will come back here for a grant to maybe start a business. There are not many opportunities for us but we must try, what else can we do? (Interview 54)

This excerpt summarizes the tension between intersectional forms of violence and survival as a form of resistance. Survival becomes an exertion of agency despite constrained choices and threats of violence. The vignette illustrates how entrepreneurship becomes the standard pathway for survival, especially considering that most refugees are unable to receive work permits. Moreover, the positionality of queer migrant reifies the liminality of the refugee subject. In this case, xenophobic disdain toward refugees combines with homophobia to prevent access to extant networks. Issues of safety, which citizens take for granted, mark the refugee body on the street, pointing to societal tensions that seek to cast out the refugees.

The policy emphasis of entrepreneurship, combined with ethnoracial discrimination, deepens refugee disposability. The underpinning neoliberal logics of self-reliance attempt to frame refugees as potentially useful economic citizens, but in fact negatively hamper their survival outcomes. Nairobi County, for instance, is still able to receive a steady stream of revenue from business licenses but offers no protection for refugees in return. In terms of shelter, both ownership and rental tenure become sites of exploitation by landlords, communities in informal settlements, and the state. Here, land titling provides little benefit in the face of evictions and state-led xenophobic policy, as illustrated by the rounding up of Somali refugees in Kasarani stadium. Refugees are cast out of the city by both state and society. As much as this chapter has illustrated the various tendencies of implicit and explicit violence, it has also shown the resilience of refugees who manage to survive on the fringes of Nairobi despite unimaginable pressures surrounding their identity. Refugees do survive. But they should not have to endure these inhumane hardships, which operate on material, discursive, and psychic levels. Regardless of formal status, refugees are unable to avoid constant displacement—they embody liminality.

ENDLESS DISPLACEMENT?

On June 22, 2019, refugees in Calais faced record evictions in which around 1,300 people were forced to cross the English Channel. The Calais-based NGO Auberge des Migrants called this a relentless harassment of asylum seekers in France. During the pandemic, refugees faced ongoing clearance from the streets of Paris by the national police. The police referred to the refugees as health hazards who spread COVID-19 in tented settlements. Meanwhile in Kenya, the GOK has further committed to dismantling Dadaab, and the UNHCR has relinquished former camps Kambios and Ifo II to the Kenyan government. More than 80,000 refugees have been repatriated, and the population of Somali refugees in Kenya has been reduced from half a million in 2011 to around 210,000 in 2019. In March 2021, the GOK directed the UNHCR to shut down all camp operations in Kenya by the next year. These events illustrate the ongoing, cyclical, and violent nature of forced displacement.

The parallels between the queer experience and the refugee experience are hinged on liminality and dis/belonging. Beyond the analytical confines of the relative surplus population, liminality destabilizes the refugee category and resists identification on a group that is made up of multiform intersections. This is true even if we avoid discussing LGBT+ refugees who seek asylum in both Paris and Nairobi. For queer refugees in both cities, the need to prove their queerness while also hiding it from the people they live with in order to survive illustrates a literal connection between queerness and liminality. In general, liminality points to the phantasmal qualities of the refugee experience where refugees are both threats to the nation and thieves of enjoyment who are erased when they relocate to cities.

Missing from the narrative of the refugee camp, where the camp takes center stage in media depictions of migrant survival, is the recognition that the camp itself is an urban site. Sure, Dadaab and Kakuma were intentionally placed far away from Kenya's major urban centers, but in understanding neoliberal capitalism as amorphous and penetrative, the camp becomes a site of both debt and potential revenue. While the camps show us how racial states and the institutions that constitute them enact violence on refugees, major urban centers exemplify how refugees come to be placed in the messy social reality of contemporary capitalism. Analysis of the urban as both a camp and a city cannot be separated from national and international scales, and thus multiscalarity has been central to the framing of this book, particularly because refugees seem to maneuver all three levels of governance to survive.

In returning to the key questions that drove this book—What are the fantasies that govern refugees? How do refugees survive upon relocation?—I hope to have provided some satisfactory evidence of my key argument that refugee governance disguises inequalities endemic to capitalism, where the refugee crisis and the resultant self-reliant strategies are fantasies removed from material social realities of relocation. Echoing Thomas Fabian, the refugee crisis is a housing crisis; it is also a crisis of work and, fundamentally, a crisis of belonging and racial violence.

The barriers presented by race and class dovetail. On the one hand, refugees are accepted under the condition that they become productive members of society by selling their labor power or, better yet, turning themselves into entrepreneurs. On the other hand, refugees are deemed too expensive and portrayed as job-stealing migrants, thereby facilitating and justifying their rejection and ongoing displacement. This ambivalence drives the framing of refugees as liminal subjects because they are presented with an impossible situation bolstered by disciplinary logics of austerity, accumulation, and self-reliance. Both the Kenya and France cases illustrate disposability hinged on a sink-or-swim approach.

While I have presented a grim picture, it is also true that refugees fight and succeed in raising their families, scraping by on piecemeal incomes, and ultimately navigating a complex system that is designed for them to fail. In many ways the snippets of refugee survival I have shared are illustrations of just that: struggle in the face of adversity and, in some ways, the microlevel triumphs over horrid circumstances. It is important to emphasize, however, the context of death and violence that surrounds refugee survival. This reality cannot be erased in favor of a potential feel-good ending. Survival is, of course, always (and for everyone) a temporary state and only rings with importance in the context of death.

Only if survival is an actual feat—which it is for the millions of refugees on a global scale—does the term have any resonance or utility.

This book has by no means tried to articulate a direct or orderly comparative approach. In fact, the emphasis has always been on the dual-cited case study that best illustrates the convergence of vastly disparate countries, cities, and regional forms of governance. That said, the cases do diverge in unavoidable ways. France is a waning welfare state, while Kenya had few state welfare capabilities to begin with. Refugees in France struggle to access shelter owing to overcrowded housing schemes and are forced to the streets of Paris, while refugees in Nairobi automatically seek informal housing at the fringes of the city and rely on kinship ties upon relocation. In Paris, refugees face the disciplinary force of labor in light of ongoing welfare retrenchment; and in Nairobi, where there is no welfare state, refugees face violence through disciplinary forms of entrepreneurship. Despite apparent differences and histories of exclusion that tie the variegated experience of political dis/belonging and liminality, both cities are hampered by racial exclusion in the face of austerity politics and capitalist fantasies of accumulation that box out refugees.

The key theoretical thrust of this book has been upheld by contradiction. Fantasy, disposability, and liminality refer to puzzling realities where the targeted policy often results in the opposite desired outcome. For instance, the EU's policy directives on antitrafficking have resulted in more migrants being trafficked. Similarly, the EU's funding of the Libyan coast guard has also facilitated informal networks of human smuggling in Libyan detention centers. In Kenya, the so-called voluntary repatriation of Somalis in the Dadaab refugee camp in fact facilitates circuitous and irregular forced displacement. Thus, I have emphasized both the illusory dimensions of refugee governance and its material consequences. As a result, I have been preoccupied by the register of the fantasy and the ideological currents that underpin neoliberal governance. For me, the pure dream of success in capitalism through disciplinary tropes such as bootstrapping or hard work props up a system that disadvantages the poorest and most marginalized. This is a result of ideological work that contradicts and fogs the social realities of joblessness, housing insecurity, and a permanent state of dis/belonging.

Refugee governance rests on displacement, detention, and deportation, and any challenge to this multiscalar regime would require an acknowledgment of the inequalities under the governing logics of contemporary capitalism. In placing refugee governance under logics of austerity and accumulation, we in turn learn more about capitalism's inherent exclusion and maneuverability through the instilling of disciplinary force. We also receive stark reminders of capitalism's illogical yet constantly forward-moving desire for accumulation. Capitalism's benevolent mask, hinged on liberal fantasies of freedom and justice, reveals the ways in which the racialized poor are incongruent with imaginaries of accumulation. Refugees are liminal because they are never in place—they embody what Bhabha terms experiences of dislocation and dispossession.

Race, Fantasy, and International Political Economy

My overall aim in writing this book was to understand refugees through a political economy lens. When I started researching this topic in 2013 in South Africa, my scope was small and looked solely at queer refugee dislocation and survival in Cape Town. What has developed since then is the framing of all refugees as queer subjects who lack political belonging and are barred from basic desires including love, kinship, community, shelter, and work. We have this massive never-ending "crisis" where year after year more and more people are being forcibly displaced. But what good is the word *crisis* when displacement (on multiple scales) is a never-ending reality in our world today?

Hence, I have maintained that the refugee crisis is a crisis only because capitalism itself is crisis prone. In developing the concept of the refugee fantasy, I have paid attention to the ways that the political Left and Right have framed refugees. Both the liberal Left and the Right see refugees as an external issue. Liberals see the role of the state as benevolent, and the Right sees it as border securitizing. In practice, refugee policies are a milieu of both instances in the context of a harder neoliberalism based on exclusion, policing, and border control. It is important to remember that one of the key fantasies of neoliberalism is individualism and freedom—we should not forget that third-way approaches that entrenched neoliberalism were forwarded by those whom we would recognize as Left centrists, such as Tony Blair, Bill Clinton, and even Nelson Mandela. Sure, this commitment to social liberalism fades in and out amid a polarized political landscape. But what remains are still fantasies of benevolent nations that treat refugees with fairness and justice. In this context of border violence and neoliberal governance, despite the remnants of benevolence, we are seeing increased urban, national, and regional commitments to prevention-based policies that cast out refugees. On the urban scale, for those refugees who somehow make it to Paris and Nairobi, the reality is disposability and widespread social exclusion.

My emphasis in the book has been on the governing logics of neoliberalism, because refugee governance is trapped between two related but countervailing desires: accumulation and austerity. I refer to these as fantasies of neoliberalism because refugees, unable to sell their labor power, cannot fuel capital accumulation.

Regardless, the fact that refugees are *potential* workers drives refugee acceptance or rejection even though most refugees are relegated to street or slum living in Paris and Nairobi. In opposition, the other governing logic is austerity, where those refugees who cannot transform themselves into viable labor power are not accepted. In framing accumulation and austerity as disciplinary logics of governance in capitalism, I highlight that it does not matter whether refugees are workers, but that even humanitarian aims like refugee assistance are trapped in these compulsions and fantasies.

It is worth reiterating that the fantasy operates on the register of the immaterial but is also intimately tied to the social reality of political belonging, shelter, and work. Returning to where I started in the introduction, the fantasy is pure dream, but it functions by force and forges its own encapsulated reality. Refugees in this fantasy world are the permanent thieves of enjoyment. At the same time, the fantasy (or the refugee subject) works to consolidate the nation and protect the interests of those who are deemed deserving citizens in a context of widespread poverty in both Europe and East Africa. Thus, it is unsurprising that the onset of the Syrian refugee crisis coincided with Brexit and alt-populism all over Europe. This intersection of refugee crises and right-wing populism was further contextualized by countries such as France undergoing multiple rounds of austerity in the eurozone crisis. In Kenya, it is unsurprising that the degree of refugee acceptance coincides with the amount of funding available. In the 1990s the Dadaab refugee camp was—in relative terms—flushed with global aid funding. With diminished funding, refugees have increasingly become a target for government-led attacks and societal xenophobia; thus, Kenya continues to deal with the aftereffects of structural adjustment and poor economic prospects for the burgeoning relative surplus populations in its urban centers.

My contribution to the field of International Political Economy through this book has rested on this idea of the fantasy, as I believe that some aspects of governance operate on the level of irrationality and jingoism. I focus on some libidinal aspects of political economy because there is some degree of enjoyment that allows people to treat others as unwanted. Laws that exclude and demonize all sorts of migrants are rooted in fairness and justice, and yet the results of their applications are often harm and violence. My focus on the fantasy in this book considers our current lived reality of an increasingly unpredictable and counterintuitive world where the libidinal overtakes the rational. Freud believed that libidinal desires are related to survival and sexual instincts, and these base instincts of state and society are evident in the ways that refugees are treated as nonhumans and undeserving others in both camps and cities.

While the fantasy elements of refugee governance compose one key prong of my analysis, my second and related contention dealt with how refugees survive in contemporary capitalism. Here, I drew inspiration from feminist political economy that connected the everyday to the national and global dimensions of survival. Refugee exclusion is not just delegated to the realm of policy, but it is a lived social reality, and here I emphasized both race and sexuality in understanding disposability. The fantasy of the refugee is fueled by race and racialization. Not only are refugees portrayed by the media and the government as destabilizing barbarians, but they are also seen as potential stocks of low-skill labor—a group that could (and should) do the work that no one else wants to. Refugees are thus disposable in two ways: (1) in their attempts to enter their nations of relocation and (2) in their inability to find long-term work or shelter, if/when they do make it to a major city.

In framing disposability, I pulled extensively from the works of Kalyan Sanyal and Gargi Bhattacharyya. My point is to see refugees as members of an edge population that does not even have the chains of wage slavery to break. Refugees, like waste collectors, rickshaw drivers, extremely low-wage sex workers, and other groups that might form what Marx refers to as the lumpenproletariat, are outside capitalism or are part of piecemeal and somewhat capitalism. This liminal space speaks to the nature of contemporary capitalism, too, where more and more people are redundant to the needs of capital accumulation. Disposability exceeds the various issues of informal work, where, despite the lack of labor rights, many people are able to survive. Instead, disposability highlights the bottom of the barrel: capitalism's ability to see potential in bodies that are not even selling their labor on the market. This type of disposability is best illustrated by the camps, and the experiences of those in Kakuma and Dadaab and in detention centers in Libya show us the incongruent and unexpected ways that capital penetrates impoverished and destitute spaces for potential accumulation and experimentation. These liminal spaces exist in tension with the governing logics of contemporary capitalism. People who are here are mostly forgotten, but every now and then new avenues of experimentation are placed on them. At the same time, people in these spaces do survive. They are emblematic of human connection, kinship, and desire amid an overarching structure of misery.

Urban Futures

My work parallels that of theorists who centered refugees in their analyses, such as Hannah Arendt, Giorgio Agamben, and Zygmunt Bauman. These theorists saw the plight of refugees as reflective of the various issues in wider society. For instance, Arendt's [1943] 2017 essay *We Refugees* argues that the statelessness of refugees is an indication of the failures of the nation-state via the denial of territory for them. Using Arendt's language, I agree that refugees represent the avant-garde of their people, but for reasons entirely grounded in the violence of contemporary capitalism. Undoubtedly, *Governing the Displaced* centers contemporary (and so-called) refugee crises; however, I also hope to point readers to the wider context of precarity with particular attention to urban inequality.

What we do know is that forced migration is endless. Despite the legal apparatus of identifying and protecting refugees, states are expelling asylum seekers and preventing the forcibly displaced from entering their territories. In the context of the pandemic, borders have rigidified, and refugees have been cast as public health hazards. New forms of detention and deportation have emerged—for example, the UK is aiming to deport refugees to Rwanda, following in the footsteps of the Australian model. White European/white settler states are bold-faced in their racism under the premise that the nation's coherence must be protected. In effect, the treatment of refugees is reflective of all other racialized others within a territory. Detention, deportation, and the denial of rights is a raced project. Undoubtedly, a strong antimigrant current cuts across the societal justification for Brexit and other forms of nation-based populism, and it is these *feelings* and portrayals of migrants as thieves of national enjoyment that have allowed them to be mistreated for so long. At the same time, the violence that refugees face is a red flag to all those who live at the edge of political belonging in supremacist states. Indeed, and to echo Arendt, we are all refugees.

One of the reasons that states want to prevent migrants from arriving at their borders is because of extant crises in their cities. This book has been concerned with what happens to refugees when they do—sometimes miraculously—make it to Paris or Nairobi. While I do not want to flatten the various complexities of survival, refugees in both cities must become self-reliant either as low-wage/piecemeal workers or, better yet, as entrepreneurs. In Paris, refugees faced cyclical displacement embedded in the EU Dublin process; and in the furor of increased migration in 2016, France accepted only 27 percent of its asylum claimants. Syrian and Afghan refugees received asylum status, largely along racial lines, far more often than any claimants from Africa. On the ground, refugees compete for beds with Paris's burgeoning homeless or rough-sleeping population. In turn, refugees face ongoing police violence as they attempt to survive on extremely small amounts of welfare payments. The Paris case revealed the twinned issues of shelter- and work-related insecurity. Queer refugees further showed us hidden forms of violence and exploitation, where some refugees who relied on kinship networks to survive had no place to come out to and others were pushed into precarious sex work.

The statistics in Nairobi-Kenya are far less clear, and this is likely because refugees are not allowed to live in Nairobi and must seek shelter and assistance in camps. Before conducting my fieldwork in Nairobi, I falsely assumed that because Paris had some semblance of a welfare state, refugees would easily be able to access shelter and work, even under the auspices of ongoing neoliberalization. While many refugees in Kenya face extreme violence, the fact that many people in Nairobi live in informal settlements allowed refugees to access food and (often very precarious) shelter because they were embedded in a community where ties of ethnicity and kinship allowed them to survive. This does not mean that refugees do not face social violence and are seamlessly embedded in informal settlements.

Indeed, refugees face eviction, high rents, and physical and gender-based violence from both the police and community members because of their status and foreign origins. Refugee governance in Nairobi is characterized by ideological self-reliance, where refugees must become entrepreneurs if they wish to reside in urban areas. The GOK continues to shut down the camps, within the global context of austerity, and thus the ideal refugee subject either becomes an entrepreneur or finds some semblance of paid income (tenuous and difficult as it is)—or does not exist at all. Racism and xenophobia are problems not solely in the EU; as the Nairobi case illustrates, they are reflective of a global (though uneven) rise in bordering, exclusion, and policing along ethnic and racial lines. Market logics prevail; however, the burgeoning number of people on the edge has reignited an aggressive and militarized state that uses physical force to quell unrest. Refugees face these forms of violence in obvious ways because they do not belong—they are politically wasted people who are virtually unprotected as they attempt to relocate.

As I have maintained throughout this book, the urban is both the site of survival and the most palpable site of refugee governance. Although Paris and Nairobi cannot be emblematic of the violence that urban refugees face around the world, they do point us to potential futures of urban misery. With unabated climate change, ongoing conflict, and the continued targeting of particular groups of people, calling forced displacement a crisis is an abject misnomer because it is in fact a reality that cannot be avoided in contemporary capitalism. Any solution to forced displacement starts and ends with abolishing the current mode of racialized and territorialized production. The production of refugees exists because of social cleavages of scarcity, inequality, and racialization and also because people struggle to survive and are rendered surplus to the needs of capital to the point of violent redundancy. Refugees are easy scapegoats who are stripped of political belonging and kept in limbo.

So, what about the future? I have been silent on climate refugees and internal displacement, but with 2022 being the hottest year on record it is not unfathomable that previously habitable places in both the global North and the global

South will become uninhabitable, creating widespread forced displacement into cities that allow a reprieve from climactic change. It is also apparent that major global cities and wealthy countries are no longer cushioned from this type of widescale displacement, whether they will be producing refugees or will become even more incapable of managing those who had no choice but to flee their communities. Undoubtedly, the brunt of the violence to come will be felt by the global majority of racialized people; however, it is abundantly clear that refugees no longer exist on the fringes of the political imaginary in distant camps, where they suffer from national or regional politics.

The plight of refugees is multiscalar and inseparable from the logics of global capital. While it might be reductive to echo Arendt and say that we are all refugees, the violence of forced displacement is palpable for us all. Urban misery, and by this I mean shelter insecurity, poverty, and the stripping away of people's political belonging, is the future of our communities. Who belongs, who gets excluded, and who ultimately deserves to live is, as it has always been, a battle for hearts and minds, and it fulfills some political purpose. The future is pure dream, and future fantasies of governance will have to contend with intersecting systemic crises. The plight of refugees is the canary in the coal mine, the indicator of neoliberalism's unraveling. We have entered the liminal space where we are collectively collapsing under the weight of neoliberalism's cold corpse amid fantasies of global authoritarianism. At the same time, perhaps the solution lies in the everyday practices of social reproduction assisted by bonds of connection and community. Perhaps the queer safehouse I visited in Nairobi does illustrate instances of joy and possibility in an otherwise difficult situation. While structures of oppression always exist, we cannot ignore the ways that people survive. Desires for control, fantasies of exclusion are often met with communal desires of connection, aid, and possibility. While the future looks bleak, we might still ask, Who survives and how?

Notes

INTRODUCTION

1. Rayhan Uddin, "Russia-Ukraine War: These European Politicians Welcome Ukrainian Refugees but Not Muslim Ones," *Middle East Eye,* March 7, 2022, https://www.middleeasteye.net/news/russia-ukraine-war-right-wing-welcome-refugees-not-muslims.

2. Business and Human Rights Resource Centre. "Jordan: NGO Reports Poor Working Conditions and Degrading Treatment for Migrant Workers in Garment Factory in Al Hassan Industrial Zone," February 12, 2017, https://www.business-humanrights.org/en/latest-news/jordan-ngo-reports-poor-working-conditions-and-degrading-treatment-for-migrant-workers-in-garment-factory-in-al-hassan-industrial-zone/.

3. The law is named after billionaire philanthropist George Soros, who is allegedly supporting some sort of Muslim invasion to destabilize Hungary and the European Union, according to Orban.

4. Helen Nugent, "The Number of People Fleeing Their Homes Has Doubled in a Decade," *World Economic Forum,* July 5, 2022, https://www.weforum.org/agenda/2022/07/global-displaced-conflict-refugees/.

5. Patrick Kingsley, "Mediterranean Death Rate Is Highest Since 2015 Migration Crisis," *New York Times,* September 3, 2018, https://www.nytimes.com/2018/09/03/world/europe/mediterranean-migrants-deaths.html.

6. Aderanti Adepoju. "Migration Dynamics, Refugees and Internally Displaced Persons in Africa," United Nations–Academic Impact, accessed April 12, 2023, https://www.un.org/en/academic-impact/migration-dynamics-refugees-and-internally-displaced-persons-africa#:~:text=The%20refugee%20map%20in%20Africa,million)%20of%20the%20world's%20refugees.

7. Angelique Chrisafis, "French PM Manuel Valls Says Refugee Crisis Is Debilitating Europe," *The Guardian,* January 22, 2016, https://www.theguardian.com/world/2016/jan/22/french-pm-manuel-valls-says-refugee-crisis-is-destabilising-europe.

8. "Nowhere Else to Go: Forced Return of Somali Refugees from Dadaab Refugee Camp, Kenya," Amnesty International, November 14, 2016, https://www.amnesty.org/download/Documents/AFR3251182016ENGLISH.PDF.

9. See a refugees international rejoinder by Izza Leghtas and David Kitenge, "What Does Kenya's New Refugee Act Mean for Economic Inclusion," May 4, 2022, https://www.refugeesinternational.org/reports/2022/4/29/what-does-kenyas-new-refugee-act-mean-for-economic-inclusion.

10. Eleanor Penny, "Can Europe Make It?," openDemocracy, November 5, 2016, https://www.opendemocracy.net/en/can-europe-make-it/we-don-t-have-refugee-crisis-we-have-housing-crisis/.

11. See the Europa report: European Union Agency for Asylum, "Latest Asylum Trends Annual Overview 2021," accessed April 10, 2023, https://euaa.europa.eu/latest-asylum-trends-annual-overview-2021#:~:text=considerably%20more%20decisions.-,Recognition%20rates,applications%20was%2034%20%25%20in%202021.

12. Will Grant, "Kamala Harris Tells Guatemalan Migrants: 'Do Not Come to US,'" *BBC News,* June 8, 2021, https://www.bbc.com/news/world-us-canada-57387350.

13. See also Jessica Brandt, Bruce Jones, and Bruce Katz, "What Makes Displacement Different Today?," Brookings Institution, September 13, 2017, https://www.brookings.edu /blog/metropolitan-revolution/2017/09/13/what-makes-displacement-different-today/.

14. For France's year-on-year increase in refugees since 2018, see Macrotrends, "France Refugee Statistics 1960–2023," accessed April 10, 2023, https://www.macrotrends.net /countries/FRA/france/refugee-statistic.

1. THE LOGICS OF REFUGEE GOVERNANCE UNDER CAPITALISM

1. See Philippe Legrain, "Refugees Are Not a Burden but an Opportunity," Organisation for Economic Co-operation and Development, 2016, accessed April 15, 2023, https:// www.oecd.org/migration/refugees-are-not-a-burden-but-an-opportunity.htm.

2. See this CBC think piece on drones and surveillance on border sites: "Drone Surveillance and Crowdfunded Ransom: How Tech Is Changing Borders and Those Who Can Cross Them," CBC Radio Canada, Sept 16, 2022, https://www.cbc.ca/radio/spark /drone-surveillance-and-crowdfunded-ransom-how-tech-is-changing-borders-and -those-who-cross-them.1.6584692.

3. Holly Ellyat, "'Pack Your Bags,' Italy's New Leaders Tell 500,000 Illegal Migrants— but It'll Cost Them," *CNBC News*, June 4, 2018, https://www.cnbc.com/2018/06/04/pack -your-bags-italys-new-leaders-tell-500000-illegal-migrants—but-itll-cost-them.html.

4. "Protocol Relating to the Status of Refugees" UNHCR, January 31, 1967, https:// www.unhcr.org/5d9ed66a4.

5. See the coverage on NBC: Brookes Sopelsa, "Following Pride Event, Kenya's Gay Refugees Fear for Their Lives," *NBC News*, June 20, 2018, https://www.nbcnews.com /feature/nbc-out/following-pride-event-kenya-s-gay-refugees-fear-their-lives-n885136.

6. "The Jungle May Be Gone but Solidarity Lives on in Calais," Amnesty International, June 2019, https://www.amnesty.org/en/latest/news/2019/06/the-jungle-may-be-gone -but-solidarity-lives-on-in-calais/.

7. "France Received Record 100,000 Asylum Claims in 2017," France 24, September 2018, https://www.france24.com/en/20180108-france-record-100000-asylum-requests -2017-migrants-macron; OFPRA (French Office of the Protection of Refugees and Stateless Persons), "Statistics France: Asylum Europe Database," Asylum Information Database, 2018, https://www.asylumineurope.org/reports/country/france/statistics.

8. A banlieue is an autonomous administrative entity adjacent to a large city—a suburb that is also a stand-in for low-income housing projects in the Parisian context.

9. Andrew McCarthy, "France's No-Go Zones: Assimilation-Resistant Muslims Are the Real Refugee Problem," *National Review*, November 19, 2015, https://www.national review.com/2015/11/frances-fifth-column-muslims-resist-assimilation/.

10. Henry Kamm, "Yuguslav Refugee Crisis Europe's Worse since 40s," *New York Times*, July 24, 1992, https://www.nytimes.com/1992/07/24/world/yugoslav-refugee -crisis-europe-s-worst-since-40-s.html.

11. Here the pivot to camp alternatives is clear: "Policy on Alternatives to Camps," UNHCR, July 22, 2014, https://www.unhcr.org/uk/protection/statelessness/5422b8f09 /unhcr-policy-alternatives-camps.html.

12. World Bank Group, "Growing African Cities Face Housing Challenge and Opportunity," press release, December 1, 2015, https://www.worldbank.org/en/news/press -release/2015/12/01/growing-african-cities-face-housing-challenge-and-opportunity.

13. Here are some interesting facts about Kibera: "Kibera Facts and Information," Kibera Org, accessed April 13, 2023, https://www.kibera.org.uk/facts-info/.

2. THE FANTASY

1. See European Commission and OECD, *How Are Refugees Faring on the Labour Market in Europe?* (Brussels: European Commission and OECD, 2016).

2. Lucius Coulote and Daniel Kopf, "Out of Prison & Out of Work: Unemployment among Formerly Incarcerated People," Prison Policy Initiative, 2018, accessed April 20, 2023, https://www.prisonpolicy.org/reports/outofwork.html#fn:15.

3. Worth Rises, "Immigration Detention: An American Business," 2018, accessed April 20, 2023, https://worthrises.org/immigration.

4. Jouissance is also referred to as excessive pleasure, like eating till you burst, or what Dean (2006) suggests, as the difference between friendship (pleasurable) and love (pleasure with agony).

5. It parallels what Lacan refers to as the *objet petit a*—the thing that slips away or the leftover that embodies the lack. The *objet petit a* is what Žižek ([1989] 2009) refers to as the original lost object or void. It is the thing that sets off desire, but it is also a void. *Objet petit a* points to our desires—for example, it is the light that shines on the thing we desire, the basis of enjoyment.

3. DISPOSABILITY

1. See the podcast, "Ruth Wilson Gilmore Makes the Case for Abolition," *The Intercept*, 2020, accessed April 23, 2023, https://theintercept.com/2020/06/10/ruth-wilson-gilmore-makes-the-case-for-abolition/.

2. See Brenna Bhandar's article, "Organized State Abandonment: The Meaning of Grenfell," *Critical Legal Thinking*, 2018, accessed April 23, 2023, https://criticallegalthinking.com/2018/09/21/organised-state-abandonment-the-meaning-of-grenfell/.

3. A CEPS working paper notes how refugees, while a small and potentially insignificant population, could have a potential impact on aggregate wages where many of the refugees are low-skilled men. See Mikkel Barslund, Mattia Di Salvo, and Nadzeya Laurentsyeva, "The Impact of Refugees on the Labour Market: A Big Splash in a Small Pond?," CEPS, 2018, https://www.ceps.eu/wp-content/uploads/2018/10/Refugee%20labour%20market%20shock_0.pdf.

4. Marx uses the word *Trieb* in a similar fashion as Freud, pointing to capitalism's endless compulsions for crisis.

5. A discussion of the money relation exceeds the scope of this book, but it is through money that labor is obfuscated and the money commodity is fetishized. Laborers are paid in the form of money, only to return some of that money to the capitalist (in general), thereby facilitating a double exploitation of labor time.

6. For an illustration of the draconian measures supported by Salvini's government coalition, see Cecilia Butini, "There's No End in Sight for Mateo Salvini's War on Migrants," *Foreign Policy*, August 21, 2019, https://foreignpolicy.com/2019/08/21/theres-no-end-in-sight-for-matteo-salvinis-war-on-migrants-league-liga-open-arms-rescue-ships-mediterranean-libya/.

7. I observed this at a refugee legal clinic in Paris on June 12, 2017. The refugees were trying to find shelter and could not access beds designated for homeless people. The paralegal was not being callous but was simply suggesting this as one way for refugees to avoid living on the street.

8. Alexander Seale, "What Macron Said to the Malian 'Spider-man' Hero in Paris about Citizenship Was Incredibly Misguided," *Independent*, May 29, 2018, https://www.independent.co.uk/voices/mamoudou-gassama-mal-saves-boy-balcony-emmanuel-macron-france-immigration-a8374171.html.

9. Carl Wittman, *Refugees from Amerika: A Gay Manifesto*, Back2StoneWall, 1970, accessed April 23, 2023, http://www.back2stonewall.com/2018/03/gay-independence-carl-wittmans-refugees-amerika-gay-manifesto-1970.html.

4. THE REFUGEE FANTASY AND THE EUROPEAN FRONTIER

1. A decade-long curve (2008–2019) is available for download for both Greece and Italy from Statisa, "Unemployment Rate in Italy from 2008 to 2020," accessed April 23, 2023, https://www.statista.com/statistics/531010/unemployment-rate-italy/; "Unemployment Rate in Greece from 2008 to 2020," Statista, accessed April 23, 2023, https://www.statista.com/statistics/531010/unemployment-rate-Greece/.

2. David Shariatmadari, "Swarms, Floods, and Marauders: The Toxic Metaphors of the Migration Debate," *The Guardian*, August 10, 2015, https://www.theguardian.com/commentisfree/2015/aug/10/migration-debate-metaphors-swarms-floods-marauders-migrants.

3. Abbe Pierre and Feantsa, "Sixth Overview of Housing Exclusion in Europe," May 2021, accessed April 23, 2023, https://www.fondation-abbe-pierre.fr/documents/pdf/rapport_europe_2021_gb.pdf. This has been exacerbated by the pandemic, where "the experiences of service providers fulfilling basic needs speak for themselves: the health crisis, successive lockdowns, and abrupt end to various industries (hospitality, culture, tourism, etc.) have plunged millions of people into poverty, particularly unemployed people, those in insecure or seasonal work, young people and students, older people, and those no longer eligible for benefits and failed asylum seekers" (118).

4. According to the UNHCR, at the height of the crisis, France accepted the most refugees at 252,264, Germany at 216,943, and Sweden at 142,207.

5. Even in Sweden, what we are seeing are housing crises in terms of affordable rental units. Reuters Staff, "Dysfunctional Swedish Housing Market behind Ouster of PM Lofven," Reuters, June 23, 2021, https://www.reuters.com/article/sweden-housing-idINL5N2O51RM.

6. See various migration reports at Migration and Home Affairs in "Migration," European Commission, accessed April 23, 2023, https://ec.europa.eu/home-affairs/what-we-do/policies/european-agenda-migration/background-information_en.

7. Jennifer Rankin, "Human Traffickers Using Migration Crisis to Force More People into Slavery," *The Guardian*, May 19, 2016, https://www.theguardian.com/world/2016/may/19/human-traffickers-using-migration-crisis-to-force-more-people-into-slavery. Rankin also reports that around ninety-six thousand children claimed asylum at the height of the migration crisis.

8. "Libya: Horrific Violations in Detention Highlight Europe's Shameful Role in Forced Returns," Amnesty International, July 15, 2021, https://www.amnesty.org/en/latest/press-release/2021/07/libya-horrific-violations-in-detention-highlight-europes-shameful-role-in-forced-returns.

9. Certain portions of the budget can be spent on refugee camps and relocation work in Turkey and in other countries in Africa and the Middle East in order to reduce migratory flows. Internal funding remains the highest at €3.9 billion. In 2017, the AMIF and the Internal Security Fund received €1.7 billion more in funding than in 2015. Funding outside the EU included €500 million for the Madad EU trust fund for Syria, €1 billion for the emergency trust fund in Africa, another €1 billion for the creation of a refugee center in Turkey, and around €300 million for other security and border control agencies.

10. For more on this topic, see the European Commission document *Migration and Borders: Commission Awards Additional 305 Million to Member States under Pressure*, December 18, 2018, and the European Commission document *EU Budget for the Future*, 2018.

11. "The Common European Asylum System," European Commission, accessed April 23, 2023, https://home-affairs.ec.europa.eu/policies/migration-and-asylum/com mon-european-asylum-system_en. This quotation is found on the EU Commission Fact Sheet on the CEAS—a summary document to explain the CEAS to anyone needing more information. This is important because the exclusionary discourse is baked into the cake, so to speak. It is explicit. The humanitarianism that accompanies longer-form documents is not present here either, apart from reference to the Geneva Convention requirements, which seem to constrain the CEAS in general.

12. The Dublin Convention was signed in 1997 and became a regulation in 2003 through further extension to all member states. Dublin III seeks to balance the issues in Dublin II. Namely, family reunification is considered of central importance; if asylum seekers have family members in particular member states, they are more easily able to transfer to a member state regardless of point of entry. In addition, Dublin III allows for a right to a personal interview for those asylum seekers who are being designated a transfer. It also requires all member states involved in the asylum case to explain why the individual is being transferred back. There is also an expanded section on how to deal with minors and dependent persons, as well as a discretionary clause permitting member states to allow certain applicants to stay on a case-by-case basis.

13. The full regulation can be found here: https://eur-lex.europa.eu/LexUriServ /LexUriServ.do?uri=OJ:L:2013:180:0031:0059:EN:PDF.

14. "The Eurodac System," Euroda, 2010, accessed April 23, 2023, https://eur-lex .europa.eu/EN/legal-content/summary/eurodac-system.html.

15. *Greece: Violence against Asylum Seekers at Border*, Human Rights Watch, 2020, 1, https://www.hrw.org/news/2020/03/17/greece-violence-against-asylum-seekers-border.

16. European Commission, "President Jean-Claude Juncker's State of the Union Address," *Europa Online*, 2017, accessed April 23, 2023, https://ec.europa.eu/commission /presscorner/detail/en/SPEECH_17_3165.

17. European Commission, *EU Budget for the Refugee Crisis and Improving Migration Management*, 2018, https://op.europa.eu/en/publication-detail/-/publication /162493fe-04a9-11e8-b8f5-01aa75ed71a1/language-en.

18. The proposal can be found on the European Commission website under "Migration and Home Affairs," https://ec.europa.eu/home-affairs/what-we-do/policies/asylum /examination-of-applicants_en.

19. European Parliament, "Meeting Tajani-Kurz: Migration Is Europe's Biggest Challenge and the Austrian Presidency Has to Provide Concrete Solutions," June 19, 2016, https://europarl.europa.eu/former_ep_presidents/president-tajani/en/newsroom /incontro-tajani-kurz-migrazione-e-sfida-piu-grande-da-presidenza-austria-risposte -concrete.html.

20. Fiona Maxwell, "Tusk Claims Victory on Migration Deal," *Politico*, June 30, 2018, https://www.politico.eu/article/tusk-migration-xenophobia-claims-victory-over-deal/.

21. As table 4.2 illustrates, the top six member states reject far more claims than they accept. Acceptance rates rose by only 6 percent between 2014–2015 and 2015–2016. In France, the recognition rate from 2014 to 2016 improved from 21 percent to 25 percent, while Italy's acceptance rate decreased from 57 percent to 43 percent. Again, Germany has made the greatest improvement in acceptance rates, from 40 to 56 percent; however, these increases, on average, do not reflect the imminent needs of asylum seekers entering the region.

22. See the EU Emergency Trust Fund for Africa report, *Trust Fund for Stability and Addressing Root Causes of Irregular Migration and Displaced Persons in Africa*, 2019, https://ec.europa.eu/trustfundforafrica/sites/euetfa/files/eu_emergency_trust_fund _for_africa_20-12-2018.pdf.

23. For more on Denmark's zero-asylum-seeker policy, see Weronyka Strzyzynska, "Zero Asylum Seekers: Denmark Forces Refugees to Return to Syria," *The Guardian*, May 25, 2022, https://www.theguardian.com/global-development/2022/may/25/zero-asylum-seekers-denmark-forces-refugees-to-return-to-syria.

24. For Sweden's reduction of asylum claimants, see Dale Gavlak, "New Swedish Government to Tighten Migration Policy," *VOA*, October 27, 2022, https://www.voanews.com/a/new-swedish-government-to-tighten-migration-policy-/6808370.html.

25. See European Parliament, *Reintegration of Returning Migrants* (Brussels: Europarl, 2017); European Parliament, *Labour Market Integration of Refugees: Strategies and Good Practices* (Brussels: Europarl, 2016); European Parliament, *Employment and Social Affairs*, https://www.europarl.europa.eu/RegData/etudes/STUD/2016/578956/IPOL_STU(2016)578956_EN.pdf. Also see Eurostat, *Asylum Quarterly Report: Statistics Explained* (Brussels: Eurostat 2017), https://ec.europa.eu/eurostat/documents/12544011/12980988/Asylum+Quarterly+Report+Q3+2017.pdf/a12ab8b0-fe8a-9b3a-8cc5-d73f9b607106?t=1625511349613.

26. See the full report here: https://www.oecd.org/els/mig/migration-policy-debates-13.pdf.

27. The EU baseline for housing affordability hovers around 35 percent of total household income.

28. Find the updated report for 2022 including the data at the peak of the migration crisis here: "Migrant Integration Statistics—Housing," Europa Online, 2022, accessed April 23, 2023, https://ec.europa.eu/eurostat/statistics-explained/index.php?title=Migrant_integration_statistics_-_housing.

29. "Delivering a Dignified Housing Response to Ukraine," Housing Europe, March 29, 2022, https://www.housingeurope.eu/resource-1680/delivering-a-dignified-housing-response-to-ukraine.

30. See *Social Protection Statistics—Social Benefits 2019*, Eurostat, https://ec.europa.eu/eurostat/statistics-explained/index.php/Social_protection_statistics_-_social_benefits#Expenditure_on_social_protection_benefits_by_function.

31. "The External Dimension of the New Pact on Migration and Asylum: A Focus on Prevention and Readmission," European Parliament, 2019, accessed April 23, 2023, https://www.europarl.europa.eu/RegData/etudes/BRIE/2021/690535/EPRS_BRI(2021)690535_EN.pdf.

5. DISPOSABILITY AND SURVIVAL IN PARIS

1. "French PM Valls Says 'No Room for More Refugees,'" *France24*, November 25, 2015, https://www.france24.com/en/20151125-france-manuel-valls-refugees-migrants-europe.

2. This analysis of Calais fits in the wider intellectual tradition of biopolitics, where refugees are understood as the tensions of population management. One population (say Europeans) needs to be protected while others (refugees in Calais) require qualification, measurement, and appraisal within a hierarchy.

3. Lucy Williamson, "Homeless in Paris," BBC Special Feature, January 25, 2018, https://www.bbc.co.uk/news/resources/idt-sh/Paris_homeless.

4. These statistics are always in flux, and the numbers of urban refugees in Paris in particular cannot be confirmed, but they do provide a general sense of how many refugees are in the city/region/country. The wider report can be found in OFPRA and European Commission 2018. See also INSEE 2017a.

5. The following is a brief overview of the turn toward neoliberalism in France. From 1945 to 1974, the French economy was one of the largest in Europe under dirigisme and France was an active welfare state. From 1974 to 1983 the OPEC (Organization of the

Petroleum Exporting Countries) crisis and the demise of the Bretton Woods system caused the French economy to slow down—this led to the abandonment of dirigisme and paved the way for neoliberal experimentation. From 1983 onward, the neoliberal framework defined through the removal of state intervention also led to some cuts in public expenditure (Kus 2006).

6. For information about the entire housing process in France see this overview by the Asylum Information Database (AIDA), "Regular Procedure," April 8, 2022, https://asylumineurope.org/reports/country/france/asylum-procedure/procedures/regular-procedure/.

7. Pseudonym used.

8. For an illustration of this crackdown, see Aurelien Breeden, "Outcry in France After Police Clear Paris Migrant Camp," *New York Times*, November 24, 2020, https://www.nytimes.com/2020/11/24/world/europe/police-paris-migrant-camp.html.

9. For an update on the ADA card, see Tiffany Fallon, "Everything You Need to Know about the New ADA Card," *InfoMigrants*, August 21, 2019, https://www.infomigrants.net/en/post/18955/france-everything-you-need-to-know-about-the-new-ada-card.

10. The director informed me that they filed as a language training NGO for refugees to receive some funding, but they also provide shelter, employment, and psycho-social support.

11. Gay dating app that is often a platform for sex workers and escorts.

6. REFUGEE GOVERNANCE AND ENCAMPMENT FANTASIES IN KENYA

1. Refugee status without impediment or the political baggage of proving one's claim for asylum.

2. See the UN briefing note on Somalis fleeing in 2022 here: https://www.unhcr.org/news/briefing/2022/12/638f13ae4/drought-conflict-force-80000-flee-somalia-kenyas-dadaab-refugee-camps.html.

3. See "EU to Give Migrants in Greece €2000 to Go Home," *BBC News*, March 12, 2020, https://www.bbc.com/news/world-europe-51859007.

4. "Annual Report 2021," *Refugees International*, 2021, https://static1.squarespace.com/static/506c8ea1e4b01d9450dd53f5/t/63a1e9475f30831746b5b74e/1671555406930/Annual+Report+2021+%E2%80%93+FINAL+%E2%80%93+12.20.22.pdf.

5. See UNHCR Kenya 2016 for the full document.

6. For Nathan's take on turning refugee camps into smart cities at the World Economic Forum, see Tara Nathan, "How to Turn Refugee Camps into Smart Cities," *World Economic Forum* August 31, 2017, https://www.weforum.org/agenda/2017/08/can-we-turn-refugee-camps-into-smart-cities-e5281afc-7213-40f6-bf13-d304e20c8943/.

7. For an update on Kenya's plan to shut down call camps by 2022, see "Kenya to Close 2 Refugee Camps Next Year," *DW*, April 30, 2021, https://www.dw.com/en/kenya-to-close-2-refugee-camps-next-year/a-57382561.

7. DISPOSABILITY AND ABANDONMENT IN NAIROBI

1. A type of loan arrangement which is interest free. People put money into a pot at pre-decided intervals and when need arises from a contributor they can withdraw from the pot given that they replace the money within a given timeframe.

2. See the story reported by Reuters by Kevin Mwanza, "Despair as Bulldozers Destroy Hundreds of Homes in Kenya's Biggest Slum," Reuters, July 23, 2018, https://www.reuters.com/article/us-kenya-slum-demolition-idUSKBN1KE045.

3. *Gay* is used as a general term to reflect the whole spectrum of queerness among the people who live in the safehouse.

4. Conversation with cis gay male refugee from Uganda after our LGBT safehouse activity, near Nairobi, May 21, 2018.

5. Pseudonym. Lisa is a woman in her mid-fifties whose husband, a journalist, was killed in Sudan. As a single mother, she has raised five children.

6. Kiva Microfunds is a nonprofit microfinance organization that connects lenders in the global North to refugees and other poor people in the global South. Although Kiva does not charge interest on these loans, the lenders (field partners) in Nairobi often set exorbitant interest rates.

7. M-PESA is operated by Safaricom, which in turn is owned by Vodafone. It is Kenya's most ubiquitous peer-to-peer fintech money transfer service. It eliminates large banks and other operation systems such as point of sale and credit/debit card machines. It also facilitates the informal economy, including debt.

References

INTERVIEWS AND OTHER DATA

Email correspondence 1. Email from Case Number C(2018)35405, January 4, 2018.

Email correspondence 2. Email exchange with the Citizens' Enquiries Unit, March 13, 2018.

Focus group A. Conducted with female-identifying refugees on daily finance practices, Nairobi, July 6, 2018.

Focus group B. Conducted with refugees in a safehouse near Nairobi, May 21, 2018.

Interview 1. Frontex employee, conducted online, February 1, 2018.

Interview 3. Representative from ECRE's public relations, conducted online, March 12, 2018.

Interview 4. Representative from ECRE's public relations, conducted online, March 15, 2018.

Interview 7. EASO employee, conducted online, March 19, 2018.

Interview 8. Retired Professor specializing in housing issues. Paris, May 25, 2017

Interview 10. Employee of the large social housing governance organization (does not want it to be named explicitly). Paris, June 7, 2017.

Interview 13. City of Paris Official, Paris, May 23, 2017.

Interview 14. Director of an LGBT right organization, Paris, June 5, 2017.

Interview 15. Official from the national level in one of the relevant departments that manage refugee, immigration, and asylum affairs, Paris, June 15, 2017.

Interview 16. Employee at a housing and refugee assistance organization that also employed legal assistants, social workers, and academics, Paris, May 15, 2017.

Interview 17. Employee at a housing and refugee assistance organization that also employed legal assistants, social workers, and academics, Paris, May 15, 2017.

Interview 18. Volunteers with a social justice NGO that operates only in the 19th arrondissement, Paris, June 13, 2017.

Interview 19. Representative from a homelessness NGO, Paris, June 9, 2017.

Interview 20. Refugee participant from a legal aid clinic, Paris, June 1, 2017.

Interview 22. National and Municipal LGBT homelessness organization, Paris, June 8, 2017.

Interview 23. Director of a refugee language training school in a Parisian university, May 18, 2017.

Interview 24. Employee at FTDA, Paris, June 21, 2017.

Interview 25. Employee at CALM NGO, Paris, June 12, 2017.

Interview 26. Refugee participant, Nairobi, June 12, 2018.

Interview 28. Employee at a refugee rights organization, Nairobi, June 14, 2018.

Interview 29. Employee at International Refugee Rights Council operating nationally in Kenya, Nairobi, June 25, 2018.

Interview 31. Refugee assistance department of a large international NGO, Nairobi, May 23, 2018.

Interview 33. Employee at IRC, Nairobi, June 27, 2018.

Interview 34. Employee at IOM, Nairobi, June 27, 2018.

Interview 35. Employee at EU-funded aid organization in Nairobi, Kenya, July 13, 2018.

Interview 36. Video conference interview with academic expert working in the UK, May 15, 2018.

Interview 38. Refugee participant in Nairobi, May 25, 2018.

Interview 40. Conducted with a refugee participant who was visiting the Refugee Affairs Secretariat, Nairobi, June 6, 2018.

Interview 41. Conducted with an official (employee) at the Refugee Affairs Secretariat, Nairobi, June 6, 2018.

Interview 42. Volunteer at local refugee housing NGO, Nairobi, June 6, 2018.

Interview 43. Video conference with an international research organization conducting work on refugee development issues, March 13, 2018.

Interview 45. Refugee participant from a safehouse near Nairobi, May 21, 2018.

Interviews 46 and 47. Refugees were interviewed after a focus group on microfinance and share lending (N = 12), Nairobi, July 6, 2018.

Interview 48. Follow-up interview with refugee from Focus Group B, near Nairobi, May 21, 2018.

Interview 49. Director of an international (European) aid organization focusing on LGBT refugee issues, Nairobi, May 28, 2018.

Interview 50. Refugee participant, Nairobi, May 21, 2018.

Interview 51. Conversation with cis gay male refugee from Uganda after our LGBT safehouse activity, near Nairobi, May 21, 2018.

Interview 54. Refugee participant from Uganda, Nairobi, May 25, 2018.

Participant observation 1. Refugee assistance clinic, Paris, May 15, 2017.

BOOKS AND OTHER SOURCES

Aalbers, Manuel, and Brett Christophers. 2014. "Centering Housing in Political Economy." *Housing Theory and Society* 31 (4): 373–394.

Abbe Pierre Foundation. 2018. *Report on the State of Inadequate Housing in France*. Paris: Abbe Pierre Foundation.

Agamben, Giorgio. 1998. *Homo Sacer: Sovereign Power and Bare Life*. Meridian: Crossing Aesthetics. Stanford, CA: Stanford University Press.

Alami, Ilias and Adam Dixon. 2020. "State capitalism(s) redux? Theories, tensions, and controversies. *Competition and Change* 24 (1): 70–94.

Amis, Philip. 1984. "Squatters or tenants: the commercialization of unauthorized housing in Nairobi." *World Development*, 12 (1); 87–96.

Amnesty International. 2017. *A Blueprint for Despair: Human Rights Impact of the EU-Turkey Deal*. London: Amnesty International.

Angelil, Marc, and Cary Siress. 2012. "The Paris Banlieue: Peripheries of Inequality." *Journal of International Affairs* 65 (2): 57–67.

Arendt, Hannah. 1991 [1951]. *The Origins of Totalitarianism*. New York: Harcourt INC.

Arendt, Hannah. 2007. *The Jewish Writings*. Chicago: University of Chicago Press.

Arendt, Hannah. 2017. "We Refugees." *International refugee law*, Routledge: 3–12.

Arnold, Dennis, and John Pickles. 2011. "Global Work, Surplus Labor, and the Precarious Economies of the Border." *Antipode* 43 (5): 1598–1624.

AU (African Union). 1969. *Constitutive Act of the African Union*. Addis Ababa: African Union. https://au.int/sites/default/files/pages/34873-file-constitutiveact_en.pdf.

Baboulias, Yiannis. 2019. "The Next Syrian Refugee Crisis Will Break Europe's Back." *Foreign Policy*, October 4, 2019.

Balibar, Etienne, and Immanuel Wallerstein. 1991. *Race, Nation, Class: Ambiguous Identities*. London: Verso.

Barou, Jacques. 2014. "Integration of Immigrants in France: A Historical Perspective." *Identities: Global Studies in Culture and Power* 21 (6): 642–657.

Barutciski, M. 1994. "EU States and the Refugee Crisis in the Former Yugoslavia." *Refuge* 14 (3): 32–36.

Bauman, Zygmunt. 2004. *Wasted Lives: Modernity and Its Outcasts.* Cambridge: Polity Press.

Benet-Gbaffou, Claire, and Sophie Oldfield. 2014. "Claiming 'Rights' in the African City." Chap. 25 in *The Routledge Handbook on Cities of the Global South*, edited by Sue Parnell and Sophie Oldfield. London: Routledge.

Berlant, Lauren. 1997. *The Queen of America Goes to Washington City.* Durham, NC: Duke University Press.

Bernadot, M. 1999. "Chronique d'une institution: la Sonacotra." *Societes Contemporaines* 33/34:38–55.

Bernards, Nick and Susanne Soederberg. 2021. "Relative surplus populations and the crises of contemporary capitalism: Reviving, revisiting, recasting." *Geoforum* 126 (2021): 412–419.

Bhagat, Ali. 2017. "Forced (Queer) Migration and Everyday Violence: The Geographies of Life, Death, and Access in Cape Town." *Geoforum* 89 (Winter): 155–163.

Bhagat, Ali. 2018. "Queer Necropolitics of Forced Migration: Cyclical Violence in the African Context." *Sexualities* 23 (3): 361–375.

Bhagat, Ali. 2022. "Governing refugees in raced markets: Displacement and disposability from Europe's frontier to the streets of Paris." *Review of International Political Economy* 29 (3), 955–978.

Bhagat, Ali. 2023. "Queer global displacement: Social reproduction, refugee survival, and organized abandonment in Nairobi, Cape Town, and Paris." *Antipode* Online First. https://doi.org/ 10.1111/anti.12933.

Bhagat, Ali, and Leanne Roderick. 2020. "Banking on Refugees: Racialized Expropriation in the Fintech Era." *Environment and Planning A: Economy and Space* 52 (8). https://doi.org/10.1177/0308518X20904070.

Bhagat, Ali, and Susanne Soederberg. 2019. "Placing Refugees in Authoritarian Neoliberalism: Reflections from Berlin and Paris." *South Atlantic Quarterly* 118 (2): 421–438.

Bhattacharyya, Gargi. 2018. *Rethinking Racial Capitalism: Questions of Reproduction and Survival.* London: Rowman and Littlefield International.

Blatt, David. 2013. "Immigrant Politics in a Republican Nation." In *Post-colonial Cultures in France*, edited by Alec Hargreaves and Mark McKinney, 56–72. London: Routledge.

Bonjour, Saskia, and Doutje Lettinga. 2012. "Political Debates on Islamic Headscarves and Civic Integration Abroad in France and the Netherlands: What Can Models Explain?" *Journal of Immigrant and Refugee Studies* 10 (3): 260–278.

Bowie, Malcolm. 1991. *Lacan.* London: Dosti.

Bruff, Ian. 2014. "The Rise of Authoritarian Neoliberalism." *Rethinking Marxism* 26 (1): 113–129.

Butler, Judith. 2004. *Undoing Gender.* New York: Routledge.

Byrnes, Melissa. 2013. "Liberating the Land or Absorbing a Community: Managing North African Migration and the Bidonvilles in Paris's Banlieues." *French Politics, Culture, and Society* 31 (3): 1–20.

CAHF (Centre for Affordable Housing Finance in Africa). 2019. *Assessing Kenya's Affordable Housing Market.* Nairobi: CAHF.

Chehayeb, Kareem, and Sarah Hunaidi. 2019. "Turkey's Deportation Policy Is Killing Syrian Refugees." *Foreign Policy*, August 8, 2019.

Clarke, Simon. 1978. "Capital, Fractions of Capital and the State: Neo-Marxist Analysis of the South African State." *Capital and Class* 2 (2): 44–77.

Clarke, Simon. 1983. "State, Class Struggle and the Reproduction of Capital." *Kapitalistate* 10/11: 113–130.

Clarke, Simon. 1991. "States, Class Struggle, and the Reproduction of Capital." In *The State Debate*, edited by Simon Clarke, 183–203. London: Palgrave Macmillan.

Clemens, Michael. 2018. "How Europe Can Stop African Migration." *Politico*, October 12, 2018. https://www.politico.eu/article/europe-can-stop-african-migration-symposium-experts/.

Cohen, Robin. 1995. *The Cambridge Survey of World Migration*. Cambridge: Cambridge University Press.

Council of the European Union. 2019. *Limite—Libya and the Surrounding Area: Current Situation and Need for Immediate Action*. Brussels: European Union.

Crisp, Jeff, Tim Morris, and Hilde Refstie. 2012. "Displacement in Urban Areas: New Challenges, New Partnerships." *Disasters* 36 (1): S23–S42.

Darrow, Jessica. 2015. "Getting Refugees to Work: A Street-Level Perspective of Refugee Resettlement Policy." *Refugee Survey Quarterly* 34 (1): 78–106.

Davies, Thom, Arsha Isakjee, and Surindar Dhesi. 2017. "Violent Inaction: The Necropolitical Experience of Refugees in Europe." *Antipode* 49 (5): 1263–1284.

Davis, Mike. 2006. *Planet of the Slums*. New York: Verso.

Dean, Jodi. 2006. *Zizek's Politics*. New York: Routledge.

Dean, Jodi. 2011. "Claiming Division, Naming a Wrong." *Theory & Event* 14 (4): 14IS–4PY.

Dean, Jodi. 2013. "Complexity as Capture—Neoliberalism and the Loop of Drive." *New Formations: A Journal of Culture/Theory/Politics* 80–81 (1): 138–154.

Dean, Tim. 2003. "Lacan and Queer Theory." In *The Cambridge Companion to Lacan*, edited by Jean-Michel Rabate, 238–253. Cambridge: Cambridge University Press.

Dikec, Mustafa. 2006a. "Guest Editorial: Badlands of the Republic? Revolts, the French State, and the Question of Banlieues." *Environment and Planning D* 24 (1): 159–163.

Dikec, Mustafa. 2006b. "Two Decades of French Urban Policy: From Social Development of Neighbourhoods to the Republican Penal State." *Antipode*: 38 (1) 60–84. https://doi.org/10.1111/j.0066-4812.2006.00565.x.

Dikec, Mustafa. 2011. *Badlands of the Republic: Space, Politics, and Urban Policy*. London: John Wiley & Sons.

EASO (European Asylum Support Office) 2016. "EASO guidance on reception conditions: operational standards and indicators." Accessed April 23, 2023: https://euaa.europa.eu/sites/default/files/publications/EASO_Guidance_on_reception_conditions_-_operational_standards_and_indicators%5B3%5D.pdf

The Economist. 2018. "European Countries Should Make It Easier for Refugees to Work." April 21, 2018.

Edelman, Lee. 2004. *No Future: Queer Theory and the Death Drive*. Durham, NC: Duke University Press.

Engels, Friedrich. 1872. *The Housing Question*. https://www.marxists.org/archive/marx/works/1872/housing-question/. Accessed April 17, 2023.

Engels, Friedrich. (1942) 2010. *The Origin of the Family, Private Property and the State*. London: Penguin Classics.

Enright, Theresa 2013. "Mass transportation in the neoliberal city:The mobilizing myths of the Grand Paris Express." *Environment and Planning A: Economy and Space* 45 (4): 797–813.

Enright, Theresa, and Ugo Rossi. 2017. *The Urban Political: Ambivalent Spaces of Late Neoliberalism*. London: Springer.

EU Parliament. 2016. *The Implementation of the Common European Asylum System.* Brussels: Department for Citizen's Rights and Constitutional Affairs.

Eurofound. 2016. *Inadequate Housing in Europe: Costs and Consequences.* Luxembourg: Eurofound.

European Commission. 2016a. *An Economic Take on the Refugee Crisis: A Macroeconomic Assessment for the EU.* Luxembourg: European Commission.

European Commission. 2016b. *Action Plan on the Integration of Third-Country Nationals.* Brussels: European Commission.

Fanon, Frantz. (1952) 1986. *Black Skin, White Masks.* London: Pluto Press.

Fanon, Frantz. (1986) 2011. *The Wretched of the Earth.* London: Grove Press.

FEANTSA (European Federation of National Organisations Working with the Homeless). 2018. *Third Overview of Housing Exclusion in Europe.* Paris: Abbe Pierre Foundation and FEANTSA.

Fields, Barbara. 1990. "Slavery, Race and Ideology in the United States of America." *New Left Review* 118 (1), 95–118.

Fields, Karen, and Barbara Fields. 2012. *Racecraft: The Soul of Inequality in American Life.* London: Verso.

Fitzgerald, David Scott, and Rawan Arar. 2018. "The Sociology of Refugee Migration." *Annual Review of Sociology* 44 (1): 387–406.

Fourcade-Gourinchas, Marion, and Sarah Babb. 2002. "The Rebirth of the Liberal Creed: Paths to Neoliberalism in Four Countries." *American Journal of Sociology* 108 (3): 533–579.

Gabor, Daniela, and Sally Brooks. 2017. "The Digital Revolution in Financial Inclusion: International Development in the Fintech Era." *New Political Economy* 22 (4): 423–436.

Germain, Felix. 2014. "A 'New' Black Nationalism in the USA and France." *Journal of African American Studies* 18 (3): 286–304.

Germain, Felix. 2016. *Decolonizing the Republic: African and Caribbean Migrants in Post-war Paris.* Detroit: Michigan State University Press.

Gilmore, Ruth Wilson. 2002. "Race and Globalization." In *Geographies of Global Change: Remapping the World*, edited by Ronald Johnston and Michael Watts, 261–271. New York: Wiley-Blackwell.

Government of Kenya. 2014. *Kenya National Housing Survey.* Nairobi: Republic of Kenya.

Government of Kenya, UNHCR, and Government of Somalia. 2013. *Governing the Voluntary Repatriation of Somali Refugees Living in Kenya.* Nairobi: UNHCR, GOK, and GOS.

Grabska, Katarzyna. 2006. "Marginalization in Urban Spaces of the Global South: Urban Refugees in Cairo." *Journal of Refugee Studies* 19 (3): 287–307.

Gupta, Tania Das, and Franca Iacovetta. 2000. "Whose Canada Is It? Immigrant Women, Women of Colour and Feminist Critiques of 'Multiculturalism.'" *Atlantis* 24 (2): 1–4.

Habitat for Humanity. 2015. *Housing Review 2015.* Habitat for Humanity: Nairobi.

Hage, Ghassan. 2012. *White Nation: Fantasies of a White Supremacy in a Multicultural Society.* London: Routledge.

Hall, Samuel, and African Centre for Migration and Society. 2018. *Free and Safe Movement in East Africa: Research to Promote People's Safe and Unencumbered Movement across International Borders.* Johannesburgh: Samuel Hall.

Hall, Stuart. 1980. "Race, Articulation and Societies Structured in Dominance." In *Sociological Theories: Race and Colonialism*, edited by UNESCO, 305–345. London

Hancock, Claire. 2017. "Feminism from the Margin: Challenging the Paris/Banlieues Divide." *Antipode* 49 (3): 636–656.

Hart, Gillian. 2018. "Relational Comparison Revisited." *Progress in Human Geography* 42 (3): 371–394.

Harvey, David. 1982. *Limits to Capital*. Oxford: Blackwell.

Harvey, David. 2001. *Spaces of Capital*. London: Routledge.

Harvey, David. 2003. *Paris, Capital of Modernity*. New York: Routledge.

Harvey, David. 2008. "The Right to the City." *New Left Review* 53:1–20.

Hazan, Eric. 2010. *The Invention of Paris: A History in Footsteps*. London: Verso.

Hennessy, Rosemary. 2000. *Profit and Pleasure*. New York and London: Routledge.

Holloway, John. 1994. "Global Capital and the National State." *Capital and Class* 52 (1): 23–49.

House, Jim, and Neil Macmaster. 2006. *Paris 1961: Algerians, State Terror, and Memory*. Oxford: Oxford University Press.

Housing Europe. 2017. *The State of Housing in the EU 2017: Housing Is Still Europe's Challenge*. Brussels: Housing Europe.

Huchzermeyer, Marie. 2007. "Tenement City: The Emergence of Multi-storey Districts through Large-Scale Private Landlordism in Nairobi." *International Journal of Urban and Regional Research* 31 (4): 714–732.

IFC (International Finance Corporation). 2018. *Kakuma as a Marketplace*. Nairobi: IFC.

IKEA Foundation. 2018. *Refugees and Their New Communities Thriving Together*. Nairobi: Ikea Foundation.

IMF (International Monetary Fund). 2016. *The Refugee Surge in Europe: Economic Challenges*. Geneva: IMF.

INSEE (National Institute of Statistics and Economic Studies). 2017a. *Migrations residentielles: 60% des arrivals dans la metropole du Grand Paris ont entre 15–29 ans*. Paris: INSEE Analysis.

INSEE. 2017b. *Unemployment. Conjoncture in France (INSEE Employment Survey)*. Paris: INSEE: French Developments.

Jack, William, and Tavneet Suri. 2011. "Mobile Money: The Economics of M-Pesa." NBER Working Paper. https://www.marketlinks.org/sites/marketlinks.org/files/resource/files/The%20Economics%20of%20M-PESA.pdf.

Jaji, Rose. 2012. "Social technology and refugee encampment in Kenya." *Journal of Refugee Studies* 25 (2): 221–238.

Jaji, Rose. 2014. "Religious and Ethnic Politics in Refugee Hosting: Somalis in Nairobi, Kenya." *Ethnicities* 14 (5): 634–649.

Jazouli, Adil. 1992. *Les années banlieues*. Paris: Seuil.

Jessop, Bob. 1990. *State Theory: Putting the Capitalist State in Its Place*. London: Polity Press.

Kairu, Pauline. 2018. *East Africa Host Countries at a Crossroads: Are Refugees Welcome or Not?* Nairobi: East African.

Kenya National Bureau of Statistics. 2016. *Kenya Demographic and Health Survey of 2014*. Nairobi: Government of Kenya.

Kenyan Refugees Act. No. 13 of 2006. 2006.

Kibreab, Gaim. 2003. "Citizenship Rights and the Repatriation of Refugees." *International Migration Review* 37 (1): 24–73.

Kipfer, Stefan. 2016. "Neocolonial Urbanism? La renovation urbaine in Paris." *Antipode* 48 (3): 603–625.

Kirszbaum, Thomas, and Patrick Simon. 2001. *Racial and Ethnic Discrimination in Access to Social Housing*. Paris: Groupe D'etude et de Lutte Contre Les Discriminations.

Kus, Basak. 2006. "Neoliberalism, Institutional Change and the Welfare State: The Case of Britain and France." *International Journal of Comparative Sociology* 47 (6): 488–525.

LeBaron, Genevieve, and Adrienne Roberts. 2010. "Toward a Feminist Political Economy of Capitalism and Carcerality." *Signs: Journal of Women in Culture and Society* 36 (1): 19–44.

Macdonald, Laura, and Arne Ruckert. 2009. "Post-neoliberalism in the Americas: An Introduction." In *Post-Neoliberalism in the Americas,* edited by Laura Macdonald and Arne Ruckert, 1–19. London: Palgrave Macmillan.

MacFarquhar, Neil. 2010. "Banks Making Big Profits from Tiny Loans." *New York Times,* April 14, 2010, 3.

Macharia, Keguro. 2018. "Domesticating Trump." In *The Fire Now: Anti-racist Scholarship in Times of Explicit Racial Violence,* edited by Azeezat Johnson, Remi Joseph-Salisbury, and Beth Kamunge, 175–189. London: Zed Books.

Mader, Philip. 2018. "Contesting Financial Inclusion." *Development and Change* 49 (2): 461–483.

Marcuse, Herbert. 1966. *Eros and Civilization: A Philosophical Inquiry into Freud.* Boston: Beacon Press.

Martinovic, M. 2016. "Refugees Reloaded—Lessons from Germany's Approach to Bosnian War." *Deutsche Welle,* February.

Marx, Karl. 1992. *Capital Volume 1: A Critique of Political Economy.* London: Penguin Classics.

Mastercard and Western Union 2017. *Smart Communities: Using Digital Technology to Create Sustainable Refugee Economies.* Nairobi: Mastercard, Western Union, and UNHCR.

McIntyre, Michael. 2011. "Race, Surplus Population and the Marxist Theory of Imperialism." *Antipode* 43 (5): 1489–1515.

McNevin, Anne. 2013. "Ambivalence and Citizenship: Theorising the Political Claims of Irregular Migrants." *Millennium* 41 (2): 182–200.

Melamed, Jodi. 2015. "Racial Capitalism." *Critical Ethnic Studies* 1 (1): 76–85.

Merrill, Heather. 2011. "Migration and Surplus Populations: Race and Deindustrialization in Northern Italy." *Antipode* 43 (5): 1542–1572.

Mezzadra, Sandro, and Brett Neilson. 2012. "Between Inclusion and Exclusion: On the Topology of Global Space and Borders." *Theory, Culture & Society* 29 (4/5): 58–75.

Mitchell, Don, and Nik Heynen. 2009. "The Geography of Survival and the Right to the City: Speculations of Surveillance, Legal Innovation, and the Criminalization of Intervention." *Urban Geography* 30 (6): 611–632.

Mittelman, Robert, and Leighann Neilson. 2011. "Development Porn? Child Sponsorship Advertisements in the 1970s." *Journal of Historical Research in Marketing* 3 (3): 370–401.

Moch, Leslie Page. 2012. *The Pariahs of Yesterday: Breton Migrants in Paris.* Durham, NC: Duke University Press.

Morris, Julia. 2021. "The Value of Refugees: UNHCR and the Growth of the Global Refugee Industry." *Journal of Refugee Studies* 34 (3): 2676–2698.

Mwesigwa, Alon. 2018. "99% of Fintech Funding in E. Africa Goes to Kenyan Apps." *The Observer,* April 20, 2018, 1.

Nally, John, Susan Lockwood, Taiping Ho, and Katie Knutson. 2014. "Post-release Recidivism and Employment among Different Types of Released Offenders: A 5-Year Follow-up Study in the United States." *Journal of the South Asian Society of Criminology and Victimology* 9 (1): 16–34.

Nanima, Robert. 2017. "An Evaluation of Kenya's Parallel Legal Regime on Refugees, and the Courts' Guarantee of Their Rights." *Law Democracy and Development* 21 (1): 1–30.

Ndungu, Jeremia. 2013. "Donor-Driven Neoliberal Reform Processes and Urban Environmental Change in Kenya: The Case of Karura Forest." *Progress in Development Studies* 13 (1): 63–78.

Neilson, Brett. 2018. "The Currency of Migration." *South Atlantic Quarterly* 117 (2): 375–396.

New York Times. 1991. "Aid Donors Insist on Kenya Reforms." November 27, 1991.

Newell, Peter. 2006. "Race, Class, and the Global Politics of Environmental Inequality." *Global Environmental Politics* 5 (3): 70–94.

Njeru, Jeremia. 2013a. "'Donor-Driven' Neoliberal Reform Processes and Urban Environmental Change in Kenya: The Case of Karura Forest." *Progress in Development Studies* 13 (1): 63–78.

OECD (Organisation for Economic Cooperation and Development). 2016. *Development Aid at a Glance: Statistics by Region.* Geneva: OECD.

OECD. 2017. *Working Together for Local Integration of Migrants and Refugees in Paris.* Paris: OECD.

OFPRA (French Office for the Protection of Refugees and Stateless Persons). 2016. *Activity Report* [in French]. Paris: OFPRA.

OFPRA. 2018. *Annual Report on Migration and Asylum 2017.* Paris: OFPRA

Omi, Michael, and Howard Winant. 1994. *Racial Formation in the US: From the 1960s to the 1990s.* New York: Routledge.

Oswin, Natalie. 2008. "Critical Geographies and the Uses of Sexuality: Deconstructing Queer Space." *Progress in Human Geography* 32 (89): 89–103.

Owens, Patricia. 2017. "Racism in the Theory Canon: Hannah Arendt and 'the One Great Crime in Which America Was Never Involved.'" *Millennium: Journal of International Studies* 45 (3): 403–424.

Peck, Jamie. 1998a. "Workfare: A Geopolitical Etymology." *Environment and Planning D* 16 (1): 133–161.

Peck, Jamie. 1998b. "Workfare in the Sun: Politics, Representation, and Method in U.S. Welfare-to-Work Strategies." *Political Geography* 17 (5): 535–566.

Peck, Jamie. 2012. "Austerity Urbanism: American Cities under Extreme Economy." *City* 16 (6): 626–655.

Peck, Jamie, and Adam Tickell. 2022. "Neoliberalizing Space." *Antipode* 34 (3): 380–404.

Peck, Jamie, Nik Theodore, and Neil Brenner. 2011. "Postneoliberalism and Its Malcontents." *Antipode* 41 (1): 94–116.

Picciotto, Sol. 1991. "The Internationalisation of Capital and the International State System." In *The State Debate*, edited by Simon Clarke, 214–224. London: Macmillan.

Povinelli, Elizabeth. 2011. *Economies of Abandonment: Social Belonging and Endurance in Late Liberalism.* Durham, NC: Duke University Press.

Pradella, Lucia, and Rosanna Cillo. 2015. "Immigrant Labour in Europe in Times of Crisis and Austerity: An International Political Economy Analysis." *Competition and Change* 19 (2): 145–160.

Prashad, Vijay. 2003. *Keeping Up with the Dow Joneses: Debt, Prison, Workfare.* Cambridge, MA: South End Press.

Pratt, Geraldine, Caleb Johnston, and Vanessa Banta. 2017. "Liftimes of disposability in surplus entrepreneurs in Bagong Barrio, Manila." *Antipode* 49 (1): 169–192.

Rajaram, Prem. 2017. "Refugees as Surplus Population: Race, Migration and Capitalist Value Regimes." *New Political Economy*, 23 (5): 627–639.

RCD (Reception Conditions Directive). 2013. *Directive 2013/33/EU of the European Parliament and of the Council.* Brussels: European Parliament.

RCK (Refugee Consortium of Kenya). 2019. "Refugees, Asylum Seekers and Returnees." Accessed March 6, 2019. https://www.rckkenya.org/refugees-asylum-seekers-and -returnees/.

RefugePoint. 2018. "Madiha Ali delivers statement about self-reliance." Accessed April 23, 2023. https://www.refugepoint.org/refugee-self-reliance-initiative-excom/#:~:text =Most%20refugees%20say%20they%20want,stay%20is%20temporary%20or%20 permanent.

Ribot, Jesse, and Nancy Peluso. 2003. "A Theory of Access." *Rural Sociology* 68 (2): 153–181.

Roberts, Adrienne, and Susanne Soederberg. 2014. "Politicizing Debt and Denaturalising the 'New Normal.'" *Critical Sociology* 40 (5): 657–668.

Robinson, Cedric. 1983. *Black Marxism: The Making of the Black Radical Tradition.* London: Zed Press.

Roderick, Leanne. 2014. "Discipline and Power in the Digital Age: The Case of the US Consumer Data Broker Industry." *Critical Sociology* 40 (5): 729–746.

Rono, Joseph Kipkemboi. 2002. "The Impact of Structural Adjustment Programmes in Kenyan Society." *Journal of Social Development in Africa* 17 (1): 81–98.

Ross, Kristin. 2015. *Communal Luxury: The Political Imaginary of the Paris Commune.* London: Verso Books.

Roy, Ananya. 2017. "Dis/possessive Collectivism: Property and Personhood at City's End." *Geoforum* 80: A1–A11.

Sala-Pala, Valerie. 2010. "Differentialist and Universalist Antidiscrimination Policies on the Ground: How Far They Succeed, Why They Fail: A Comparison between Britain and France." *American Behavioural Scientist* 53 (12): 1788–1805.

Salter, Mark. 2013. "Part I: Research Design." In *Research Methods in Critical Security Studies: An Introduction,* edited by Mark Salter and Can E. Multu, 15–25. London: Routledge.

Sanyal, Kalyan. 2007. Rethinking Capitalist Development: Primitive Accumulation, Governmentality, and Post-Colonial Capitalism. New Delhi: Routledge India.

Sassen, Saskia. 2005. "The Global City: Introducing a Concept." *Brown Journal of World Affairs* 11 (2004) 27–35.

Shilliam, Robbie. 2018. *Race and the Undeserving Poor.* Newcastle upon Tyne: Agenda Publishing.

Sieff, Kevin. 2017. "'What Other Choice Do I Have?'—How Debt-Ridden Refugees Are Being Forced to Return to a War-Zone." *Washington Post*, December 15, 2017.

Silver, Hilary. 1993. "National Conceptions of the New Urban Poverty: Social Structural Change in Britain, France, and the United States." *International Journal of Urban and Regional Research* 17 (3): 336–354.

Singh, Nikhil Pal. 2017. "On Race, Violence, and 'So-Called Primitive Accumulation.'" In *Futures of Black Radicalism*, edited by Gaye Theresa Johnson and Alex Lubin, 102–145. London: Verso.

Smith, Andrea. 2010. "Queer Theory and Native Studies: The Heteronormativity of Settler Colonialism." *GLQ* 16 (1–2): 41–68.

Soederberg, Susanne. 2013a. "Universalising Financial Inclusion and the Securitisation of Development." *Third World Quarterly* 34 (4): 593–612.

Soederberg, Susanne. 2013b. "The US Debtfare State and the Credit Card Industry: Forging Spaces of Dispossession." *Antipode* 45 (2): 493–512.

Soederberg, Susanne. 2014. *Debtfare States and the Poverty Industry: Money, Discipline and the Surplus Population.* London: Routledge.

Soederberg, Susanne. 2018. "The Rental Housing Question: Exploitation, Eviction, and Erasures." *Geoforum* 89 (Spring): 114–123.

Squire, Vicki. 2017. "Governing Migration through Death in Europe and the US: Identification, Burial, and the Crisis of Modern Humanism." *European Journal of International Relations* 23 (2): 513–532.

Taylor, Marcus. 2012. "The Antinomies of Financial Inclusion: Debt, Distress and the Workings of Indian Microfinance." *Journal of Agrarian Change* 12 (4): 601–610.

Taylor, Marcus. 2016. "Risking Ventures: Financial Inclusion, Risk Management and the Uncertain Rise of Index-Based Insurance." *Research in Political Economy* 31 (1): 237–266.

Tomsic, Samo. 2020. *The Labour of Enjoyment: Towards a Critique of Libidnal Economy.* Berlin: Walther Konig.

UN-Habitat. 2017. Policy Paper 1: "The Right to the City and Cities for All." Geneva: United Nations.

UNHCR (United Nations High Commissioner for Refugees). 2009. *UNHCR Policy on Refugee Protection and Solutions in Urban Areas.* Geneva: UNHCR.

UNHCR. 2012. *Promoting Livelihoods to Build the Self-Reliance of Urban Refugees in Nairobi.* Nairobi: UNHCR, DRC, FEG consulting.

UNHCR. 2017a. *Alternatives to Camps: Making It Work—Key Action #6 Building Sustainable Livelihoods.* Geneva: UNHCR.

UNHCR. 2017b. "Kalobeyei Settlement." UNHCR Kenya. https://www.unhcr.org/ke/kalobeyei-settlement.

UNHCR. 2018a. *Figures at a Glance—Statistical Yearbooks.* Geneva: UNHCR.

UNHCR. 2018b. *Microfinance Programmes in UNHCR Operations—Innovative Microlending in Kenya Kiva Zip and Refuge Point.* Nairobi: UNHCR.

UNHCR. 2020. *Figures at a Glance—March 2020.* Nairobi: UNHCR.

UNHCR Kenya. 2015. *Voluntary Repatriation of Somali Refugees from Kenya Operations Strategy 2015–2019.* Nairobi: UNHCR and Government of Kenya.

UNHCR Kenya. 2016a. *Comprehensive Refugee Response Framework: From the New York Declaration to a Global Compact on Refugees.* Nairobi: UNHCR and Government of Kenya.

UNHCR Kenya. 2016b. *Kenyan Comprehensive Refugee Programme 2016.* Nairobi: UNHCR and Government of Kenya. https://www.unhcr.org/ke/wp-content/uploads/sites/2/2016/05/Kenya-Comprehensive-Refugee-Programme-document-KCRP-20161.pdf.

UNHCR Kenya. 2019–2020. *Kenyan Comprehensive Refugee Programme: Programming for Inclusive Solutions and Sustainable Development.* Nairobi: UNHCR and the Government of Kenya.

Veney, Cassandra. 2007a. *Forced Migration in East Africa: Democratization, Structural Adjustment, and Refugees.* New York: Palgrave: Macmillan.

Veney, Cassandra. 2007b. "Local Host Communities: Responses to Refugees." In *Forced Migration in Eastern Africa*, edited by Cassandra Veney 105–149. New York: Palgrave Macmillan.

Wacquant, Loïc. 2008. *Urban Outcasts: A Comparative Sociology of Advanced Marginality.* Cambridge: Polity.

Wacquant, Loïc. 2010. "Crafting the Neoliberal State: Workfare, Prisonfare and Social Insecurity." *Sociological Forum* 25 (2): 198–220.

Walia, Harsha. 2021. *Border and Rule: Global Migration, Capitalism, and the Rise of Racist Nationalism.* Chicago: Haymarket Books.

Wesling, Meg. 2008. "Why Queer Diaspora?" *Feminist Review* 90 (1): 30–47.

Western Union. 2017. "Mastercard and Western Union Explore Digital Model for Refugee Camps." Press release.

WFP (World Food Programme). 2017. "WFP Cuts Food Rations for Refugees in Kenya amidst Funding Shortfalls." Briefing World Food Programme, October 2, 2017.

Wilson, Japhy. 2013. "The Shock of the Real: The Neoliberal Neurosis in the Life and Times of Jeffrey Sachs." *Antipode* 46 (1): 301–321.

Wolfe, Patrick. 2001. "Land, Labor, and Difference: Elementary Structures of Race." *American Historical Review* 106 (3): 866–905.

World Bank. 1994. *Kenya: Structural Adjustment in the 1980s.* Nairobi: World Bank.

World Bank. 1999. *Kenya Case Study.* Geneva: World Bank.

World Bank. 2018. "Record High Remittances to Low and Middle-Income Countries in 2017." Press Release.

World Economic Forum. 2018. *These Countries are Most Supportive of Taking in Refugees.* Brussels: World Economic Forum.

World Refugee Survey. 1994. *World Refugee Survey—1994.* United States Committee for Refugees: New York.

Wright, Melissa. 2013. *Disposable Women and Other Myths of Global Capitalism.* London: Routledge.

Yates, Michelle. 2011. "The Human-as-Waste, the Labor Theory of Value and Disposability in Contemporary Capitalism." *Antipode* 43 (5): 1679–1695.

Žižek, Slavoj. (1989) 2009. *The Sublime Object of Ideology.* London: Verso.

Žižek, Slavoj. 1993. *Tarrying with the Negative.* Durham, NC: Duke University Press.

Žižek, Slavoj. 2016. *Against the Double Blackmail: Refugees, Terror, and Other Troubles with Neighbours.* London: Penguin.

Index

Note: A page number followed by a "t" indicates an item in a table.

Aalbers, Manuel, 24
Abbe-Pierre, 61
accumulation, capital: and the capitalist state in general, 32–33, 43; credit-led, particularly in Kenya, 36–37, 112, 114, 120; and the French case for disposability of refugees, 80, 83, 84, 85, 96, 100; Marx on, 48–49; and neoliberal refugee governance, 5, 8, 9, 10, 17, 18, 19–20, 24–25, 30, 33–34, 35, 39, 40, 41, 46, 53, 136, 137–38, 138–39, 140; and race, 43–44, 52, 54; and welfare, 38
Action Plan on the Integration of Third County Nationals, The, 74
ADA (refugee allowance in France), 94, 96
Afghan refugees, 17, 62, 72, 73t, 85, 90t, 100, 141
Africa: city growth in, 30; investing by EU to prevent future migration from, 63, 70–71, 103; and poverty imagery, 110–11; UNHCR's attention to, 28. *See also* African migrants; East Africa/Horn of Africa; North Africa; sub-Saharan Africa; *and specific countries and groups of refugees*
African Centre for Migration and Society, 28
African migrants, 5, 25, 70–71, 72, 90, 90t, 141; framed as undesirable and racialized, 2, 10, 16, 51, 65, 90; in France, 54, 83–85; sub-Saharan, 25, 42, 85
African Union Convention on Refugees, 27–28
African Union's Convention Governing the Specific Aspects of Refugee Problems, 106
Agamben, Giorgio, 22, 140
AIDS, 55
Albanian migrants, 85, 90t
Algerian migrants, 83
Algerian War for Independence from France, 83
Aliot, Louis, 79
Al-Shabaab, 103
alt-right, 6, 9, 11, 66, 79, 90. *See also* Right, political; white supremacy
Althusser, Louis, 8, 58

AMIF. *See* Asylum Migration and Integration Fund
Amis, Philip, 119
Amnesty International, 6
anti-ghetto law, 87
antisemitism, 55
Arabs. *See* Middle East; Muslims
Arar, Rawan, 16
Arendt, Hannah, 21, 140–41, 143
Artists for Refugees, 120
asylum claims, "authenticity" of. *See* refugees, authenticity vs. inauthenticity of
Asylum Migration and Integration Fund (AMIF), 65, 70, 148n9
Auberge des Migrants, 135
austerity: in the EU, especially after the Great Recession, 60, 65, 76, 86, 89, 98, 139; and the Lacanian concept of enjoyment, 39; Marx on, 49; and neoliberal refugee governance, 5, 6, 9, 11, 17, 18, 19–20, 24–25, 30, 31, 32, 34, 37, 38, 40, 41, 46, 85, 96, 111, 119, 136, 137, 138–39; pressures of, forcing closure of camps, 29, 142; and race, 41–42, 44, 54, 99; and the Right, 33
Australian model of refugee deportation, 141
Austria, 26, 67, 71, 72t, 76
"authenticity" of refugees. *See* refugees, authenticity or inauthenticity of
authoritarianism, 21, 47, 62, 143; neoliberal, 18, 25, 27, 31–32, 60, 82

Babb, Sarah, 85
Bakker, Isabella, 15
Bangladeshi refugees, 90t
banlieues, 25–26, 29, 84, 87–88, 89, 93, 146n8
Bauman, Zygmunt, 50, 114–15, 140
Belgium, 77
Benet-Gbaffou, Claire, 120
Berlant, Lauren, 57
Bhabha, Homi, 41, 56, 138
Bhattacharyya, Gargi, 8, 44, 53, 74–75, 89, 140
Biden, Joe, 9
biometric technology. *See* surveillance, refugee